THE **COMPLETE IDIOT'S GUIDE**® TO

Starting a Food Truck Business

by Alan Philips

ALPHA

A member of Penguin Group (USA) Inc.

ALPHA BOOKS

Published by the Penguin Group

Penguin Group (USA) Inc., 375 Hudson Street, New York, New York 10014, USA • Penguin Group (Canada), 90 Eglinton Avenue East, Suite 700, Toronto, Ontario M4P 2Y3, Canada (a division of Pearson Penguin Canada Inc.) • Penguin Books Ltd., 80 Strand, London WC2R 0RL, England • Penguin Ireland, 25 St. Stephen's Green, Dublin 2, Ireland (a division of Penguin Books Ltd.) • Penguin Group (Australia), 250 Camberwell Road, Camberwell, Victoria 3124, Australia (a division of Pearson Australia Group Pty. Ltd.) • Penguin Books India Pvt. Ltd., 11 Community Centre, Panchsheel Park, New Delhi—110 017, India • Penguin Group (NZ), 67 Apollo Drive, Rosedale, North Shore, Auckland 1311, New Zealand (a division of Pearson New Zealand Ltd.) • Penguin Books (South Africa) (Pty.) Ltd., 24 Sturdee Avenue, Rosebank, Johannesburg 2196, South Africa • Penguin Books Ltd., Registered Offices: 80 Strand, London WC2R 0RL, England

International Standard Book Number: 978-1-61564-162-8
Library of Congress Catalog Card Number: 2011938637

14 13 12   8 7 6 5 4 3 2 1

Interpretation of the printing code: The rightmost number of the first series of numbers is the year of the book's printing; the rightmost number of the second series of numbers is the number of the book's printing. For example, a printing code of 12-1 shows that the first printing occurred in 2012.

Printed in the United States of America

Publisher: *Marie Butler-Knight*

Associate Publisher: *Mike Sanders*

Executive Managing Editor: *Billy Fields*

Executive Acquisitions Editor: *Lori Cates Hand*

Development Editor: *Jennifer Moore*

Senior Production Editor: *Janette Lynn*

Copy Editor: *Cate Schwenk*

Cover Designer: *Rebecca Batchelor*

Book Designers: *William Thomas, Rebecca Batchelor*

Indexer: *Tonya Heard*

Layout: *Brian Massey*

Proofreader: *John Etchison*

ALWAYS LEARNING   PEARSON

This book is dedicated to my mother, Diane Cohen, the woman who made me believe anything is possible. Through your sacrifice and limitless love I know and see the world. This has made everything in my life possible. Everywhere I go you're in my mind and heart. You blessed me with limitless desire and loved me without expecting anything in return. I know we used to listen to "I Will Survive," but no more just surviving. Now it's time to live life to the fullest, and we're just getting started.

Contents

Appendixes

Introduction

As I write this, I'm sitting on a plane flying to Hawaii for a consulting project. I can't help but be amazed at how I arrived here. I started out much as I envision you, filled with passion and chasing a dream. I've earned the right to spend my days pursuing my passion to serve, feed, and entertain people in the most creative ways I can imagine. My arrival at this nirvana manifested through countless hours of hard work and commitment to my personal vision. At one point I was so obsessed with my dream, I wrote countless letters to celebrity chefs and restaurateurs begging them for jobs. I wrote so many letters and made so many phone calls that I recall one luminary welcoming me to his office under the moniker "Mr. Persistent."

Following your passion for food and hospitality will be hard work, but it will take you on a spectacular journey, teach you countless lessons, and expose you to amazing opportunities and people. The key is to recognize the opportunities, seize them, and enjoy every moment along the way. Your enjoyment will directly affect the experience you provide to your customers.

At the core of the food truck business and its current revolution is the chance to open doors and expose your talent. If you're passionate about food and hospitality, a truck can be your entry into this world. They provide a platform for the next generation of foodies, entrepreneurs, and chefs to turn their love into a business—at half of the traditional investment. Blogs, social media, and press can then potentially turn you into the newest sensation faster than you can fill up your tank. Just look at the venerable Kogi BBQ Truck. It started out as a drunken late-night conversation but wound up igniting a revolution and, along with that, a Los Angeles–based empire.

The journey you're about to embark on is your chance to contribute your voice and talents to the conversation. It's a ticket to the game with front row seats because of the media hype surrounding trucks. But with great power comes great responsibility. The truck you choose to create will be an extension of you and your views, and in turn, your reputation. You only get one reputation, so protect it with your life. Just as you can establish yourself as a player in the food business, you also can negatively impact your future with unsavory practices or a low-quality product.

The most important advice I can give you is to be authentic, honest, and always put the customer first. Create a truck that speaks to who you are and what you love. Customers will know if you're being true to yourself, and it will directly affect people's enjoyment of your product. Don't cut corners or try to take advantage of anyone in your business affairs. Treat everyone as you would your mother or grand-mother. And never forget that your customers are the most important part of your truck business. Make sure, no matter what, that your customers leave your truck happy. Sometimes that might mean losing money or swallowing your pride, but word of mouth and buzz will determine your fate. A customer is 10 times more likely to talk about a bad experience than a good one.

Welcome. You are about to become the proud owner of a food truck, the most exciting opportunity in the modern hospitality business and also, quite possibly, the most delicious. Ladies and gentlemen, start your engines and fire up those stoves; it's going to be an extraordinary journey.

How This Book Is Organized

Our journey is divided into four parts. That means you have four major steps to complete before becoming a food truck entrepreneur.

Part 1, Food Truck Basics, provides a breakdown of the fundamentals of the business. You'll learn the history of the revolution to give you a feel for the marketplace, and then the business behind creating your rig.

Part 2, The Mobile Food Mogul, takes that knowledge and begins to put it into practice. You'll take your ideas and put them into a plan, get your financing together, and understand the regulations that affect your day-to-day operation.

Part 3, Getting Road Ready, shows you what to do with your truck, from staffing it with the most incredible employees ever to hit the road to laying out your kitchen and making sure your food is not only delicious but safe, too!

Part 4, Growing Your Business, helps you protect your truck business like the new-born baby it is, growing it so it can expand through marketing efforts, building your clientele, and monitoring your financial performance.

Extras

Along the way you'll find the following sidebars containing extra nibbles of helpful information:

TRUCK TALES

The street has more stories than a library, and you need to know what's happening directly from the source.

TIP

I spent years learning this stuff so you don't have to. This is your chance to get the inside info.

BEEP! BEEP!

Like a warning horn for your mobile business, these alert you to potential threats to your truck.

DEFINITION

An explanation of words and terms you may not be familiar with but will need to know in your new business.

Acknowledgments

Sharing and appreciation are fundamental to a fulfilling existence. I know no greater joy than giving part of myself to another human being. I've always loved the hospitality business but I can't say I've always known why. This past year I figured it out. I realized that my life's work is to appreciate the blessings I have every moment and share them endlessly with as many people as possible. That was my thought while writing this book, and I hope it comes through in the text. More important, it wouldn't have been possible for me to be able to see or share it without the help of some extraordinary people.

Thank you to Rita Battat Silverman and Leap Over It Productions, my literary agent and agency. You're singlehandedly responsible for my involvement in this book. From nowhere Rita popped into my life and made a dream come true.

To Randy Ladenheim-Gil, my incredible editor. I wouldn't have been able to complete this without your countless hours of work and support. Thank you so much for your generosity and understanding.

To Pavlos Sierros, operator of Souvlaki GR, thank you for the countless hours you spent giving me insight into your truck operation. To Michael Mazzolla, your assistance in writing and researching this book was incredibly valuable. I can't wait to read your first book and see your first movie.

To my teacher, adviser, and friend David Ghiyam, thank you for guiding me through the daily obstacles of life and helping me to get closer to the light. That strength is what gives me the ability to pursue my true purpose.

Danny Zelouf, Jason Behfarin, Josh Dardashtian, Sam Afra, Josh Shames, and Derek Feinman, great friends with great appetites. My ability to be in the food business is directly linked to the confidence you inspired in me through our shared love of food and the many memorable times we have spent together.

Barbara Levites. What can I say? You're the best aunt ever. Thank you for being the most selfless person I know. To Jerry Cohen and Mona Philips, your arrival in my life has made it more fulfilled; thank you for always backing me up in good times and bad.

No one works harder and no one understands how to build a team better than Jason Apfelbaum. A lot of the lessons you taught me are in this book. Thank you for making CO-OP and Viktor & Spoils a reality and keeping it together while I pursued this dream.

Rob Levites, I know you're my cousin, but you're more like my other brother. So many good times and so many lessons; thank you for showing me what it means to be a man.

Grandma Lally, your official pasta taster is all grown up. You taught me to love food and I will always love you and miss you.

To my father, Frank Philips. You said it and I hope I'm doing it: "Play in the biggest game possible." Thank you for your love, advice, and encouragement. You have always made me believe I could accomplish anything.

To my brother, Jason Philips, I aspire to one day be as good a father as you and as kind a man. You share and don't even know you're sharing. And my sister, Claudia Borg, you're the reason my name is on this book and you have tirelessly supported my career. But your true merit is as a family member, sister, mother, and daughter. I respect you in ways you could never imagine.

To Gelareh Mizrahi, my soul. Your arrival in my life has deeply enhanced every day and given it so much more meaning. You are an incredibly kind and loving partner, and that love brought the light back into my life. Through your heart and eyes I rediscovered my true self. Thank you for your patience and support during this process. Every day with you is a blessing filled with pleasant surprises. I'm so excited for our life together.

Special Thanks to the Technical Reviewer

The Complete Idiot's Guide to Starting a Food Truck Business was reviewed by an expert who double-checked the accuracy of what you'll learn here, to help us ensure that this book gives you everything you need to know about running a food truck. Special thanks are extended to Gigi Pascual, owner/founder of the Buttermilk Truck in Los Angeles (www.buttermilktruck.com).

Trademarks

All terms mentioned in this book that are known to be or are suspected of being trademarks or service marks have been appropriately capitalized. Alpha Books and Penguin Group (USA) Inc. cannot attest to the accuracy of this information. Use of a term in this book should not be regarded as affecting the validity of any trademark or service mark.

Food Truck Basics

Mobile food carts have been around longer than you might think, and just when engines started purring so did appetites. The modern food truck revolution is a gourmand's fantasy with no limits. From French fry trucks to mobile meatball meccas, food trucks are here to stay!

In this part, I explain what caused the tremendous growth of the modern food truck and give you a brief sampling of the types of trucks out there. Then I talk about the business behind the trucks, from choosing the right concept and food to selecting a type of rig. After that, we can get busy with what to look for when purchasing and customizing your truck. Finally, I discuss where you can park your truck once you have it. You can't park anywhere you want anymore, and building your spots is crucial to your success.

So buckle up, get focused, and let's get busy making your ideas and passion into a deliciously profitable enterprise.

The Food Truck Revolution

In This Chapter

- Tracing the evolution of a food industry phenomenon
- Grasping the factors that drive food truck growth
- Finding the right food truck for you

My first experience with food trucks was a delectable dose of Americana. I was four years old and playing in the park with my friends. As I played on the swings, slide, and jungle gym, I patiently waited for the bell—the bell of the ice-cream truck!

That jingle was the highlight of my many days at the park. Who cared about slides and swings when you could taste the succulent sweetness of vanilla soft serve? I thought for hours about what combination or special treat I would choose. I became partial to Creamsicle Push Pops and King Cones, usually with a side of Nerds candies and Watermelon Big League Chew. We are all creatures of habit. Though I wanted to venture off into the latest Teenage Mutant Ninja Turtles green ice-cream creation, I was tied to what I knew and loved. Who could bear the thought of wasting my hard-earned allowance on some second-rate ice-cream treat? Not me, not then, not now.

But more than the food, there was something out of this world about the experience of the ice-cream truck. Nowadays marketers might call it *aspirational*, but the ice-cream truck made my day magnificent. Waiting for the truck to show up, its arrival, eating my goodies in the grass, and the truck's eventual departure was about far more than just an ice-cream cone. The colors, sounds, and interactions with friends and neighbors made the ice-cream truck an unforgettable food experience.

That's the same type of experience you can create with a food truck business. As you find out about the nuts and bolts of inventing, operating, and marketing your very own food truck business, always keep in mind the most important factor between being moderately and wildly successful: creating an emotional connection between the customer and your food, and giving them an unforgettable experience.

Fast-forward to the present day, and urban centers teeming with food trucks. They're the hottest food trend of the decade and the most exciting new segment of the food industry. The ice-cream truck remains, but now it's the Van Leeuwen Ice Cream Truck in downtown New York City, serving homemade Red Currant ice cream prepared with fresh cream and oak barrel–aged vanilla.

Not only has the ice-cream truck evolved into a gourmand's dream, but it sits alongside a virtual streetside food court serving Korean tacos, souvlaki, falafel, schnitzel, waffles, pizza, dumplings, and every other type of food imaginable (and some even unimaginable). Gone are the days of candy bars, ice-cream cones, and prepackaged sandwiches at construction sites. In this chapter, I explore the food truck phenomenon and how to find the right truck to begin your business.

What Is a Food Truck?

A food truck is a mobile kitchen, canteen, or catering truck that sells food or drinks. Some trucks, such as ice-cream trucks, sell mostly frozen or prepackaged food, but many restaurants-on-wheels have full kitchens with equipment specific to the creation of their specialty. Many cater to individual items or particular meals, such as breakfast, lunch, or late-night grub. The trucks usually park in high-traffic zones in urban centers, or at events like carnivals, festivals, and football games. Many trucks move to different locations throughout the day in order to maximize business. Food trucks are a beacon of experimental cuisines and new ideas. The low barrier to entry makes a food truck the perfect testing ground for the newest and most exciting concepts in the food business.

TIP

Don't confuse food trucks with food carts. Although both are mobile kitchens set up to sell food to local pedestrian traffic, the difference lies in how they travel. Food trucks move from place to place on their own power, while food carts are either towed by another vehicle or pushed by the person running the cart.

A food truck revolution is underway, and not only does it taste incredible, it's an opportunity for entrepreneurial magic. So let's take a look at where this revolution began.

How It All Began

Los Angeles was ground zero for the food truck revolution. The mobile food business began there with taco trucks back in 1910, thanks to the influx of Mexicans into California, with East L.A. receiving the highest concentration of immigrants. The taco truck became a staple of the SoCal landscape over the years, with an estimated 7,000 trucks operating in 2010. But it wasn't until a self-described failure, 30-year-old Mark Manguera, had his "aha" moment, that the modern food truck revolution was officially born.

Manguera's story begins after a late night of drinking. Mark and his sister-in-law, Alice Shin, decided to head to one of Los Angeles's many taco trucks. As he enjoyed the greasy goodness, a thought popped into his mind: combine Korean BBQ and tacos.

This simple idea, the fusion of these Korean and Mexican staples, was a match made in food truck heaven. Many people would have abandoned the idea along with their hangover the next day, but Manguera didn't. He believed in following his dream. He was willing to put his money, hard work, reputation, and everything else he had on the line to follow his passion and become his own boss.

Mark partnered with a local chef, the incredibly talented Roy Choi, and purchased a taco truck. The truck took a while to catch on. After several weeks of parking in different locations, including the busiest part of West Hollywood, and not getting any customers, they began going to clubs and giving free samples to the bouncers, who helped spread the word. Their first big break came when they got the idea to contact food bloggers about the tacos. This led them into the world of social media and an eventual use of Twitter to announce the truck's location.

The outcome of Mark's passion and hard work is the Kogi Korean BBQ taco truck. Kogi is a Los Angeles food phenomenon that inspires rabid dedication from its fans. Every time the truck reaches its destination, hundreds of people line up to taste their standard menu items and Chef Choi's rotating specials. Kogi set the example for many entrepreneurs to jump into the food truck business. They've even garnered nationwide attention among foodies and the food press.

For our purposes, the most powerful thing about Kogi was that they showed the potential of the food truck industry to many incredibly talented people. Not only that, they formulated a blueprint for the industry. The floodgates had opened, and the revolution was just beginning.

> **TRUCK TALES**
>
> Kogi chef Roy Choi was named to *Food & Wine* magazine's best new chefs in 2010 and was honored by *Bon Appetit* in 2009. Currently, Kogi has five food trucks and has recently opened its first bricks-and-mortar restaurant. Kogi's massive buzz on social networking services, including its 85,000 Twitter followers, led *Newsweek* to call Kogi "America's first viral eatery."

As we begin this journey together, there are a couple of questions I'd like you to ponder. How did this Kogi phenomenon come to life? Was it the food, Spicy Pork Tacos, Kimchi Quesadillas, and Short Rib Sliders? Was it the marketing, a family of Twitterers posting truck locations combined with trendy downtown Los Angeles slang? Was it the design? The trucks are actually pretty simple for the world of food trucks, white with a fairly tame Kogi logo. Was it the culture? Kogi involved their fans in the naming of their trucks and sometimes brings along a DJ to spin for those waiting to dine. Was it connections? Manguera's wife, Caroline, was a food, beverage, and hospitality specialist with Four Seasons hotels. Was it the combination of high-end food at street-level prices?

What's Driving the Growth?

Food trucks have been around for a century, satiating the need for food far and wide, but why the revolution now? What happened that took the lowly food vendor from street meat and dirty water dogs to the top of the culinary food chain? Here are the factors that lit the food truck fire.

The Recession

The hospitality/food business is one of the largest industries in the world. It's filled with some of the hardest-working and most creative minds around today. When the economy tanked a few years ago, a couple of things happened to the industry. First, more people lost their jobs or couldn't find work. Traditionally people flock to the food industry during times of economic hardship. They want to find a career they're passionate about, need part-time work, or want to become their own bosses. A restaurant costs a minimum of $500,000 to open, but a food truck can cost less than $100,000. Which do you think is a better place to start? A food truck is the perfect entry-level project for an entrepreneur looking to test the waters with an incredible new idea.

Second, Americans love to eat out. But what happens when you want to eat out when your income has declined? You look for cheaper options, such as food trucks. Food trucks aren't just less expensive, however. Food trucks tend to focus on specialty items, often from the youth or ethnic background of the truck creator. This is exactly the type of comfort food people are looking for when the rest of their lives is uncertain.

So why don't Americans just go to McDonald's or Burger King for a cheap meal? Modern young professionals are very conscious of what they put into their bodies. Gourmet food trucks are clearly more appealing to this demographic than calorie-laden, over-processed fast food. Food trucks make most of their food from scratch with high-quality, fresh ingredients. Therefore customers are getting something that is better quality and healthier at a similar price.

Technology

The next element of the perfect food truck storm is technology. The advent of social media (Facebook, Twitter, and Foursquare) and the ubiquitous nature of the Internet made for the perfect platform for marketing food trucks.

Using social media was like adding gasoline to the food truck fire, allowing trucks to communicate with their followers hourly and announce their location in real time. For customers, the game of finding the trucks and having the latest information about them became almost as important as the meal itself. Social media, combined with the spread of information through food blogs and other websites, made gourmet food trucks an overnight trend.

TIP

Technology gave food trucks a voice to establish their brand. It wasn't only what they were saying, but also the language they were using in the message. Successful trucks created their own culture through the use of social media, which established a strong connection between the truck and their customer.

Foodie Culture and Social Media

Long gone are the days of Julia Child demonstrating classic French food to housewives. Over the past 15 years, food has become theater and chefs celebrities. We're more conscious then ever of what we're consuming, and we love to talk about it. Cheeses, cured meats, wines, burgers, meatballs, cupcakes, exotic olive oils, and even the grossest foods in the world: you name it, and I promise you there's a magazine, television show, or blog dedicated to discussing its taste, aroma, and the best place in the world to eat it.

Food trucks are no exception. Celebrity chef Tyler Florence hosts the Food Network show *The Great Food Truck Race*, where food trucks compete against one another. A search of the term "food truck" on the food blog Eater.com generates more than 1,000 results. Our culture has embraced the food truck as a testing ground for the future of the food industry and, more important, a regular stop for gourmet goodness.

Combine all of these factors and you have all the ingredients necessary to create a mouthwateringly profitable revolution. The question is, how do you get your piece of the pie?

TRUCK TALES

The Fojol Bros. of Merlindia specialize in the cuisine of Merlindia and Benethiopia, mythical places they created in a marketing move that has made their food truck one of the most popular in Washington, D.C. Kipoto, Dingo, Gewpee, and Ababa Du wear neon jumpsuits, mustaches, and turbans while selling spicy cyclones, lassipops, palakpaneer, and chicken Masala.

The cuisine is actually a mix of Indian and South Asian foods served over a choice of basmati rice or their special breads. The food is authentic and delicious, but packaged with whimsical theatrics in order to attract attention and differentiate their product. The truck was launched during the Obama inauguration. As millions of people flooded the nation's capital, the Fojol Bros. drove around the city blasting marching band music from their 1965 Chevy step van. Today, the truck is welcomed by a line of patrons every time they pull up.

D.C. law mandates that there must be a line when they park, and the Fojol Bros. have made a game out of the regulation. They encourage customers to start a dance party where they want to park, and the person who starts the party gets a free meal.

If the Fojol Bros., four twenty-somethings, can invent a new cuisine and a mythical place where it originates, you, too, can conceive a fabulous new food business.

The World of Food Trucks

The following sections explore the many types of food trucks dominating the scene.

Taco Trucks: The Original

Taco trucks were one of the original food trucks on the scene. With thousands of taco trucks in existence, you could stop at a new one every day for years and never repeat. The mighty taco truck has spread far beyond its Los Angeles origins, with trucks throughout the United States and abroad. The two dominant forms are the classic Southern California style and Fusion, the Kogi style.

Classic taco trucks offer some of the best Mexican food available, with specialties ranging from pescuezos (chicken necks) to onboard suadero (rotisserie pork and pork fat seasoned with onion, lime juice, salt, and adobo). Taco trucks represent all aspects of classic Mexican cuisine. Some restaurants, like the El Gallito chain, park their own food truck in front of their bricks-and-mortar business to showcase specialty items. The Gallito truck specializes in Birria de Chivo, a traditional Jaliscan goat stew made of shredded goat mixed with roasted chilis, toasted cloves, and fresh oregano. Wrap it up in a tortilla, wash it down with a cold Modelo, and go back for more.

Fusion trucks tend to combine another cuisine such as Asian with the standards of tacos, protein, veggies, and sauce wrapped in a hard or soft tortilla. I've already discussed the importance of the Kogi truck to the food truck revolution, but there are countless similar trucks throughout the country. In New York you find the Korilla & Kimchi BBQ Trucks; in Dallas the Ssahm BBQ Truck takes to the road; and in Portland, Oregon, the fleet of Koi Fusion trucks are customer favorites. The Fusion tacquerias seem here to stay and are crossing over into bricks-and-mortar restaurants, essentially defining a new cuisine.

TIP

Many people would tell you to avoid a crowded market like taco trucks, but being part of a trend can be great. It can help grow your business, and people tend to go for the foods they know they'll enjoy. The only precaution is to make sure your product is absolutely fantastic, because if it isn't, other taco trucks down the road are only too happy to pick up your customers.

Pizza Trucks: It's All About the Ovens

Pizza is one of the most popular foods in America, and pizza trucks are one of the fastest-growing segments of the food truck industry. Strolling out of my door at lunchtime in Manhattan's Financial District, I bump into the Eddie's, Jianetto's, and Vinny Vincenz pizza trucks. Eddie's Pizza's bricks-and-mortar operation has been around in a New York suburb for decades, and its fan base expanded when HBO's *Entourage* featured it. Its New York City truck specializes in the thin crust variety and has average waits of over an hour during the busy part of the day. Jianetto's has a more diverse menu of Grandma slices, a Sicilian-style slice served with dots of plum tomato sauce above the cheese. And Vinny Vincenz serves classic New York–style slices for $1 each. Who needs to go to the pizza parlor when the pizza parlor can come to you?

The main concern when starting a pizza truck is product differentiation and quality. Look for inspiration from someone like Casey's Pizza in San Francisco, which focuses on a well-prepared pie using only the best ingredients, or California Pizza Kitchen, which has built a chain through the use of unusual toppings and combinations.

BEEP! BEEP!

Some pizza trucks prebake their product offsite and then finish it on the truck. I advise against that practice. You'll end up with a better-quality product if you bake it all at once, even if it takes a little more time. Customers will notice the difference.

Dessert Trucks: Nighttime Sweetspots

It was only a matter of time until deliciously decadent sweets made their way into the food truck game. On the night before Halloween 2007, direct from some underfed college student's dreams, came Dessert Truck. The vehicle, which parks outside New York City college dormitories, serves pastries you would have to go to cooking school to learn how to concoct. Jerome Chang, the creator of Dessert Truck, went to the French Culinary Institute and left a job in the world-famous restaurant Le Cirque to establish his own brand, selling Warm Chocolate Cake and Espresso Panna Cotta. He has since expanded to a permanent location on the fashionable Lower East Side.

The idea for Dessert Truck came from a chance snack that Chang and his roommate, Columbia Business School student Chris Chen, came up with in their apartment. A combination of toast, Nutella, caramelized bananas, and sea salt ignited their passion for sweets on the street. Chen and Chang chose a truck because it had more space than a cart and lower overhead than a storefront. They invested about $60,000 to purchase and design their truck. They prepare their items in a kitchen during the day and sell their desserts at night.

Other dessert trucks include Cupcake Stop, specializing in nostalgic cupcakes, including Betty Crocker–style cake with buttercream icings or exotic flavors like chocolate caramel pretzel. Flip Happy Crepes, an old-fashioned trailer in Austin, Texas, serves French crepes; and Wafels & Dinges, who doles out Brussels Wafel, the "mother of all wafels" with sweet and savory artisanal toppings.

TIP

Dessert trucks have more limited sales options. Not that many people are looking for cupcakes at lunchtime. Dessert trucks flourish where students are looking for a quick sugar fix or couples are strolling after a nice dinner. To maximize revenue, many successful dessert trucks focus on delivery, catering, and providing sweets to savory truck operators.

Ice-Cream Trucks: Good-Bye, Good Humor

Oh, how the ice-cream truck has changed! Generally the lines in front of the Van Leeuwen Ice Cream truck are so long that you'd think they were giving it away, but that's only until you get a taste. Ben Van Leeuwen's off-white postal truck, decorated like a shabby chic Italian farm house, has a loyal following of folks looking to satisfy their sweet tooth.

Ben is a youthful former Good Humor Truck driver, who makes his ice cream from local, hormone- and antibiotic-free milk and cream. He combines his 18 percent butterfat ice cream with special ingredients such as Michel Cluizel chocolate and Tahitian vanilla beans. A farm in Sicily harvests the nuts in the pistachio ice cream and all the toppings are organic. In addition, Van Leeuven uses biodegradable cups, napkins, spoons, and straws. The Van Leeuwen truck is the haute cuisine answer to ice-cream trucks, a product of the Whole Foods generation.

Van Leeuwen is joined by many other gastronomists in his attempt to put his old employer out of business. Two standouts are the Coolhaus Truck in Los Angeles, specializing in creations like coffee toffee ice cream covered in red velvet cookies, and the King Kone, which delivers soft serve and flavored shaved ices to your doorstep.

> **TIP**
>
> The ice-cream business is great in the summertime, but business chills when the weather turns cold. If you're planning an ice-cream truck, assume your business will be seasonal, or find a warm-weather climate.

Dumpling Trucks: Simply Delicious

What do you get when you combine high-quality ingredients and tasty dipping sauces with a celebrity chef? The Rickshaw Dumpling Truck, of course. Rickshaw is a *reverse truck* Kenny Lao and David Webber created after building their dumpling empire on a bricks-and-mortar location. When you have a restaurant as well as a truck, you can share overhead and have fewer start-up costs, which means more profit for you. During slow months, you don't have to take out your truck. Having a bricks-and-mortar establishment, even if it's small, is a massive advantage in creating a successful food truck business.

> **DEFINITION**
>
> A reverse truck is a food truck business that began as a bricks-and-mortar food operation.

Dumplings are the perfect food truck item. Most of the prep is done off the truck, with the dumplings just steamed or fried on board. They lose none of their freshness, cook quickly, and are easily served and eaten alongside a salad and a dipping sauce. Done right, dumplings are simple, fresh, clean, and, most important, authentic.

David and Kenny consulted with celebrity chef Anita Lo when formulating their concept. Kenny used to sell dumplings out of the back of his truck at farmers' markets in New Hampshire. They're a passion that comes straight from his heart, and it shows. David is a businessman with a fascination for efficiency, and that shows, too. Combine their skill sets with their desire, and you have the odd couple of food trucks: Felix and Oscar have nothing on these guys.

TIP

To make fresh dumplings correctly takes a lot of time and manpower. The key to your profitability is controlling your labor costs for the prep work. If you can put together a good system for that, you're one step closer to your dream.

Burger Trucks: Look Out Mickey D's, We're the Burger Kings!

The Latin Burger and Taco Truck was launched in early 2010 by Ingrid Hoffman of the Food Network, along with her boyfriend, Jim Heins. It was one of the first gourmet trucks in Miami and is best known for the Latin Macho Burger, with a patty made of blended chorizo, chuck, and sirloin topped with Oaxaca cheese, caramelized onions, avocado sauce, and red pepper mayo. The result is an over-the-top, melt-in-your-mouth creation that proves burgers have a home in the food truck game.

Burger trucks have taken hold throughout the country. In New York, E-squared Hospitality, the group behind the enormously successful BLT restaurants, has the Go Burger Truck. La Cense Beef, a grass-fed beef company, has created a truck to promote their brand of beef. And in Los Angeles, Baby's Badass Burgers are being featured on the Travel Channel and CBS. The ladies of Baby's Badass sell burgers such as the Au Natural and the Covergirl, referring to the owners' feminine charms.

TIP

Propane is the key to the burger business on a truck. Grills (burgers) and fryers (fries) use a lot of propane, so you'll need to work the cost of extra tanks into your numbers.

Mediterranean Trucks: New York's Taco Truck

Souvlaki, gyros, and falafel have always been favorites in the world of street food. Nowadays a new breed of Med trucks are taking hold, such as the 2010 *Vendy Award–* winning Rookie of the Year, Souvlaki GR.

DEFINITION

The **Vendy Awards** is an annual award ceremony organized by the non-profit street vendor project. The event celebrates New York's street vendors and awards prizes in categories such as "rookie of the year" to top street vendors.

Souvlaki GR specializes in the signature street food of the founders' beloved homeland, Greece. With a commitment to only the freshest handmade ingredients, the company has created the ultimate Greek food truck. Their signature souvlakis are available on sticks or wrapped in hand-rolled pitas, and served alongside signature salads such as the Prassini, featuring chopped greens, dill, and feta cheese in a lemon/olive oil dressing.

TRUCK TALES

Mediterranean trucks are Manhattan's answer to the taco trucks of Los Angeles. Moshe's Falafel and Taim Mobile are engaged in truck-to-truck combat for New York's best falafel truck, both serving some of the crispiest falafel, smoothest hummus, and freshest salads in Manhattan.

The types of trucks mentioned here are just samplings of the many possibilities for food on wheels. Just because you don't see your favorite cuisine on the list, don't be discouraged. Part of what makes the food truck industry so successful is that people aren't afraid to experiment and take a risk. Whatever you choose, make it yours by letting your personality show.

The Least You Need to Know

- Food trucks have been around for years, but trucks today are offering more of a lifestyle choice than just a quick meal.
- Because start-up costs aren't excessive, truck operators can bring new ideas and experimental touches to their offerings without as much risk as bricks-and-mortar restaurants.
- From tacos and desserts to Asian Fusion and falafel, there's a type of truck for every taste.

Secrets of Food Truck Success

In This Chapter

- Choosing your concept
- Considering start-up costs
- Creating a business based on volume
- Accounting for the intangibles that make good food great

Success in the food truck business is in large part determined by the decisions you make at the beginning of the process. As you develop your business you will make hundreds of small decisions, but the early ones affect all the others that follow. Early decisions about your concept and how you execute food production will determine whether you succeed or go bust.

For example, you might make the best burritos in the world and are certain your burrito recipe is the perfect food truck concept. But when you really start to apply your product to the food truck business, things don't look so rosy. Here's why: when you make your burritos at home it takes you about 10 minutes to make each burrito, with a total cost of $8 apiece because you use special meats and cheeses. You may have a great product, but it costs a lot to make and takes a long time (10 minutes is a long time in the food truck business). This is a recipe for disaster in the food truck business. In Chapter 2, I discuss the importance of thinking with your head, not your heart, when developing your food truck concept. Remember, you're a business-person now.

Understanding the Business Model

The business model of food trucks is fairly simple: choose a simple concept and sell as much food as you can in as little time as possible. Sounds easy, doesn't it? But what happens when it rains and nobody comes by the truck? Or you get a flat tire? Or an employee doesn't show up and you have to fill in yourself despite other commitments? All these variables make seemingly simple ideas complicated, and that's why you need systems in place to take all these variables into account.

Projecting Food and Labor Costs

Controlling your food and labor costs is your key to profitability. Your food cost is determined by how much it costs you to purchase the food for your menu over a set period of time. This includes food that you don't sell, also known as waste. Your food cost should be targeted at or below 30 percent of *gross sales* (after taxes and gratuities have been deducted) and your *percentage of waste* should be no more than 5 percent of gross sales.

DEFINITION

Gross sales, also called **gross revenues**, are your sales minus taxes and gratuities.

Percentage of waste is the wholesale value of food purchased divided by total food sales.

I recommend serving fresh food every day, so it's very important that you closely control your purchasing and keep a record of sales. Good sales records will help you make accurate forecasts. Labor cost should average around 30 percent of gross sales as well. So to prepare, cook, drive, and serve the food for your concept, it should cost you no more than 30 percent of your gross revenues.

To determine your food cost, without taking into account any secondary factors such as waste, you need to figure out what you believe is an acceptable price to charge. Let's say for this exercise that you plan to charge $10 for a burrito. You need to get pricing from your suppliers to determine the cost of all your ingredients. If your cost is below $3 for the ingredients, or 30 percent of the cost of food, you're off to a good start.

But you probably won't be selling only one kind of burrito. You might serve a lobster burrito whose ingredients cost $3.50, or 35 percent, and a chicken burrito that costs only $2.50, or 25 percent, to make. You're okay as long as the average of all the burritos you sell is no greater than 30 percent of the price you charge for it.

> **TIP**
>
> You must also take into account secondary factors such as waste and menu mix when determining your "true" food cost, but for now let's stick with the "simple food cost."

After you've determined whether the concept you've chosen is practical from a food cost perspective, you have to look into labor. Average trucks have anywhere from two to six workers. For this exercise, let's assume that you aren't working in the truck yourself, though if you are, you should pay yourself as an employee. A food truck employee will make an estimated $20 per hour, depending on your location and the level of skill required for your concept, with a minimum of six-hour shifts.

Estimating Average Sales

To calculate your labor cost, you need to generate a simple forecast of how much you expect to sell in an average week. Follow these steps:

1. Estimate how many items you expect to sell for a week.

2. Multiply the number of items sold from Step 1 by the amount you plan to charge for that item.

3. Multiply the result from Step 2 by 80 percent. This deducts 20 percent from your total to account for things like slow seasons, rainy days, and overly optimistic estimates.

This gives you your estimated gross weekly sales.

If you estimate that you will sell 2,000 burritos a week and plan to charge $10 per burrito, you multiply 2,000 by 10 to get 20,000. Next, you multiply that by .80 to get an estimated gross weekly sales of $16,000.

For the sake of simplicity, the preceding instructions assume that you sell a single item at a single price. In reality, you will probably sell multiple items at different prices. To account for this, repeat steps 1 through 3 to calculate the estimated gross weekly sales for each item, and then add these totals together to generate your total estimated gross weekly sales.

Estimating Labor Costs

You need to pay staff to prep, cook, and serve this amount of food, and you need to calculate these costs.

1. **Determine the number of staff hours of prep time per week.**

   It's fairly common for most food trucks to require three hours of prep daily, by a minimum of three people, for a total of nine staff hours per day (three hours × three people). If your truck operates seven days a week, your weekly prep time is 63 hours.

2. **Determine the number of staff hours on the truck per week.**

   If you have two shifts—11 A.M. to 3 P.M. and 5 P.M. to 9 P.M.—that's a total of eight hours. If you have three people on the truck for each shift, your total number of staff hours on the truck per day is 24. Multiply this number by 7 to get your weekly total, which is 168.

3. **Add together your weekly staff prep hours from Step 1 and your weekly staff truck hours from Step 2 to get your total weekly staff hours.**

   In this example, you add 63 and 168 to get a total of 231.

4. **Multiply the total staff hours by the hourly pay rate.**

   If you pay your staff $20 an hour, your total weekly labor costs, excluding payroll taxes, are $4,620.

Determining Whether You Pass the Test

Your labor costs shouldn't exceed 30 percent of your gross total sales. To calculate whether your estimates are in line with this guideline, follow these steps:

1. **Divide your total weekly labor costs by your gross weekly sales and round up to the nearest hundredth.**

   In this example, total weekly labor costs are $4,620 and gross sales are $16,000. If you divide 4,620 by 16,000 and round up to the nearest hundredth, you get .29, or 29 percent.

2. **Pat yourself on the back if your estimated labor costs are less than 30 percent—so far your estimates are in line with running a successful food truck business. If your labor costs exceed 30 percent, you need to rethink your business plan.**

   If your labor costs are above the accepted range, it is important you look into the number of steps involved in preparing and serving your food items. Other than the preparation of food, the labor on a truck is standard. In order to cut labor costs, you may want to look into simplifying your menu by cutting items or ingredients. Also make sure that you're using foods multiple times on your menu. For instance, if you're using chicken in a burrito, use the same chicken in your taco. Another way to cut labor costs is purchasing pre-prepared items such as pre-made tortillas rather than homemade. Just make sure you are not sacrificing the final product. Balance is the key to making this work.

Testing Your Production Time

Later in the book I show you how to streamline your production process (see Chapter 14), but for now let's do a test. Go to your home kitchen and *prep* your item. After you've prepped the item, make 20 orders of it in a row. If you're able to make 20 plates in a row at the same quality level in less than 5 minutes per plate using minimal equipment, you've got a shot on a food truck.

 DEFINITION

To **prep** a menu item means to do everything you could do to a menu item prior to a customer placing an order for it, such as seasoning chicken in preparation for grilling it.

Hitching Your Truck to Three Revenue Streams

Food trucks can be a source of three streams of revenue. In a business that has such razor-thin margins, you must have a concept that utilizes all three of them, as follows:

- **On-truck sales:** The primary source of revenue. Sales from customers coming up to the truck and purchasing food should account for 60 percent of your revenue. The expected profit margin from these sales is 15 to 20 percent.

- **Catering:** The second, and most profitable, revenue center involves selling packages or orders of food for 10 or more people per head or per tray. The profits for catering can be up to 50 percent of the total revenue, so a catering component is crucial to your truck's success and should account for 30 percent of your business.

- **Delivery:** Depending on where you're parked, you should be able to make deliveries to local businesses and individuals. Delivery should represent 10% of your business and will have the same profit margin as on-truck sales (15 to 20 percent).

Estimating Commissary Costs

Your commissary is where you park, clean, and stock your truck. It's also where you do all your prep work and—for some concepts—the majority of your cooking. You also store your food and dry goods at your commissary.

Some food truck operators use their homes as their commissaries. New York City has some great commercial commissaries, such as Casablanca in Hunts Point, but there are many sub-par ones as well. The most important point is that you have access to a commercial kitchen outside of your truck. Health departments inspect commissaries regularly. It's of the utmost importance for food safety purposes as well as the quality of your product that you use a high-quality commissary.

A New York City commissary costs about $650 per month just to park your truck. To park and have basic access to a kitchen runs a minimum of $1,200 a month and goes all the way up to $2,500 for one truck. In California a commissary runs from $500 to $1,200 for basic water, electricity, and parking. No matter where you open your truck, your commissary's quality and related costs will be integral to the success of your truck.

Choosing an Authentic Concept

You are your concept. If you spent your entire life cooking Italian food, don't tell me you want to open a Chinese food truck. Unless you have an incredible competitive advantage or Chinese chef partner, the percentages say you won't succeed.

A food truck takes on the personality of its owner. As one food truck owner told me, "This is not like a restaurant where the chef can hide in the kitchen." As a food truck owner, chef, or server, you're front and center with your customers, and they want it that way.

BEEP! BEEP!

You need to be open, interactive, and authentic in every aspect of your truck business. If you aren't, your customers will know, and not only will they not come back, they'll blog about it!

No one wants to eat at a corporate food truck. When the guy who writes a food blog and reviews four trucks a week on Yelp shows up, he wants to see you, or at least your brother. He wants to know that you're making the same meatball recipe your grandmother made 50 years ago. Not only that, he wants to know that you're going to the same butcher in Brooklyn and that you make the sauce every morning using Grandma Lally's ladle. As a truck operator you need to create an authentic connection with your customers, and then maintain that connection with hard work and honesty.

Your truck must be true to your beliefs. Choose a concept that represents who you are, and not what you think you should be or want to be. Look to your roots as an individual or a family, and then apply that to your choice of concept.

Making Sure You Have Sufficient Start-Up Capital

I devote two chapters to the financials of the food truck business (see Chapters 6 and 7), but looking at the basics, you need to consider the minimum capital requirements to get your business started. It is going to cost you at least $50,000 to start a food truck business, but I recommended that you budget at least $100,000.

Where will all that money go? Here are some of the big-ticket items:

- **A high-quality truck and mobile kitchen.** You could spend less, but what's the point if it's going to cost you the same amount in repairs and lost sales later on?

- **Enough operating capital to help you get through the start-up period.** It's going to take a while for you to build your business to the point where it turns a profit; until that time, you need to have reserve funds available to cover all your expenses.

- **Your weekly paycheck.** If you don't pay yourself anything while you're getting your business off the ground, you might create your own personal financial problems, which will hurt the business.

TIP

After you come up with a budget for your project, add 20 percent to that total. This gives you some financial breathing room and is probably a more realistic figure anyway.

Don't go overboard and spend too much money creating your food truck business. Some people spend $250,000 or more on their truck, which doesn't make sense for two reasons. The first is that the return on investment isn't high enough to justify the cost. Why spend $250,000 to make $1,000 dollars a week in profit? The second is that people don't like expensive food trucks. The truck business is a countercultural movement, and anything that yells big and expensive is against everything the industry stands for. Most people will take an authentic truck over an expensive one any day of the week.

Generating Volume, Volume, Volume

The key to the food truck game is volume—selling as much as you can. The check at most food trucks is no more than $20 per person. At 10 percent profit, you're making around $2 per person on every item sold. In order to make $100 dollars, you have to sell 50 of whatever it is you're slinging. You aren't spending $100,000 on a truck business to make $100 dollars a day, so you need to be able to attract and serve large volumes of business.

Identifying Your Spots

The key to selling large volumes of food is identifying and building your spots. Within each neighborhood are areas where food trucks are known to park or people are known to eat a particular meal, such as lunch. You need to identify a location that has good business but isn't oversaturated. You also need to establish positive relationships with the businesses on the street so they don't become hostile to your presence.

Once you identify a few potential spots, you have to begin to establish a presence there. This might involve being there every day—or certain days of the week—at a particular time. Additionally, you must advertise it to the local community and businesses. Let them know through social media and flyers that you plan to be around the neighborhood. Offer complimentary samples during your first couple of weeks to establish that you have a good product. Deliver complimentary food baskets to businesses in the neighborhood. See Chapter 5 for an in-depth look at finding the best spots for your food truck business.

Creating an Assembly Line

To service the volume required to sustain your business, you must create an assembly line system. An assembly line is the process in which parts, or in our case food, is added to a product in sequence.

TRUCK TALES

The assembly line developed by Ford Motor Company between 1908 and 1915 enabled mass production at reasonable prices. The McDonald Bros, Maurice and Richard, are rumored to have been the first to apply it to a restaurant in the early 1940s. It was called the Speedee Service System, and restaurateurs from all over the United States tried to duplicate it. The key was to become less dependent on skilled cooks by making unskilled labor responsible for just one part of the cooking process. Unskilled labor is paid less and takes less money to train, and using the system got food out quicker while tasting just as good.

Your assembly line involves cooks and servers working in unison to place, prepare, and deliver orders in a timely fashion. For a food truck, that means under five minutes from order to delivery.

If you have four people on your burrito truck, here's how your assembly line might look:

1. The server takes the customer's order at the truck window, hands the order off to the cooks, and accepts payment from the customer.

2. One cook heats the tortilla and cooks the meat and then hands the order off to the next cook.

3. The second cook fills the tortilla with the vegetables, beans, sauce, and cheese and hands it off to the third cook.

4. The third cook wraps the tortilla, puts it in the serving container, and hands it to the server.

5. The server calls out the name of the order and hands it off to the customer.

If one member of the team isn't doing his or her job well or fast enough, the entire system will break down, and you'll lose a customer. Lose enough customers and you'll be out of business. If you deliver enough high-quality meals quickly, you just might turn a profit. Chapter 14 delves into these issues in more detail.

Getting from Place to Place Efficiently

Getting in and out of your spots in as little time as possible is critical to the success of your truck. The less time you spend during each part of your operation, from prep to travel to sales, the more money you make. The more time you spend, the more labor cost, fuel cost, propane cost, and food waste you'll have. Spending 30 extra minutes during each stage of your day could cost you an extra $300 to $400. Failing to be prepared can easily cut daily profits by 30 to 50 percent.

To maximize efficiency and profitability, you must have a plan. You need to think of every detail *before* you start moving forward, not after. How long will it take you to prep? How long will it take you to travel? Once you park the truck, how long will it take you to get set up? Will you have to send someone ahead with the truck to get the parking spot early and then deliver the food? How long will it take you to break down the truck and move to the next shift?

I recommend creating a timeline for your day. Take a piece of paper or use a spreadsheet program and literally break down the entire process into 15 minute increments, and assign very specific tasks to each quarter hour. What needs to be happening at the commissary from 6 to 6:15 A.M.? What about from 7:16 to 7:30 A.M.? What needs to be happening on the truck from 5 to 6:30 at night?

Next, assign every task to a particular person. After you've made the assignments, you need to provide each worker with a clear schedule, breaking down their specific duties for the day.

The hardest part of this process is proactively and positively managing and motivating your workers to stay on schedule. This is a skill I talk about in Chapter 12.

Achieving Consistency

Market research indicates that the primary reason people choose where they're going to eat is the location of the establishment. The second most important factor is the consistency of the food. Consistency—making the food item the same again and again exactly the same way—is the key to restaurant success. McDonald's Big Macs are the same at every location.

Customers like to know what they're getting, how much of it they're getting, what they're paying for it, and that it's going to be served exactly the way they want it. That's the key to repeat business, and the more repeat business you have, the more successful you'll be.

You can ensure consistency of your product through recipes, sampling, training, hands-on management, and great people.

Perfecting Your Recipes

You need to handle every aspect of every menu item you sell precisely the same way each and every time you make it. If you're cooking burritos at home for friends or family, it's okay to switch brands of salsa or try a different type of cheese. It's also okay to change the quantity of beans you add to the tortilla. But when you're serving food from your food truck, all these things—from the brand of salsa and type of cheese to the amount of each ingredient you use and how long you grill the meat— must be handled exactly the same way for each burrito you serve. If you served your burrito with a slice of orange as a garnish the last time a customer ordered it, he is going to expect an orange garnish the next time he orders it as well.

You need exact specifications for everything from the look of the plate to how much lettuce goes on your burger. Your recipes are your lifeblood and your trade secrets. Anyone who prepares your food must know exactly what to do to prepare all of your menu items.

Sampling Your Food

You, and only you (because this is your dream), must constantly sample your products. You need to test at least two items daily to make sure the taste, texture, and presentation are perfect. You should also do this randomly during different points in the process. This will give you a true sense of the customer's experience, as well as enable you to pinpoint any possible issues within the process.

TIP

You can also test your product using secret shoppers. These can be friends or even a paid service who dine "undercover" at your truck a couple of times and provide you with feedback on the product and service. Secret shoppers provide an unbiased view of your business and product from the consumer's point of view.

Training Your Staff

You need to actively train any employee prior to their taking a role in your business. You need to teach them the exact methods you use to prepare your product. To ensure uniform training of your staff, create an employee manual that outlines all the processes of your business. It should include photos of the physical plant and step-by-step instructions for preparing food. Additionally, it should provide standard language for answering customer questions and referring to menu items.

Finally, employees should be empowered in the art of *service recovery*. People make mistakes, and fixing the situation with a customer through a complimentary check, drink, or discount is the fast track to making a customer for life.

DEFINITION

Service recovery describes the paradox that a service or product failure can offer the chance for a business to receive higher customer satisfaction than if the problem had never occurred.

For details on the training process, refer to Chapter 12.

Taking Charge

All ships need a captain, and either you or your manager are the captain of your food truck. You're accountable for all the decisions made by everyone involved in your business, so you must be there, leading by example. If you aren't on hand and included in all aspects of your creation, you won't realize your dream of creating a successful food truck. You need to have knowledge of all aspects of the business, and you must be able to fill in for any of your employees at a moment's notice. Your presence will make everyone work a little bit harder and ensure that your customers receive the best product every time.

Hiring Great People

The people you choose to represent and execute your business are critical to it becoming a success. You're looking for 51 percenters, a term I'm borrowing from restaurateur Danny Meyer. He doesn't believe in pursuing the so-called 110-percent employee; that's about as realistic as working to achieve the 26-hour day. You're looking for employees who will go that extra step every time to get the job done, with skills divided 51/49 between emotional hospitality and technical excellence.

Meyer says a 51-percenter has these five core skills:

- **Optimistic warmth:** Genuine kindness, thoughtfulness, and a sense that the glass is always at least half full.

- **Intelligence:** Not just "smarts" but rather an insatiable curiosity to learn for the sake of learning.

- **Work ethic:** A natural tendency to do something as well as it can possibly be done.

- **Empathy:** An awareness of, care for, and connection to how others feel and how one's actions make others feel.

- **Self-awareness and integrity**: An understanding of what makes you tick and a natural inclination to be accountable for doing the right thing with honesty and superb judgment.

My recommendation when hiring is to choose people you like. The first minute you meet someone you get an initial feeling in your gut about that individual. That feeling says either "I like this person" or "I don't like this person." Trust that instinct.

You're going to spend a tremendous amount of time with these people, and if you don't like them the truck will become unbearable. More important, good people who like each other combine to form a great team that makes an awesome product—every time!

Adding Value

Magnificent food and fabulous service are sometimes enough, but in today's hyper-competitive hospitality environment you need something else—something intangible that differentiates you from the crowd. I call these intangibles emotional attachment and personality.

Creating an Emotional Attachment

There are tons of fast-food restaurants in the world. Two of my favorites are Roy Rogers and White Castle. Why do I love them? It definitely isn't because they're the most popular. It probably isn't because they have the best food, although I do enjoy them on occasion. It's because my grandmother used to bring me White Castle hamburgers and my mother used to bring me Roy Rogers fried chicken. I have an emotional attachment to these brands.

Turning on the Personality

So you have a great product and a great brand—do you need anything else? Yes, an associated personality. People don't want to talk to your brand, they want to talk to a person. The person makes it real; the person has emotions, struggles, and a story. You are that person. You are your truck. Would you prefer to go to a great restaurant or a good one where the owner knows you and takes care of you? Most people would choose the latter. There's no substitute for a personal touch.

How do you translate that to a food truck? Two ways: you are present, and you pleasantly surprise your guests.

You are present. You should be on or around your food truck 80 percent of the time it's open. If you can't be, you need to find a strong manager who's outgoing and can take on this role for you, although I strongly advise against the latter. Just keep in mind that no one will care more about your truck or your customers than you.

You pleasantly surprise your guests. The pleasant surprise is an art form that has been perfected by great hosts since the beginning of time. Here's an idea of how it works. You have a great business going on your pizza truck. One guy shows up at your truck every day of the week. He buys the same lunch every day, pays, doesn't say much, and goes back to work. One day he shows up and places his order. He puts his hand into his pocket to pay for the food and *bam*—you tell him lunch is on you today. Instantly a huge smile comes over his face and he thanks you. You've made him feel special, and that means more than you can possibly imagine.

The business of hospitality is all about servicing your guests and making them feel exceptional. You've just made a customer for life. Not only that, he's now a walking advertisement. He goes back to his office, friends, and family to tell everyone how incredible your pizza is and that he'll "hook them up" if they go there. You're on your way to food truck success!

The Least You Need to Know

- You are your concept. A food truck takes on the personality of its owner.
- Controlling food and labor costs is the key to profitability.
- Choosing the right spot for your food truck will make or break it.
- Giving people something extra with their meal creates customers for life.

The Right Concept and Food

In This Chapter

- Picking a clearly defined food niche that works for you
- Determining your customers and where you'll find them
- Making sure your menu and your concept work together
- Finding the right pricing strategy

In the food truck business there's no such thing as the "right" concept and food, there's just the right concept and food *for you*. Our mantra for defining what's right for your truck is *Do You*—in other words, stay true to who *you* are. Over the years I've spoken with many ultra-successful people, and that's the one concept that connects all of their stories. In Chapter 3, I help you decide how to select the best menu for *your* food truck concept.

Staying True to Who You Are

Successful people stay true to who they are, their roots, and their values. They choose a path and product they believe in with every inch of their humanity. To be successful, you need to follow their lead. If you try to create a truck that's not representative of you and your skills, the customer will know, and I can guarantee you that it won't lead to success.

Here are a few examples of food truck entrepreneurs who stayed true to themselves and succeeded:

- **Souvlaki GR** is run by a Greek immigrant who serves authentic and fresh Greek food.

- **Rickshaw Dumpling Truck**, the product of a partnership between an Asian American chef and an expert management consultant, serves tasty Asian dumplings with modern branding and efficiencies.

- **Van Leeuwen Ice Cream Truck**, run by a former Good Humor ice-cream man, uses locally sourced gourmet ingredients.

- **GastroPod** is owned by a gourmet chef with experience in Europe's and America's most avant-garde kitchens. He serves experimental and seasonal comfort food from a 1962 Airstream trailer.

Can you see that all these trucks somehow make sense? The proprietors' beliefs, passions, and personalities are inseparable from their products. If they're hip, their truck is hip; if they love dumplings, they sell dumplings.

This isn't rocket science. It's actually the exact opposite; it's the science of simplicity.

Picking Your Niche

Great food truck brands have a clearly defined niche. Successful food trucks, and that's the only kind we care about, do one thing and do it really well. Whatever the item you've chosen to sell, your brand should be centered on showcasing and promoting it. The simpler the idea the better; not only does this keep your operational costs down, it enables you to focus your marketing and branding message.

To start, let's break down trucks into the following categories:

- **Cuisine trucks:** These businesses focus on a particular cuisine, like Greek or Mexican.

- **Item trucks:** These trucks focus on an item like pizza, tacos, cupcakes, or burgers. They are the most common type of truck and, I believe, the most effective. By focusing on being the "best in your world" at one specific item it will be easier to control costs, target your marketing efforts, and establish a following.

- **Meal trucks:** These trucks serve menu items consisting of a particular meal, such as breakfast, lunch, or dessert.

You can achieve success with any of these types of trucks as long as you execute them correctly. Whatever type you choose, you have to know that you can be the best in your world. That means looking at your target area and making sure you're able to make the best version of that item. There's no point in setting out to be the second-best taco truck in downtown Cleveland. Nobody wants to eat at the second-best taco truck; they want the best. Studies prove that the returns for first of anything are exponentially higher than those for second. Just take a look at this weekend's movie box office returns. Most of the time, the movie that comes in first makes two or three times what the second place one does.

Now that you know the importance of determining your niche, how are you going to figure it out? Try not to complicate that idea. Instead, focus on the simplest aspects of your idea as you develop it.

TIP

Whenever you're making a decision about your truck and you don't know what to do, sit down, take a deep breath, and try to keep it as simple as possible. Then choose the simplest solution and go with it. Overcomplicating your truck will lead to failure.

For example, if you grew up in an Italian family and love cooking Italian food, particularly meatballs (everyone in your family raves about them), one option is to consider opening an Italian food truck. You could sell chicken parmigiana, pizza, meatballs, spaghetti, salad, garlic rolls, tiramisu, and so on. But keep in mind that your specialty is meatballs, not the best chicken parmigiana, pizza, and tiramisu. So why complicate your life by making all that other stuff?

Your diamond is your meatball, and you should focus solely on it. In other words, you should focus on creating a meatball truck, not an Italian food truck. By simplifying your concept, your food and labor costs will be lower, your marketing message and target market will be more defined, and you can focus on being the "best in the world" at meatballs.

But what if there's an Italian restaurant that's famous for its meatballs where you're planning to park your truck? Can you be better than them? And even if you can, is it worth the time and energy making it known that you are?

Because you have a truck, you can put your key in the ignition and find a place to park where there's less competition. So you hit the streets, do some research, and you know what? There's a better location—a parking lot between three office buildings, with one shopping center within walking distance and no Italian restaurants nearby. Now you have the best product in a location with a need. You have further defined your niche.

The point isn't defining *a* niche, it's defining *your* niche. You don't have to be the best in the entire world; you just have to be the best in *your* world.

You've now determined your product niche, but you're only halfway done nailing down your concept.

Determining Your Cultural Perspective

Back in the day it would have been okay to define your niche and go to work, but food trucks are a microcosm of modern business. They showcase many aspects of the future of the business world, including social media, mobility, and micro markets. This brings us to layer two in defining your concept: determining your cultural perspective.

In today's hypercompetitive business landscape, having a good product is definitely the most important factor, but how you communicate about that product, and how the product itself looks and feels, is becoming almost as significant.

TRUCK TALES

The Mud Truck, a coffee truck in Manhattan with multiple locations, sells coffee, but they're also selling a lifestyle. They're the anti-establishment coffee retailer, which is perfect, considering their target market in downtown Manhattan. They even speak the language of their customers, referring to the ambiance around their truck: "The smokers smoked, the dogs had bones, and it played sweet soul music," according to their website. Since its inception, the Mud Truck has spun off into bricks-and-mortar locations, apparel, and wholesale coffee.

Think of Ben & Jerry's Ice Cream; do they just sell ice cream? Nope. Ben & Jerry's sells a cultural perspective; they're socially responsible, and that comes directly from the associated personalities of Ben and Jerry. When a truck speaks on Twitter or is written about on food blogs, it needs to have a point of view and a voice.

What you say is as important as *how* you say it. If you're located in the downtown area of a city and most of your customers are going to be under the age of 30, you need to talk like they do. You should even be referencing their favorite music, TV shows, and movies, maybe even creating a menu item that's the favorite of a local indie rock band or food writer. Our pals Ben and Jerry did that with the bands Phish and the Grateful Dead. They knew their target market really loved their music, and the bands shared their cultural perspective, so they developed Phish Food and Cherry Garcia.

Think back to your world—the people, places, and things you and your soon-to-be customers interact with every day. Once you find your cultural perspective, identify cultural elements that can integrate this perspective into your customer experience. This will provide a second layer to your food truck brand that speaks to your core clientele. That core must identify themselves with your brand over your competitors. It's the same reason people drink Starbucks or Dunkin Donuts coffee. Either you're a Starbucks person or a Dunkin person; rarely is someone both.

In order to choose your cultural perspective, you need to look at your target market to see what makes them tick. Then you have to look at yourself and see what defines you. Make a list of 10 lifestyle characteristics of your target market and then make that same list about yourself. Then compare the lists and analyze the areas in which there are similarities. Once you identify the similarities, narrow them down to two or three and choose the one you believe applies most accurately to the food business.

Let's say you're planning a burger truck and you've determined that you and your target market both love rock music and computer games. Common sense tells you computer games wouldn't be the ideal marketing partner for hamburgers, but rock music just might work. Maybe your burger truck could be called Rock Burger or Zeppelin Burger, and the logo and menu could be reflective of rock culture and icons. You can play rock music in your truck and be known for parking outside all the major rock concerts.

Identifying a nonfood connection with your customer is vital to the success of your truck and is critical in defining your branding and marketing efforts.

Knowing Who You're Feeding

Would you open a lobster roll truck in a college town?

Let's look into this. I know of a lobster roll truck that does $13,000-plus in revenues every single day. That's a lot of money for a truck; sounds like a good business to me.

Their *average cover* is around $20 per head, and in the right location the rolls sell like wildfire.

DEFINITION

In food truck terms, a **cover** is what one person purchases at your truck. If you did 60 covers, you served 60 people. Your **average cover** is the typical amount that a person spends when dining at your truck. You can figure this out by taking the total revenue for a time period and dividing it by the number of people you served during that time.

I attended Cornell University, in Ithaca, New York. Ithaca is frigid eight months of the year, and it's mostly inhabited by college kids with very little disposable income. They spend what money they do have on chips, pizza, sandwiches, soda, and beer. A lobster truck selling an expensive item that's in high demand primarily during the summer months doesn't seem like it would work there. So even though a lobster roll truck can make a lot of money, the demand probably doesn't exist among students with little money in freezing cold Ithaca, New York.

A better location for a lobster roll truck would be a high-end beach resort or affluent urban neighborhood during the summer months. Both of these locations have heavy foot traffic and clientele with disposable income. This is an example of allowing macro trends, such as weather and income levels, to build your business. You never want to be fighting the currents. Instead, you want to ride the wave to success.

Profiling Your Food Truck Clientele

The lobster roll example makes it clear that you need to define your *target market* and match your concept to that market. The target market combined with your product, place, promotion, and price—collectively called the 4 Ps—are the main elements that will determine whether you'll succeed or fail in the coming months. Determining your target clientele and their demand for your product is crucial to your success.

DEFINITION

A **target market** is a group of customers that you aim your marketing efforts and product at. They are your ideal customers.

It actually took the people who run the Kogi food truck months before they were able to create awareness within their target market. They were using traditional media to advertise their business, but it turned out their clientele was on the Internet, using blogs and social media, which is actually where most of the clientele for food trucks hang out.

Based on my research, here are some estimates about the typical food truck customer:

- Approximately 90 percent of food truck customers are below the age of 45, with the core group between the ages of 25 and 45.

- The core group (age 25 to 45) is highly active on the Internet and social media.

- Approximately 60 percent of customers are male; this is due to the nature of the food (Although the food is made with high-quality ingredients, it tends to be heavier and greasier, which seems to appeal more to men.)

TIP

The core group of food truck customers spend hours online each day. They actively seek out the newest and most interesting experiences through niche blogs like Eater.com and online newsletters like Urbandaddy, Thrillist, and Dailycandy.

Most food truck customers are looking for an exotic and rewarding food experience that will both satisfy their craving and provide a story that they can tell their friends. Many may even write their own blogs about their experiences at food trucks and will probably post pictures and reviews on social media pages like Facebook. They aren't highly price sensitive but are definitely value oriented. If they feel like a truck is ripping them off or taking advantage of them in any way, they'll be extremely vocal about it.

It's very important to develop a focused group of customers who will tout your truck's virtues to their peers. The more regular customers you have, the quicker you'll reach your tipping point—the point when something reaches critical mass. How will you know when you reach your tipping point? When you show up to your spot and the customers are already waiting for you.

Your food truck clientele is part of the general pool of people who eat at food trucks. Let's say 100 people eat out in a neighborhood. Fifty of those people are open to eating at food trucks. These people will be your easiest targets. The key is to serve a type of cuisine or item that appeals to as many of these people as possible.

Suppose you specialize in foie gras, an uppity type of duck liver. Even if you make the best foie gras ever, it probably will only appeal to 2 or 3 of the 50 people looking to eat at a food truck.

Your choice of concept and food has a massive effect on your business at the seed level. If you can determine that you'll be able to appeal to a significant portion of this base level, you know you'll be able to survive.

> **TIP**
>
> Italian food is the most popular "dining out" cuisine in America. The most popular food items by consumption, whether at home or eaten at restaurants, are hamburgers, hot dogs, pizza, and fried chicken. Think about this and study your local market when deciding what you want to sell. It's always easier to go with the trends and tastes of the public than to go against them.

But really, who just wants to survive? You're in this to make the big bucks. You might even want some of that A-Rod money. To reach those heights of success, you need to pass the second test: can you be the best in your niche, not just against other food trucks, but as part of the general market?

You shouldn't just want to have the best burrito truck in the neighborhood. You should want to have the best burritos in the neighborhood, period. If you're able to achieve this type of critical acclaim or word of mouth, the number of customers you can draw from vastly increases, as do your future opportunities. Can you make your product and brand appealing to the point that you break out of the smaller pool of just "food truck customers" and into the ocean of everyone in your neighborhood who eats out?

Meeting a Demand

When deciding on a concept for your food truck, you must choose something that the market demands. Spend some time in the neighborhoods you plan to target and see which restaurants are busy. If you don't have time to do that, just drive around after everyone is closed to see who has the most garbage outside. The restaurant doing the most business has the most garbage to throw out.

If the pizza guy is doing well, but the Japanese guy isn't so busy, what can you infer from this observation? Go into the restaurants and try their food. As long as both products are of similar quality, it probably means there's a high demand for pizza in the neighborhood but not so many customers for Japanese. Many factors can determine this, but all that matters for your purposes is determining the underlying demand within a particular location.

Try looking for a food type that's missing in the neighborhood. Maybe there are excellent Chinese and Italian restaurants, but no burger joints. If you assume that neighborhood people like burgers, which is a pretty fair assumption for most places in the United States, then this area would be ripe for a burger truck.

The questions you're asking yourself may seem like simple ones, but you'd be surprised by how many people don't ask them. As a food truck operator, it's of the utmost importance that you do this for multiple locations. You'll need to have three or four spots that you hit regularly, so scoping out neighborhoods is crucial.

Matching Your Menu to Your Concept

Your menu is everything. You'll live and die by making the proper selections so that you're able to produce the food quickly, with low costs and high quality levels.

But that's only half the battle.

Your menu is the main sales weapon in your arsenal, so you have to present it in an appealing manner. It needs to be attractive enough to lure customers into making a purchase, and then it must maximize the amount of money they spend on that purchase.

Making the Proper Selections

Start with the basics. As I pointed out in Chapter 2, you can only make money with your truck if you keep food and labor costs below 30 percent of gross revenues (after taxes and gratuities). The only way to achieve this goal is by choosing menu items that you can produce and sell for less than that amount.

The more menu items you have, the more food you need to purchase. That means your inventory is higher, and you either have to store it or sell it. If you don't sell the food it goes bad, and you lose money. You could sell every chicken you have, but if you also have beef on the menu and it doesn't sell, there goes all your profit.

The more menu items you have, the more prep work you have to do. The more prep work you have to do, the higher your labor costs are. If your labor costs are over 30 percent, you don't make money.

Any way you slice it, you need to keep menu items to a minimum. Especially on a truck, where your margins are so critical, there's no room for items that don't sell or take too long to prep or cook. Choose a maximum of three signature items and stick to them. These items will probably have variations, like toppings or different types of meats, but you should keep those to a minimum as well. With three signature items with three variations each, you already have nine potential preparations, and that's not even counting sides, desserts, or drinks. Can you see how things can go from simple to complicated very quickly?

I highly recommend no more than 10 items on your truck menu, breaking it down as follows:

- Six main items, such as sandwiches, salads, or plates
- Two sides, such as fries and/or vegetables)
- Two desserts

The main items and sides should share ingredients in common, so that you keep the total number of ingredients you're dealing with to a minimum as well.

For instance, if you're using cheese on your burgers, use the same cheese on your side of cheese fries. Or if you're selling chili as a side, you could add a chili dog to your menu. By keeping menu items and ingredients to a minimum, and cross pollinating the ingredients in multiple items, you vastly increase your chance for long-term success.

My final recommendation for making proper menu selections is matching your food concept to your truck. In the next chapter I talk about finding the right truck. Your menu should drive the internal design of your truck. You should design your entire kitchen around the cost of producing these items. To keep costs low, don't pick items that require complex equipment to execute; it will completely throw off your start-up costs and cost way more to maintain and power.

Presenting Your Menu

The presentation of your menu is critical to getting your customers to make a purchase and maximize the revenues from that purchase. Menu psychology is real, and it works. Place a dollar sign or an item in the wrong corner, and you could cost yourself hundreds of dollars in sales and or reprinting. So let's get to the details.

Grandma's is always better. When naming items on your menu, personalize them—Aunt Gertie's Pot Roast Sandwich or Jimmy's Homemade Hot Sauce. Customers tend to want to get a taste of personalized items more than just simple pot roast sandwiches. Personalize one or two items or variations that you want to push.

Romance the description. What's the point of putting your heart and soul into making the best hamburger in the world and then just calling it a hamburger on your menu? You need to use words like "handcrafted," "triple basted," or "home cooked" to describe the item and the ingredients. Alan's Signature Burger, the special blend of brisket and Angus beef grilled on an open flame with Tillamook Cheddar Cheese, Applewood Smoked Bacon, and spicy chipotle pepper sauce seems a lot more delicious to me than "hamburger with cheese, bacon, and pepper sauce."

The top right. Customers read menus the same way they read newspapers. The information on the top right of the page is where their eyes head first. Use this area of your menu to feature your signature item, and magnify its presence by framing it and creating some extra white space around it.

Review, review, review. Nothing will make you look more foolish and cost you more money than mistakes on your menu. Make sure it's proofread at least three times prior to printing for spelling and grammatical errors. If you can't put enough time into making sure the menu is perfect, what does that tell customers about your food?

Pricing to Your Market

Pricing is a tricky business. You need to take into account three areas of concern when deciding on your pricing strategy.

Calculating the Price-Value Relationship

You want your items priced high enough that the customer believes your product is high quality, but low enough that they think they're getting good value for their money. In other words, you need to achieve a balanced price-value relationship.

You can determine your price-value relationship by analyzing your competition. Take a look at other trucks in your area. Make a spreadsheet with pricing for main items, sides, and drinks. You can also guess what an average cover would be by determining what you believe a person would generally order. Take a sample set of at least 10 of your competitors. Your pricing should fall in line with the third or fourth most expensive. That puts you a little above the middle of the pack, which is acceptable for a high-quality truck like yours, and should provide enough value to not alienate customers.

Ensuring Profitability

To make money, the average cost of all your items can't be more than 30 percent of your retail menu price. When you calculate the cost of producing your item, you should multiply it by 3.33. The result is the minimum price you should be selling the item for. With that said, you can get away with charging more for some items, and for others you'll have to charge less. The most important factor is that based on your *menu mix*, the average doesn't exceed 30 percent.

DEFINITION

Your **menu mix** is how much of your gross sales each item on your truck accounts for. If you sell $10,000 worth of food and burritos account for $2,000 of those sales, then burritos make up 20 percent of your menu mix.

Downplaying the Price for Customers

Unless you're offering the deal of the century, which doesn't send the right quality message, you should always downplay pricing on your menus. Menu psychologists tell us that dollar signs and the word *dollar* trigger the "pain of paying." You aren't in the pain business; you're in the pleasure business.

Eliminate all dollar signs and use a font that downplays the pricing. Never use a bold or larger font; the idea is to make the price an afterthought. When it comes to cents, .95 is always better than .99, but I recommend no cents at all. And if you want to sell one item more than any of your other items, it pays to put it next to something more expensive or less desirable. Customers tend to purchase items that fall in the middle in terms of pricing. If you want to really push your highest-profit item, put it on the menu next to your most expensive item.

Creating Your Brand

What makes your truck special? Are you giving 10 percent of your profits to charity? Did a famous artist paint your truck? Do you make your own bacon and sausages for your breakfast sandwiches? Are you a comedian who tells a joke to every customer? Are you a celebrity chef? These are all actual ways people have chosen to differentiate their food trucks.

> **TRUCK TALES**
>
> Fresher than Fresh Snow Cones is a truck based in Kansas City, Missouri, started by Lindsay Laricks. With her boyfriend Brady's encouragement, Lindsay took her love and knowledge of herbs and applied them to the simplest thing she could think of, snow cones. Instead of using artificial colors and sugary syrups to flavor shaved ice, Lindsay used homegrown herbs. She chose an ideal spot across from Blue Bird Bistro, a popular locavore restaurant, to park her 1957 Shasta trailer (purchased on eBay). The truck was an instant hit; the marriage of fresh, sustainable ingredients with a simple concept and passion, made for a very successful combination.

Remember that your brand must be a manifestation of yourself. First combine what you love with what you know, then take that idea and make it as simple as possible. Your brand is a combination of the product and your cultural perspective.

The name should be no more than three words and must easily identify the type of product you're serving. Also critical to a successful food truck, the brand you choose should differentiate you from your competitors and be available as a URL (Internet address), Twitter name, and Facebook page.

Testing Your Concept with a Focus Group

There's no formula for coming up with your brand name, so once you've brainstormed for a few days, take your best idea and test it out with a focus group.

Your first step is to create a one-page description of your concept. It should include:

- A mission statement
- A one-paragraph concept description
- A one-paragraph menu description

The mission statement should say, in one sentence, what you plan to create or establish. For instance, "Establish the Meatball Factory as the premier meatball food truck in Miami Beach."

The concept description is more detailed and speaks specifically to what makes your concept unique. For example:

> "The Meatball Factory will target young people during their day at the beach and after they visit nightclubs. We'll serve one type of meatball, in a bowl, as a slider, or as a hero, and three types of sauce to go along with it. I plan to do this because my grandmother made the best meatballs and they're a high-profit item. We'll attract customers by having a young rock 'n' roll image because I've spent the last five years following rock 'n' roll bands; they're what I love and I think my customers will relate to them."

Finally, describe your menu:

> "I'll serve only organic beef meatballs made with my grandmother's recipe. The sauces will be spicy tomato, creamy Alfredo, and pesto. The bread will be from a local bakery and will be picked up fresh every morning."

You should have samples of the menu items prepared for the group. Invite at least six people to be in your group. Do your best to have people who don't have a vested interest in your success and won't be afraid to tell you the truth—even if it might hurt your feelings. You can offer them some sort of compensation if you'd like, but I find that a free meal usually does the trick.

Have a list of questions for the group members to answer anonymously. You want them to give you honest feedback on your idea and food. Sugarcoated answers won't help you, so it's important you tell them that. Your questions should have number answers, along with options for additional comments.

Here's a sample of the kinds of questions you should ask your focus group:

- How would you rate each food item on a scale of 1 to 10? (With 10 being "perfectly awesome" and 1 meaning "I would never pay for this food")

- How would you suggest I improve these items?

- How would you rate my concept on a scale from 1 to 10?

- How would you suggest I improve my concept?

- Does this concept feel authentic? Does it match my personality?

- Would you pay X [insert average expected price per person] to eat at this truck?

- If not, what do you think is a fair price for the product?

- Where do you think a truck like this should park?

- How do you think we should package our food so that it's easiest to eat on the street?

You'll garner loads of information by listening to the answers to these questions. Most important, you'll find out how people react to your concept. As much as I can teach you about food trucks, the feedback you receive from unbiased people will show you the true potential of your idea. If the group doesn't like your idea, it's important that you understand why. Maybe they love the taste of the food but not the branding. Maybe they like the branding but don't like the pricing. Maybe they love it all and you'll be the next Kogi. Nobody knows ahead of time, but I can't wait to find out.

The Least You Need to Know

- Your personality and cultural perspective will determine the right type of food truck for you. The authenticity of your product is vital to your success.

- Matching your menu items to your target customer increases your chances of success.

- Balancing the price-value relationship and comparing it with the competition will help you find the right balance.

- Food truck customers are vocal about their likes and dislikes, so create a brand that makes you the best in your world.

- The right menu mix will spell success for your truck.

The Right Truck

In This Chapter

- Looking at the pros and cons of various types of trucks
- Shopping for your truck
- Customizing your truck to fit your needs
- Estimating truck costs
- Finding a commissary

There's one solid rule when you search for your truck, and you have to promise to keep repeating it to yourself during the process:

You get what you pay for.

If you try to take shortcuts, you'll pay for them later. Gas lines, generators, fryers, ovens, mileage: if you skimp on any of them, you'll lose big time. When it comes to buying a quality food truck, you have to literally put your money where your mouth is.

The "right" truck doesn't exist yet; it's the one you're going to build to perfectly match your concept. If you're selling empanadas and plan to do most of the cooking off the truck, your truck is going to need more storage and heating equipment than actual cooking equipment. If you're selling burgers and fries, your truck must be equipped with grills and fryers. Or maybe you're selling slushies; if so, you'll need the highest-capacity slushie machines to pump out loads of icy goodness.

Your marching orders are to locate a truck in the best condition possible and then customize it specifically for your needs. Used or pre-fabricated trucks won't have been built for the specific needs of your business. Trucks are usually built for general use, or past owners' uses, often with equipment you have no use for. Even if you buy an inexpensive used truck, it's highly likely you'll have to spend money customizing it to your needs.

I start from the beginning and break down the most common types of trucks employed in the food truck industry.

Types of Trucks

You can choose from three main types of food trucks:

- Chevy step vans

- Grumman Olsen step vans

- Mercedes-Freightliner Sprinter vans

Of course, people adapt other types of vehicles for use as food trucks, too, such as Airstream trailers or highly customized vehicles, but since we're talking about creating the most viable business, and these require extensive custom renovations, I don't recommend them.

BEEP! BEEP!

Many trucks come with propane and generators located inside the truck. Propane is dangerous, and having it inside your truck is a recipe for disaster. The Frites & Meats truck had their propane located in or under the truck, and it exploded, sending two people to the emergency room. Also, your generator must be housed securely outside your truck so that you can easily replace or repair it. Picture yourself in the middle of service when your generator goes. If you don't have easy access to it, you won't be able to fix it or replace it. There goes a whole day's revenues, as well as your hard-earned reputation.

The following sections consider each of the three primary types of vehicles people adapt for food truck businesses.

Chevy Step Vans

Step vans are the most economical and effective base on which to build your food truck. Also known as multistop trucks and walk-in delivery vans, step vans are light- or medium-duty trucks created for local deliveries. The following features make these vans ideal food trucks:

- They're usually designed to be driven either sitting down or standing up.

- They provide easy access between the driving area and the back.

- They usually have enough headroom to allow for an average-size adult to stand up in the cargo areas.

- They have enough space in the back to comfortably accommodate food truck equipment.

Step van trucks are also durable, have strong chassis, and tend to be less pricey than other options.

Step vans have drawbacks as well. They aren't easy to drive or park, so only trained members of your team will be able to operate them. Also, it can be difficult to find newer trucks, as opposed to Sprinter vans, which are readily available at dealerships.

TRUCK TALES

Kelvin Natural Slush Co., created by Alex Rein, a former corporate attorney who spent his childhood craving classic convenience store treats, serves all-natural frozen slushies. It's one of the most popular trucks in Manhattan and was voted Best Dessert at the 2010 Vendy Awards. Drink flavors include ginger, tea, or citrus and a choice of real fruit purée or mix-ins such as fresh chopped mint or basil. Alex's truck is a 2000 P30 Chevy step van he had customized. His advice is to make sure your equipment is bolted down tightly; his weren't in the beginning, and he had water leakage issues while traveling from spot to spot.

Step vans are available in many different sizes and models. Unless you're running a "cold" truck, selling ice cream or slushies, which requires less space for food preparation, the ideal truck is 14 feet long by 9 feet wide. A length of 14 feet gives you plenty of space for selling and prep/cooking areas, but anything longer than that will be nearly unmanageable to drive and especially difficult to park. In terms of width, you need at least 8 feet of space to create an efficient internal layout. Generally you can park in most spots with a width of up to 9 feet. If you choose a van that's smaller than 14 by 9, you'll make your working life more difficult because your interior space will be limited.

Buy a step van that runs on gasoline, not diesel. Although diesel trucks are typically cheaper, gas models are more reliable and easier to fix. And buy as new a truck as you can afford. Ideally, your truck should be no more than seven years old and should have fewer than 100,000 miles on it. Plan to spend between $10,000 and $15,000.

TIP

Before you buy a truck, make sure you know what equipment you need to be able to fit in it. The cargo area of the truck you choose must have enough space to accommodate your equipment. Visit your local restaurant supply company and identify the best and largest propane use or electric equipment. I say "largest" because propane equipment is usually small, and you want to maximize your production space. Only after you've laid out the equipment in the most efficient manner for your concept is it time to start shopping for your truck.

The majority of food trucks are repurposed step van postal trucks that were used by DHL, FedEx, or other large commercial companies. In fact, the bankruptcy of DHL, and the auction of their fleet of vehicles that followed, was a direct contributor to the food truck revolution.

Sprinters

Sprinter vans are commercial vans, chassis cabs, and minibuses sold under the brands Mercedes Benz and Freightliner. Despite the fact that they're more expensive than step vans—four to five times more expensive before customization—some entrepreneurs have started to use them for food trucks. Sprinters are easier to drive and park, which means more of your crew will be able to drive the rig. They're readily available new, and most of them are more up-to-date than step vans, which means that they're more reliable, have more advanced internal systems, and are generally more comfortable. Sprinters aren't as wide as step vans, so they don't have nearly as much space in the cargo area. A new sprinter van will run you $40,000 to $60,000.

Prefabricated Trucks

Companies like AA Cater Truck, Food Cart USA, Armenco, and Roadstoves rent, lease, and sell prefabricated food trucks. They offer one-stop-shopping, and their trucks often come with a guarantee or warranty. Rarely, though, do their deals make good financial sense for small business owners.

The goal of their business is to make money off every part of what they're selling; in saving the time and energy of managing the process yourself, you'll be spending tremendous amounts of money. A prefabricated truck customized to fit your needs will cost you well over $100,000. This huge expense makes it nearly impossible to recoup your investment without hitting a Kogi-style home run.

TIP

If you're planning to buy a used vehicle for your food truck business, spend the money to have the truck tested by a reputable mechanic prior to finalizing the deal. Spending a little bit of money in advance could end up saving you thousands of dollars down the road.

Calculating Truck Costs

For the sake of calculating costs, I am going to assume that you will buy a used step van. Purchasing your truck should cost you no more than $15,000, and if you can keep the cost to $10,000, which I recommend you do, you'll put yourself ahead of the game. The costs of customizing your rig should break down as follows:

- **Equipment for your onboard kitchen:** $15,000–20,000, depending on your menu

- **Electrical, steel, awning, and nonkitchen equipment:** $10,000

- **Labor to customize truck and install infrastructure:** $15,000–$20,000

- **Pots, pans, grease mats, bowls, hotel pans, and other kitchen goods:** $3,000

- **High-quality vinyl skin:** a major source of advertising: $5,000.

- **A brand-new Honda generator:** $6,000.

- **A POS system:** will cost you approximately $5,000. (Although more cost-effective options have recently come onto the market utilizing Apple's iPad.)

That's a total cost of $60,000 to $70,000.

Finding Your Truck

Now that you know what you should buy, you need to find out where to get it.

The main sources for step vans or used food trucks are eBay (motors.ebay.com), Craigslist (craigslist.org), truck dealers, truck auctions, and customizers. Check out all of them to find the best deal available.

Before you start looking, create a spreadsheet with price, year, mileage, model, previous use, and any other categories you deem important for choosing your truck. Having all the information in one place will make it easier for you to compare the different trucks you'll be considering.

eBay and Craigslist

On eBay search the terms "step van" or "food truck" from the main page. eBay offers auctions and "buy it now" prices for the trucks available. Use eBay's search filter so it will only bring up trucks that are within a specified distance from your zip code. No matter how good a deal seems to be, stick to trucks that are within three hours of your location, because you're going to want to see the truck and have it reviewed by a mechanic prior to finalizing your purchase. On Craigslist look in the "Cars & Trucks" section and search the same terms.

Neither Craigslist nor eBay will provide you with a guarantee for your truck. Once you purchase it, it's yours, and you have no recourse if the truck breaks down or is faulty. You should also be aware that Craigslist is infamous for vehicle scams, so be on your guard.

Truck Dealers and Auctions

A good truck dealer can provide guidance on which truck models will best suit your needs, which can be invaluable for someone just starting out in the food truck business. Also, most dealerships offer a guarantee or warranty on the trucks they sell.

The problem is that when you plan to customize the truck you buy from a dealer or, in truck terms, "chop it up," you're basically deeming any guarantee null and void. Speak with the dealer about creating a guarantee on certain parts of the truck, like the engine, chassis, transmission, and tires, so you'll have protection on the areas you won't be touching for customization.

Auctions are great places to find incredible deals, but they're a bit of a gamble. Although you are allowed to make sure it starts, you won't be able to have a mechanic check the engine and systems. Auctions are a buy "as is" proposition. I've heard of people getting spectacular deals at auction, but I've also heard horror stories of trucks needing expensive repairs.

Customizers

Customizers purchase trucks and then convert them into prefabricated food trucks. Basically, you're paying a premium to have them locate a truck for you and do all the work for you. You'd be much better off finding and purchasing the truck yourself and then bringing it to a customizer or metal shop to turn it into your food truck. The only benefit of purchasing directly from the customizer is that they'll usually offer you a guarantee on the vehicle and their work. Though it will be mighty expensive, as always, you get what you pay for. If your truck breaks down or has issues that relate to their work, they should be responsible.

See Appendix B for a list of some well-known truck customizers.

BEEP! BEEP!

It's well known in the truck business that customizers take much longer than expected to do the work—sometimes twice as long as expected. Clearly state the length of time the work should take in your contract with a customizer, along with penalties for late delivery. Waiting an extra three or six months to get your business started could end up with it never getting started at all. Even if you have a good contract, expect moderate delays and pad your pre-opening budget to account for it.

Redesigning an Existing Truck

After you've purchased your truck, the fun really begins: it's time to make it the "right" truck.

The first step in doing this is finding a customizer in your area. In most major cities and on the East and West coasts you'll find professional food truck customizers, but all you really need to do is locate a quality sheet metal shop. Sheet metal workers have the expertise and machinery necessary to customize your truck, and you should be able to find a local metal shop through a simple online search. I recommend finding someone who has experience working on trucks and is aware of local health codes.

After meeting with the customizer and making sure you're comfortable with their professionalism and expertise, you should follow up by asking them for references. Check those references to get a feel for the customizer's reliability and quality of work.

> **TIP**
>
> Make sure your customizer uses high-quality steel. The preferred type is corrosion-resistant restaurant-grade 304 stainless.

Choosing Your Equipment

Based on the work you've done on your concept, you should have a basic idea of what you'll need to pull it off.

Here are important questions to ask yourself at this point:

- **Will you be doing most of your cooking on or off the truck?**

   Are you heating up burritos, serving ice cream, or cooking egg sandwiches? Each one of these items requires very different equipment needs. Identify your needs and base your equipment on this information.

- **What is your main cooking technique for your menu?**

   If you'll be preparing a lot of fried food, you'll need a lot of fryers and probably won't use a grill or other heat source. A truck that specializes in fried foods can have up to four onboard deep fryers. You should also think about how much storage you'll need, and if it will be hot or cold storage.

- **Will you have one window or two?**

  If you have two windows, you'll be able to park on either side of the street; with only one, you'll be limited to only one side. That said, if you're going to be doing a lot of cooking on the rig, it will be virtually impossible to have two windows.

The next thing to consider before you purchase any equipment is how your assembly line will work. Take a minute to outline your *steps of service*. What happens when someone places an order? As you go over each step in the process of ordering, cooking, and serving a dish, you'll see what problems might arise and solve them before they happen. I strongly advocate practicing these steps on the truck or a space that is similarly sized to it. This will give you a real feel for how much space you have, which will help you make better long-term decisions regarding the layout of your truck.

DEFINITION

Steps of service are the basic steps that employees perform in food service businesses. You can make changes in the steps of service as needed to fit the expectations and experience you want your guests to have.

The following figures show basic layouts for a one-window and two-window food truck. Use these diagrams, along with proper measurements of your truck, as a jumping-off point for designing your truck. Take them with you to your local restaurant supply store. Sit with the supplier to find the best and largest propane- or electric-powered equipment that will fit on your truck.

BEEP! BEEP!

I highly recommend using as much electric-powered equipment as you can; electric is safer and more reliable than gas.

When you have your list of equipment and their dimensions, bring it to your customizer to review. Make sure that he or she signs off—contractually, if possible—on the fact that all the equipment will fit and function in his or her truck design. The last thing you want to do is buy equipment that doesn't work with your rig.

Recommended Truck Internal Layout #1. This is the ideal layout for a 1 window truck.

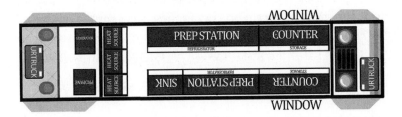

Recommended Truck Internal Layout #2. This is the ideal layout for a 2 window truck.

TIP

One of the best ways to showcase your truck's personality is through your truck's window, with all the conversation, music, and great smells coming from the kitchen. The larger the window, the more action customers can see while they wait. Remember, the customer is coming for the experience and you, so the more of you, your staff, and the cooking process the customer sees the better.

Powering Your Vehicle

The gas and electric lines on your truck must be flexible. You're a moving vehicle; anything that isn't flexible or tightly locked in place will eventually move or break.

Don't under any circumstances combine the gas lines for the generator and the truck. It may seem like a great idea to only have one tank to fill up, but if something goes wrong you lose both, you have to fix both, and you can't drive *or* cook.

Budgeting for Fuel and Maintenance

What makes your truck different from a restaurant business? You're a moving operation. Not only do you have to do standard restaurant maintenance, but you also have to maintain your truck. Here's a basic truck maintenance schedule:

- **After service every night:** Take the truck back to the commissary and thoroughly clean the kitchen and the vehicle itself. No one wants to eat from a dirty truck, inside or out. The care you show with your daily cleaning will directly relate to how successful your truck becomes.

- **Every 100 hours:** Change the oil in your generator. Review the manufacturer's guidelines for your specific model, but no matter what's recommended, I advocate changing the oil after 100 hours of operation.

- **Every six months:** Get your truck checked by a mechanic once every six months—an oil change, and checking tires, transmission, engine, and chassis.

As for fuel costs, expect to spend about $50 a day on gasoline for the generator and the truck (if it's a gas generator).

Propane costs $15 per 20-pound tank if you own the tanks, $30 per tank if you don't. You can expect to go through one and a half 20-pound tanks per day.

BEEP! BEEP!

Most cities restrict how much propane you can carry on your truck at one time. In New York City you can carry one 40-pound tank or two 20-pound tanks on your truck. Check with the local authorities before you build your truck; ignorance is no excuse when it comes to the law.

Finding an Off-Truck Kitchen (Commissary)

Locating a good licensed commissary is one of the most important aspects of creating a successful food truck. Other than your truck, the commissary is where you'll spend the most time, and it will have the most direct impact on the product you serve. Your commissary will be your off-truck kitchen, refrigerated storage facility, dry storage facility, and where you clean the inside and outside of your truck.

Most major cities have multiple licensed commissaries that service the needs of catering companies, food trucks, and other mobile food businesses. With that said, the quality of these facilities varies greatly depending upon the operator. A great way to locate a high-quality facility is to ask a respected operator or speak to the local health department.

Using a licensed commercial facility for your truck can be very costly. Two other options are to use your home kitchen or to partner with a bricks-and-mortar restaurant. If you use your own kitchen, you'll have to get it inspected and licensed by your local health department. If you own or partner with a restaurant, you'll save the significant weekly costs of belonging to a commissary, which will greatly increase your profitability. Obviously, that's your best choice if it's a possibility for you.

Depending on the size of your operation, a commissary can cost $500 to $5,000 a month.

The Least You Need to Know

- Most food trucks are converted step or Sprinter vans that you can purchase online, from dealers, or at auctions.
- Prefabricated trucks are the most expensive way to go. You're better off finding your own truck and then taking it to a customizer.
- Design your kitchen before you purchase any equipment, and then make sure that your customizer commits to making sure everything will fit and function in your truck.
- Create a budget for fuel along with a maintenance schedule to help manage your resources and keep your truck running smoothly.
- Don't overlook the importance of finding a good commissary.

The Right Location

In This Chapter

- Choosing where you *should* and where you *can* park
- Taking a strategic approach to finding the best spots for your truck
- Identifying spots to avoid
- Considering the business community for each of your spots
- Making the most of your locations

When it comes to food trucks and the restaurant business, similarities abound. The basics are the same: you must consistently put out a high-quality product with attentive service, with a side of aspirational marketing. It sounds simple, but trust me, doing this well day after day is no walk in the park.

Then comes the curve ball: in the truck business your real estate isn't fixed. Like everything in life, that's a blessing and a curse. But one thing's for sure: not having a fixed location makes things a lot more complicated. In this chapter we discuss finding the best locations to park your truck, as well as identifying locations to avoid. Then we help you figure out how to make the most of the locations you do choose.

Being Mobile: The Pros and Cons

Let's start with the blessings. You're the food equivalent of a guerrilla army. You can use your mobility to rake in the profits in ways that larger and less mobile food operations can't. If you open up in a spot that's busy for lunch but not for dinner, you can just start the engine and move somewhere else for the second half of the day. If you take a risk on a new spot and it doesn't work, not to worry; just park somewhere else tomorrow. Someone wants you to cater a party an hour away in the middle of a field? Just hop behind the wheel, and the gig and the profits are yours. Your mobility provides you with endless opportunities to generate more income.

On the flip side, being mobile creates other issues, and it's your job to minimize them. Let's start with storage: as a mobile food business, your storage is off-site, at your commissary. If you run out of buns for hamburgers, then burgers are *86'd* for the rest of the day. You have to pay extra attention to planning and creating a support system with other trucks, as well as local food businesses, making running out of food less likely, and providing you with options when and if you do.

DEFINITION

Eighty-six, or **86**, is restaurant lingo for taking an item off the menu. Generally it refers to taking something off temporarily because you ran out of that particular item, but it can also refer to removing it permanently.

Your mobility can also create issues with the stability of your business. You may have a great parking spot one day, but what ensures that you'll have it again the next? And what if a competing pizza truck or shop opens in your spot? Do you surrender it, or do you stay and fight? You aren't paying rent, so other than the goodwill of the food truck community you really have no claim to that space. That's another reason why being part of the community is so important. When you're part of a group of trucks, you work together to protect each other's interests and share a code of ethics.

When you find good spots, you have to protect and build them through hard work and fostering great relationships with the local community. Locating and cultivating the right locations for your truck is critical to your success. On that note, let's start identifying prime parking spots for your food truck.

Identifying Where You Should Park

Generally, you want to park in high-traffic and under-serviced locations, as well as places that will be in existence temporarily. The following sections identify some of the best places to park your food truck.

Office Buildings and Office Parks

High-traffic office buildings and office parks are ideal locations for the food truck business, especially at breakfast and lunch. Huge volumes of people pour into these locations during the morning and afternoon, and they're always looking for new and better options to quickly satisfy their cravings. Additionally, such places typically follow a set time schedule, which allows you to hit the breakfast and/or lunch rush of that area and then leave when the rush is over. You can maximize revenue and minimize staffing costs because you know exactly when you're going to be busy.

Office locations also offer great potential for delivery business and catering jobs.

TIP

Areas that are specifically for offices, like the Financial District of Manhattan, are more viable than ones with a lot of offices but multiple functions, like Midtown Manhattan. That's because areas that service several functions have higher rents, and the local food businesses will give you problems if you steal their piece of the customers' spend. If you can get into a spot, make sure you do everything you can to ensure that local food merchants aren't hostile.

Residential Buildings

Large residential developments, especially in budding neighborhoods, are ideal for food trucks. These areas are better for breakfast and dinner, because you can catch the traffic of people leaving for and returning from work. During the middle of the day they'll generally be slow; I don't advise targeting them for lunch.

Developing neighborhoods are often underserved by food businesses, and residents are looking for more food options. If you gain a following in a developing neighborhood, you'll become a staple and, eventually, be a prime candidate for expansion into a bricks-and-mortar location in the district. Delivery is also a prime opportunity in these up-and-coming locations.

Large Events

Concerts, sporting events, carnivals, festivals, and other events that draw large crowds are perfect for food trucks. These happenings bring tremendous volumes of people to a particular location for a set period of time. With the right location and product, they can spell massive profits for a food truck operator. Depending on the event, you may have to be invited by the organizers or pay a fee for access, but sometimes you can just park around the corner and ride the hype.

Recently food truck operators and local organizations have begun creating large events focused on bringing together groups of food trucks in a particular place and marketing it as a festival. Usually they're advertised in the food press and on food blogs and include additional live entertainment. Such events often sell group tickets that allow customers to sample items from all the trucks for one price . Although you are required to pay a fee to participate in these events, they can lead to big revenues outside of your usual spots.

Dorms and College Buildings

Students are the ideal food truck customers. They typically embrace the counterculture, love to try new things, and are looking for a quick fix to quench their hunger. Options for food in and around dormitories and school buildings is typically limited to sub-par cafeteria grub, making these ideal locations for creating a spot that could be yours for years to come. The key is to create relationships and become part of the school's culture.

TRUCK TALES

The Hot Truck has been serving the Ivy League campus of Cornell University since 1960. Founded by Bob Petrillose, it was named to differentiate it from rivals that sold only cold items. Petrillose decided soon after opening his truck that he could be much more profitable serving only one item: Pizza Subs, made from buttered French bread covered with a variety of toppings, which students affectionately refer to as a poor man's pizza (PMP). Bob sold PMPs until his passing in 2008. Since then the Shortstop Deli has run the truck.

Seasonal Locations

Boardwalks, beaches, pumpkin patches, and ski resorts are all ideal locations for food trucks. These areas become super busy during a particular time of year and generally have limited infrastructure to support the traffic they get at those times. They're generally good weekend spots because they receive a lot of leisure business on off days, making them a great balance for spots where you get more weekday traffic. The Ditch Witch in Montauk, New York, has a prime example of this type of spot. She's been supplying grub such as breakfast burritos, iced coffee, and sesame noodle salad to surfers on the Ditch Plains Beach for over 20 years.

A word to the wise: vendors often pay a lot of money to operate concessions in seasonal locations like beaches. You won't be popular with them if you cannibalize their business.

Nightspots

When people drink, they love to eat. Parking outside nightclubs and bars is a perfect option for a late-night location. Every city has areas that are packed after 10 P.M., and it's your job to locate them. I suggest parking for two to three hours before closing time. That's when people are looking for food, and you'll be there to serve them.

Food Truck Lots

With the introduction of legislation that regulates and limits locations where food trucks can park (see Chapter 8), food truck lots have begun to spring up. These are typically vacant lots located close to major office complexes. You're required to pay a rental fee for access, but there's no average rate, because these businesses are so new.

The lots operate like outdoor food courts, and it is your job to differentiate yourself from the rest of the trucks in the lot. How successful your involvement in a lot will be depends on its location, the rental fee, how many other trucks are involved, and the amount of traffic it attracts.

Determining Where You're Allowed to Park

Now that you know where you should be parking, it's time for the next step, finding out where you're *allowed* to park. Regulations differ from city to city and state to state. Generally, food trucks can park in metered parking spots, but beyond that each area has its own laws, often antiquated, that govern street vending businesses, and some actually have no regulations at all.

Recall that in Washington, D.C, the rule is that you can only solicit customers who flag you down. Although this law was created 35 years ago to govern ice-cream trucks, it's still on the books and very much enforced. Once a customer "flags you down" (whatever that means), you can serve customers, but if no one's waiting you have to leave. If you don't follow this regulation you'll be subject to "fines and potential revocation of your license." You can imagine this makes it very difficult to flourish as a food truck operator in Washington, D.C., but where there's a will there's a way, and the D.C. food truck scene is very lively.

> **TRUCK TALES**
>
> New York City recently had a massive crackdown on food trucks. A judge reinforced an antiquated regulation that states "no vendor, hawker, or huckster shall park a vehicle at a metered parking space to offer merchandise for sale from that vehicle." The police are enforcing the law, and food trucks now have little or no place to park. This is a prime example of backlash from bricks-and-mortar businesses and neighborhood groups, and only time will tell whether food trucks will be able to once again flourish in New York City.

Laws are constantly changing and being reinterpreted based on the food truck revolution. Regulations haven't and probably won't come close to catching up with the boom because politicians and business owners are still deciding whether the industry is good for their interests and those of the surrounding community. In many cities, food truckers have formed associations, such as the New York Food Truck Association (nycfoodtrucks.org) to protect themselves and fight for their rights. The success of the trucking industry has brought attention both good and bad. It's crucial that the industry work together to be viewed as a legitimate trade.

In order to find out the policies governing locations where mobile food businesses can park in your local area, contact the local department of transportation or similar governing body. (For example, in Miami it's the Department of Planning and Zoning.) In larger municipalities you might be able to find the information you need online. For example, try typing "food truck parking regulations" and the name of your city in a search engine such as Google.

In some places food truckers are being regulated out of business. Check your local parking regulations prior to jumping into the business. You don't want to spend your days fighting tickets and regulators rather than sharing your passion with your customers.

BEEP! BEEP!

When you're calculating your financials, it's important that you budget for parking violations. They're part of doing business, and tickets can run from $15 to $150, depending on where you are, and can add up very quickly. Even worse, if you don't pay your tickets you can end up with larger fines or even jail time. Be aware of local laws and do whatever you can to keep your fines to a minimum. It would be a shame if you worked all day slinging delicious food just to pay your profits to the state or city.

Considering Traffic

The key to choosing any spot for your food truck is to observe the traffic in that location. Rather than throwing caution to the wind and randomly choosing spots through trial and error, it's far better to take a strategic approach.

Pick five neighborhoods and take the time to scout them out. See what days and times they're busy and when they're slow. Observe the competition in the area and consider the following factors:

- **Parking:** Find out the local regulations and choose three spots in the neighborhood that will work for you. See what times those spots tend to be available. Based on what you observe, you may have to send someone ahead of you to hold the spot you most want.

- **Exposure to traffic:** The right location within the neighborhood can make all the difference in gaining exposure to the traffic you're looking for. It's the same reason people pay extra for corners or stores on high-traffic streets—they are exposed to more potential customers. Every day you're going to act as your own real estate broker, scouting the top spots for your business. You should also take into account where the majority of your customers are coming from. The closer you can get to that place, the easier it will be for you to service them.

- **Type of traffic:** Be on the lookout for businesses that attract similar crowds to your target customers. All the traffic in the world doesn't do you any good if the people aren't interested in the type of food you're selling. If you sell juices, smoothies, and health food, doesn't it make sense to park outside a popular gym or yoga studio? They service groups of people who are in to eating healthy.

Knowing Locations to Avoid

Just as there are prime locations to park your food truck, there are also locations you should avoid.

Low-Traffic Areas

The most obvious locations to avoid are ones without a lot of traffic. Some people like to buck the trends, believing that they alone can draw the masses with their incredible food and drinks. Please don't be one of them; if you were to succeed it would be out of blind luck. The reason store owners pay high rents in certain districts is because that's where the customers are.

All the marketing in the world won't make your food truck a success in a bad location on a consistent basis, and you need to focus on consistency. Successful food businesses are about moving a lot of product on a regular basis. Weeks of generating a minimal profit daily won't add up to a substantial profit monthly or yearly.

Restaurant Rows

Even though restaurant rows can be very busy, you should avoid them. Areas where a lot of restaurants are competing for the customers' food dollars aren't ideal for food trucks. The average restaurant owner has a bigger budget and larger facilities and will generally be very hostile to someone who isn't paying rent while trying to steal his or her customers.

The most unethical thing for a food truck is to park in front of a restaurant that serves the same cuisine—a falafel truck parked in front of a Middle Eastern restaurant, for example. I can see the logic in trying to attract those customers, but it's so incredibly wrong that obstacles are bound to arise. Anything gained through unethical practices generally is lost through the reaction from customers and the restaurant community. As a member of the hospitality community, it's your responsibility to protect and support your brothers and sisters.

Looking at Other Businesses in the Area

One of the most important considerations when choosing a location for your food truck is what other businesses are in the area. Being accepted into the community is key to your success, so do everything in your power to be seen as a positive addition to the neighborhood.

The worst thing that can happen to you as a truck operator is to be seen as the enemy. It's very easy for a restaurant owner to get angry because he or she thinks you're stealing customers during his or her busiest time of the day, especially because you aren't paying rent.

As a community member, your business must add to the long-term prosperity of your district. Not only must you be friendly, but you must become an active member of the organizations that govern commerce there. You should attend meetings and make your presence felt by becoming involved in the actions taken.

To initiate personal relationships, drop off care packages and introduce yourself to all the area merchants. Make sure that if they have an issue with you or your truck, they come directly to you rather than involving the authorities. This gives you the opportunity to remedy the situation instead of creating larger issues.

Take the time to establish mutually beneficial partnerships with local businesses. Let's say you park your sweets truck near a local pottery store that hosts children's birthday parties every Saturday or Sunday. A mutually beneficial partnership could involve your parking in front of their location on weekends and supplying the parties with cupcakes.

If you operate a sandwich truck and there's a construction site in the area that's isolated from local restaurants, strike a deal to show up every day at a certain time to sell to the crew. These are the kinds of things that help your business and also show support to the community. By focusing on helping the neighborhood—in addition to generating profits—you will experience greater long-term success.

TIP

You can leverage your Twitter following and e-mail database to build partnerships. You have customers, and other businesses would love access to them. Approach a clothing store with a similar demographic that's planning a big sale and agree to tell your customers about it if they'll allow you to sell your food outside for the duration. With the right store you'll both benefit without cannibalizing each other's business, because your products are distinctly different. If things work, out you'll get yourself an awesome parking spot and a boatload of new customers. Wait till the other stores hear about you!

Building Your Spots

After you've identified your regular parking places, it's vital that you build them, cultivating the local clientele to build regular business in that location. Even though you don't have a store, you must use the same methods as a bricks-and-mortar business to create local awareness. You want to use the cachet of the food truck while creating the perception of a restaurant that's in the same spot every day. If you do, you'll have your cake—mobility—and eat it too by being perceived as being just as reliable as competing food businesses.

Here are some methods for cultivating your business in a particular spot:

- **Social media:** Announce your exact location and the times that you'll be there each day on your Twitter, Facebook, and Foursquare pages.

- **Website:** Have a section called "Weekly Spots," preferably on the main landing page, dedicated to your regular locations, including a link to a website like Google Maps that shows exactly where you are. Check out korillabbq.com for an example of how to do it.

- **Competitions and promotions:** Establish promotions that are related to specific locations. You might want to offer complimentary cupcakes to the first 20 lunch customers every day, for example. Whatever the promotion, more customers will come when you have a line, so attracting those initial customers to drive business is critical.

BEEP! BEEP!

Although promotions are a good way to generate business, don't overdo them. Make sure your promotions don't cheapen your brand with too much discounting; you always want people to think of your product as an object of desire.

- **Menu distribution:** Drop off menus and promotional flyers at surrounding businesses. Invest in printing something that represents your brand positively and will make an impact. Include a coupon to generate a first visit to the truck.

- **Location-based e-mail lists:** Segment your e-mail lists to create separate ones for each place you park, then send an e-mail blast to the people in that location on the days you'll be there. Build your lists by offering an incentive to customers for signing up, like a free lunch or a catered private party for their office for customer #500. Enter the e-mails into a spreadsheet and use an application like enflyer.com to distribute your blasts.

TIP

Mass e-mail applications like enflyer.com and ConstantContact.com let you store addresses and send marketing materials to large groups of customers with relative ease. These types of applications generally charge a monthly fee, ranging from $30 to $250 per month, based on how often you send out your e-mails. The software also gives you in-depth information about who is opening your e-mails so you can monitor performance. With proper management these sites are well worth the investment.

- **Sampling:** The first four to six times you visit any spot, you should offer a special or free sampling of your signature items. Your goal is to create a following in that neighborhood, and what better way to get people hooked on your great product than allowing them to taste it? If you've got it, flaunt it.

- **Location-specific menu items:** Establish menu items that are only available in certain locations. For instance, if you're selling sliders, when you're parked on the Lower East Side of Manhattan offer a signature Lower East Slider only at that location. Make sure that item is particularly spectacular and you'll end up with press and customers coming from other neighborhoods just to try it.

- *Customer relationship management:* Do everything you can to know your regular customers in every location. Keep notes on their preferences, or give them something a little extra with their order. Anything you do to give them the best experience will make them your most valuable advertisers.

DEFINITION

Customer Relationship Management (CRM) is a widely implemented strategy for managing relationships with customers. Create a document explaining how all employees should interact with your customers, and require all of your employees to read it. The goal of CRM is to find and attract new customers, nurture and retain current customers, and entice former customers back.

The Least You Need to Know

- High-traffic and under-serviced areas are the best locations for food trucks.
- Knowing the local laws for every spot is your responsibility.
- Be a good member of your community; it will pay off in the short and long term.
- Cultivate the clientele in every place you park so your spots become your neighborhoods.

The Mobile Food Mogul

Now that I've covered the basics, it's time to take your ideas and turn them into a concrete business plan. No one is going to take you seriously unless you're able to clearly articulate your plan to them, and you won't find investors to back you unless you can create financial forecasts that show you can be profitable. If you want to be a mobile food mogul, you need to understand all aspects of the food business, and I'm going to explain them to you.

The next step is to get a grasp on regulations and licensing. The food business involves a tremendous amount of regulation from your local health department. These laws protect consumers from food that isn't properly handled or prepared. Because your business is on wheels, you're also subject to regulation by your local department of transportation. Knowing how to navigate these bureaucracies is crucial to your success as a food truck operator.

And just when you thought you were ready to serve, I get to my favorite subject, marketing. How are you going to get customers to show up at your truck? Because trucks are known for the way they use social media, I show you how to use Twitter, Facebook, and great public relations to become the darling of bloggers and foodies.

Preparing Your Business Plan

In This Chapter

- Finding out what makes a good business plan
- Looking at your plan from the perspective of an investor
- Projecting sales, expenses, and profits
- Choosing the right structure for your business

You don't need to be an architect to appreciate the fundamental importance of having a blueprint to build a skyscraper. Imagine trying to construct a building without detailed plans, measurements, and diagrams: how would you know what materials to buy, how many men to hire, or even how to lay the first bricks of the foundation with only a vague vision of the final structure? In building your business, you need to design similar blueprints. Such blueprints constitute your business plan.

Writing a business plan forces you to clearly define your concept, brand, menu, and market so that you know exactly where you're going and how you're going to get there. It's also the first step toward finding capital to finance your food truck, which I cover in Chapter 7. Ultimately, a well-thought-out business plan saves you time and money throughout the start-up, launch, and long-term operation of your truck; helps you anticipate problems; and keeps you from getting in your own way.

In this chapter, I show you how a good business plan can help you make important decisions about your food truck. I cover how to predict your costs, sales and profits, and the pros and cons of different ways to structure your business.

Why a Business Plan Matters

Writing a business plan forces you to make very crucial decisions about your business. It's not enough to have a vision in your head; by putting that vision down on paper, you clearly define for yourself and potential investors the details of your concept and the reality of your start-up costs and profitability.

The four most basic questions a business plan should answer are as follows:

- What is your concept?

- Where is your market?

- What are the start-up and operating costs of your business?

- How much money is your food truck going to make?

In the process of answering these questions, you'll come across others that you need to consider as well. Respond to all these questions in your business plan so that you're prepared when investors, vendors, and employees ask them later. Your business plan should clearly articulate your experience as well as your goals and ideas for making your goals a reality. The more thorough your business plan is, the better prepared you'll be to accurately predict costs and anticipate problems down the road.

TIP

Because food trucks are a relatively new industry, you need to clearly explain them as a business concept in your business plan. Here are some of the questions you should answer about food trucks in your business plan:

- What is a food truck?
- Why are you starting a food truck instead of a bricks-and-mortar restaurant?
- What's your long-term goal?
- Do you plan to have additional trucks or open actual restaurants?
- What are the local regulations regarding food trucks? Are they changing?
- Will you be working on the truck yourself or will employees be operating while you manage?

Even if you intend to finance your food truck yourself, a business plan helps you determine whether or not your idea can become a profitable business; it also serves as a useful resource you can refer to in order to make sure your decisions are consistent with your original intention and associated projections. Having this plan helps you remain focused on your goals and makes it easier to achieve them. If you can't answer basic questions about your business's identity, intended market, and projected financials, it isn't realistic to think you'll be able to build your business. Take the time to analyze things from the point of view of a potential investor. By removing your emotional attachment to your idea you'll be able to make more accurate analyses. This will save you a lot of time, energy, and money in the long run.

Describing Your Concept, Brand, and Market

In Chapter 3, I discuss the importance of having a clearly defined concept and menu that are designed with a niche market in mind. In the first part of your business plan, you must articulate what your food truck brand is going to be:

- What specifically is your concept?

- What is your niche market?

- How are you different from other food trucks and neighborhood restaurants?

In this part, don't be concerned with the financial calculations related to your business; instead, try to communicate your food truck's identity as clearly as possible and define your target market.

Your Identity

Your food truck's identity is a fusion of three components that should overlap and inform each other:

Menu theme. Do you specialize in Japanese-inspired vegetarian fare? Guatemalan tamales? Or perhaps you've reinvented the American comfort food favorites of your childhood. Whatever you choose, successful food trucks always specialize in a niche cuisine. Describe how your food is unique in the market and unique unto itself, but be sure that it's consistent with a single theme.

Personality. How will your food truck present itself? What do you envision for its design and the presentation of the food? What message do you want to communicate visually to passersby and how? How will you and your personality integrate into your concept? Whatever your vision, it should be consistent with the theme of your menu and attractive to your target clientele.

Philosophy. Every business owner has life stories, beliefs, or a philosophy that informs his or her product. This personal aspect is often his or her motivation for going into business in the first place. If you're environmentally conscious, perhaps you want your food to be locally sourced; sustainable and organic; and your plates, cups, and utensils to be 100 percent compostable. Or maybe all of your menu items are your grandmother's original recipes, and you want to honor her in your business. These personal aspects are critical for building a strong brand identity and should be reflected in your menu and design.

If your truck's menu, personality, and philosophy aren't in sync, your target clientele won't get the message. Writing out this section of your business plan helps you discover any areas of your concept that aren't consistent with your truck vision. This is the time to reconsider aspects of your menu, design, and operation to make sure everything is working toward the same goal. As you write, you'll see your food truck's identity begin to emerge. The more detailed the profile is, the more confidence you and others will have in the concept.

TIP

If you intend to seek a bank loan or private investment, be sure to include a detailed description of your business experience, especially within the food industry. You're less of a financial risk if you can demonstrate that you know what you're doing or have done it before.

Your Market

After you've clearly defined your identity, you must determine whom your brand is going to attract. Describe your target clientele in your business plan, including where these people typically eat, live, and work in your intended locations.

You want to be sure that there'll be a large enough customer base for your niche product. There's no point in selling the best Indian food in Athens, Georgia, if there's no demand for it there. Consider other food businesses near your intended locations and in the food truck market that share your menu theme or message. Ask yourself if there are enough customers to go around, and if you believe they'll want what you're selling.

With that said, some of the most successful entrepreneurs are great at identifying needs that don't currently exist. You need to demonstrate your belief in your food truck idea and then back it up with the facts behind the reason and be ready to supply them when investors ask.

> **TIP**
>
> Statistics and facts about the food truck industry and the general food market-place are very helpful in establishing the need for your product. Unfortunately, it's difficult to locate facts on the food truck business from reputable sources, in part because the industry is still very young. When looking for information for your business plan, you can use general food business resources. Check out the National Restaurant Industry Operations report for detailed facts on all segments of the business. It's produced annually by the National Restaurant Association.

Your Competition

Once you've established that there's a market for your brand, you must determine if you can be competitive within that market.

First, list your direct competitors, which consists of the nearby trucks and restaurants that offer a concept similar to yours. Compare their locations, hours, and prices to your own.

Next, list your indirect competitors—those trucks and restaurants whose products are entirely different from yours but who are still competing for the same customer base.

If you're selling vegetarian lunches, you aren't just competing with all the other vegetarian restaurants in the area (direct); you're also competing with any restaurant or food truck that's open for lunch (indirect). See Chapter 5 for more information on how to analyze the market for your desired location.

After you've listed your competition, you need to explain how and why you're going to gain a competitive advantage over them. Why is your product better? Do you have the e-mail addresses of 50,000 local residents? Do you have a ready-made catering business because of your recent position at a catering company? Whatever it is, use this opportunity to clarify for yourself and your investors why your truck will do better than the competition.

Forecasting Sales

Regardless of how mouthwatering your menu or heartwarming your message, the only thing most investors are really interested in when considering a business proposal is the bottom line. Profitability should also be your primary concern; no matter how in love you are with your concept, if it can't generate enough money to cover expenses, pay back investors, and make a profit, there's no point in even beginning the process. Everything always comes back to the bottom line. Businesses exist to make money. Unless you have a rich uncle who wants to indulge your passions, it's all about the Benjamins, baby.

Learning to project sales and costs is a valuable and necessary skill for any small business owner. Not only will you use financial projections to interest investors in your business plan, you'll also use them to predict sales and expenses every month for as long as you're in business. You can create a simple spreadsheet or use specialized software program like QuickBooks. They don't have to be perfect, and they certainly don't have to be fancy. You're just giving your best guess as to what kind of revenue your business will bring in. Although no one expects you to be Nostradamus and predict the future, you must be able to demonstrate to yourself and to any potential investors that your concept can generate enough sales to cover expenses and become profitable.

Estimate your sales forecast before determining your start-up costs so you know how much money you have available to spend. To forecast sales accurately, you should have already designed and priced your menu. Begin by determining a plausible *check average*.

DEFINITION

Your **check average** is the average amount each customer spends.

Put yourself into the shoes of your customers. Would most people have to order more than one item on your menu to be satisfied? Do you offer appetizers or side dishes? Do you expect dessert to be a big hit? Calculate an average check that includes a beverage. This number should reflect what you realistically expect the average person to order, not necessarily what you would ideally want him or her to order. If your average dish is $7, your sides are $2, and sodas are $1, a reasonable check average for the purpose of sales forecasting would be $10.

Now multiply your check average by the number of customers you expect to serve each day. Because it's impossible to accurately guess the number of customers you'll have on any given day, always pad your sales projections with the following three sets of figures:

- **A best-case scenario:** your sales if everything goes according to plan

- **A worst-case scenario:** your sales if everything goes wrong

- **A split-the-difference scenario**: your sales fall halfway between the best and worst cases

Here's what it looks like in a simple spreadsheet:

Calculating Your Daily and Weekly Check Average

	Sun.	Mon.	Tue.	Wed.	Thu.	Fri.	Sat.	Average	Total
				(Best)					
Covers	30	40	40	40	40	40	30	37	260
Ch/Av	$10	$12	$12	$12	$12	$12	$10	$11.43	$3,000
				(Worst)					
Covers	5	10	10	10	10	10	5	9	60
Ch/Av	$2	$5	$5	$5	$5	$5	$2	$4.5	$270
				(Split)					
Covers	20	30	30	30	30	30	20	27	190
Ch/Av	$6	$8	$8	$8	$8	$8	$6	$7.58	$1,440

BEEP! BEEP!

Always take the calendar and the climate into consideration when forecasting sales. If your food truck is on the streets of a northeastern city, December through February are going to slow down as people avoid walking in the snow. This must be reflected in your figures so you can prepare your business for the seasonal decline in revenue.

Forecasting Expenses

You can't expect to be profitable for at least six months after the launch of your food truck, so I can't overstate the value of a highly detailed and well-padded expense forecast. Failure to adequately anticipate every possible start-up and operating expense, as well as emergencies, can be devastating. Fortunately, you can predict most of those costs before you even write your business plan if you're diligent in doing your research.

Your business plan should include at least a full year forecast of operating expenses, including your salary and a decent cushion for emergencies, repairs, and worst-case scenarios. I prefer to break them down by week, month, and year. As I did with the sales forecast, include three sets of figures: one optimistic, one pessimistic, and one realistic. Your first-year projection must, of course, also include your start-up costs, which I show you how to estimate in Chapter 7.

> **TIP**
>
> When I say anticipate everything, I mean *everything,* down to the aluminum foil, paperclips, cleaning supplies, debt interest, postage and delivery, gasoline, payroll processing, deposit fees, employee meals, and parking. Many first-time food truckers overlook these things when they plan their businesses. The more you're able to predict now, the less surprised you will be when it's time to pay the bills.

Most of your expenses are controllable, meaning that you can lower or raise them based on your business needs. (However, keep in mind that in less experienced hands, controllable expenses can get out of hand.) Here's a partial list of controllable expenses you can budget for right now:

- **Payroll:** Beyond wages for salaried and hourly employees, you must include payroll taxes, worker's comp insurance, and benefits, some of which won't kick in until you're up and running.

- **Cost of Sales:** These are the costs of the actual ingredients that make up your products, including beverages. I'm not suggesting you compromise quality for cost, but be aware of rising food prices and adjust your ordering or menu accordingly.

- **Utilities:** Water and electricity are considered controllable expenses because all businesses have the flexibility to conserve them.

- **Operating Inventory:** This includes nearly everything that doesn't fall under cost of sales, such as cleaning supplies, order pads, uniforms, paper plates, utensils, straws, napkins, cups, and a thousand other small items that are easy to overlook when planning your start-up costs.

- **Administrative Expenses:** These include credit cards, banking and attorney's fees, phones, office supplies, and postage.

- **Marketing:** Unless you're already famous, there's no such thing as free publicity. Always budget for advertising and turn to Chapter 9 for ideas on how to design a profitable marketing strategy for your truck.

Determining Your Breakeven

Very simply, your breakeven point is when you generate enough revenue to cover all your expenses. Investors will ask you when you expect to break even, so you need to have this information ready. By determining your breakeven, you can see if your sales will be high enough to finance your operating costs.

To determine your breakeven point, you must already have done your sales and expense forecasts. If you've entered these projections into a spreadsheet, generate a line that contrasts both sets of values for one year. You can now see how much you need to make to cover your overhead. If your sales forecast consistently falls below your projected expenses, try to adjust your costs. If that isn't enough, reconsider your menu, pricing, or overall concept.

Estimating Profits

Your estimated profit is the number your investors are going to be the most interested in. Calculating it is easy: simply subtract your total projected expenses from your total projected sales. The remaining sum is your profit.

If you aren't seeing a profit, stop right there! Try to reduce your expenses to bring them under your projected sales. If you can't break even or make a profit, go back to the drawing board and revise your concept. Your prices may be too low, your menu too big, or your location inappropriate for the niche market you want to tap into. Determining your potential for profit now will save you a lot of time, money, and frustration in the short and long term.

Choosing Your Business Structure

You don't have to decide on a business structure right away, but this is a good time to begin to think about how you want to structure the ownership of your business. How you choose to register your food truck—as a sole proprietorship, a partnership, or a corporation—determines how you'll receive your income, how your business pays taxes, and who will be responsible should your business fail.

It's useful to know in which direction you want to go so you can tailor your business plan with that goal in mind. Whatever you decide, you should work with an attorney to register your business accordingly.

Sole Proprietorship

A sole proprietorship means that a single individual owns the business. If you choose to register as a sole proprietor, you'll be personally responsible for any losses or debts incurred by your business. You get to keep all the profit, but if your business loses $50,000, the bank can take your personal assets to pay the debt. It's a very risky scenario and definitely not recommended in the modern business world. With all the things that can go wrong on your truck, you want to limit your personal liability.

Partnership

In a partnership, you share ownership and risk with one or more investors and split the profits according to a predetermined agreement.

A partner may invest time, money, expertise, or a combination of all three. You can set up a partnership in many ways, but be sure you agree from day one on your roles and responsibilities, and the expectations you have for each other. You must also determine what stake your partner will have in the company and how you will share the profits.

TIP

It's crucial that you agree on a hierarchy and determine who has the ultimate authority when it comes to decision-making. There's no room in a food truck for competing egos. Choose someone who shares your vision and decide now who will be in charge.

A partnership won't protect you from personal liability; only a corporation will. A partnership with the right person is always a great idea, though it might not be under this business structure. I talk more about partnerships in Chapter 7.

Limited Partnership

A limited partnership is very much like taking on a *silent partner*. In the agreement a silent partner is protected from any financial or legal liability should the business fail and risks only his investment.

> **DEFINITION**
>
> A **silent partner** is an investor who isn't involved with the operation of the business.

Silent partners, however, have a tendency to speak up if they feel their investment is threatened. Be sure to put the terms of your agreement in writing and specify who has the authority to make decisions about the operation of the business. You don't want a panicked investor meddling in your business or fighting you for control.

Corporation

Some small business owners choose to incorporate, forming a corporate structure that owns the business and pays them a salary. Incorporation offers you a legal cushion should your food truck fail, but you'll be taxed twice: once on corporate profits and again on your income. If you're just starting out, your bank will likely require you to assume personal liability for any loans to your corporation, so your financial risk remains unalleviated even when you incorporate your business.

All things considered, I recommend incorporation. Even though it can lead to high taxation, the protection it gives you is invaluable. Having a corporation is like having another identity; it separates you personally from you the business. If something goes wrong with you the business, you the person and all your personal assets are protected. You'll live to fight another day, and that's how I like it.

Talk to your attorney about the benefits and risks of forming a corporation.

The Least You Need to Know

- Your business plan is a document you'll refer back to often, and it's a crucial instrument for approaching outside investors.
- A good business plan includes information about the concept and identity of your food truck as well as forecasts for sales, expenses, and profits.
- You need a legal structure for your food truck business, and the only way you can protect yourself personally from business losses is to incorporate.

Finding Financing

In This Chapter

- Figuring out your start-up and operating costs
- Determining how much of your own money to invest
- Approaching partners or other outside investors
- Assessing the availability of bank loans and government assistance
- Looking into sponsorship possibilities

Now that you've defined your vision in your business plan, including menu, design concept, and possible locations, it's time to secure the cash to make it a reality. Finding financing for a food truck is no easy task. Many people want to invest in hospitality businesses purely for vanity. They dream of hanging out with their friends at their very own restaurant, especially those with monotonous jobs that don't fulfill their passion. The reality is that most outside investors in restaurants and similar food businesses never see their money back.

From the perspective of investors, food trucks are more attractive than other hospitality businesses because they can be a relatively low investment with the potential for high returns and spin-offs like bricks-and-mortar restaurants. Your job is to sell outside investors on your dream: that for a small initial investment, they can get in on the next big thing in the food business. Not only that, but there will be incredible potential for expansion and growth. But no matter how good your numbers or your plan, ultimately investors will only put their money behind your business idea if they believe in and like you.

Start-up costs vary with the details of your concept, but in this chapter I help you estimate your initial expenses and set a dollar goal. Then I describe several strategies for reaching that number, including finding an investor, seeking a loan, and the pros and cons of tapping into your own personal savings. Finally I discuss some creative ways to leverage business relationships to free up capital and even extend your credit.

Knowing How Much Money You Need

Before you can borrow money or approach an investor, you have to determine how much money you're going to need. Estimating start-up costs is a challenge for aspiring and seasoned food truckers alike.

TIP

Once you accept money from investors, you have to continue to prove to them that you deserve their trust and confidence. As you manage and operate your truck, put yourself in their shoes and anticipate their concerns. Don't allow anything that can be interpreted as wasteful, unprofessional, or potentially threatening to your investors' bottom line to spur them to interfere with the way you run your business.

Your expenses are determined by the nature of your menu, locations, and the complexity of your truck's vision. There are, however, many food truck universals and one-time purchases that you can predict to help calculate your start-up total. In general, operators need between $100,000 and $125,000 to properly start a food truck, including purchasing and building a truck and operating capital to launch and manage it until it becomes profitable.

Calculating Your Start-Up Costs

Begin by listing all the inventory items, equipment, and services you require before you open for business. If your menu, design, and overall concept are clearly defined, you should be able to make reasonably accurate cost predictions. Use the following list, with my best estimates provided, to approximate a rough start-up figure if you don't know your actual expense:

Expense	Cost
Advertising	$5,000
Design	$2,500
Electrical and awnings	$10,000
General operating capital (gas, staff, salary, food and beverages, tickets, insurance)	$25,000–50,000
Inventory (ingredients, beverages, plates, utensils, napkins, etc.)	$2,500
Kitchen supplies (pots, pans, grease mats, etc.)	$3,000
Labor to customize truck	$10,000-15,000
Legal fees	$1,000–5,000
Permits (dependent on location)	$1,500–10,000
Restaurant equipment (stove, sink, fryer, refrigerators, grill, exhaust fan, etc.)	$15,000–20,000
Truck	$10,000–15,000
Truck wrapping	$5,000

Calculating Operating Capital

No matter how strong your concept, menu, and advertising campaigns are, you'll continue to need money well after you launch your truck. It's important to have conservative expectations for the amount of revenue you'll bring in during the first few months and to set aside operating capital to cover expenses during that time. Almost every new food business requires time to hone its operation, refine its menu and pricing, and build a loyal clientele. If you allow yourself an adequate financial cushion, you can use this period to perfect your concept without unnecessary stress.

When preparing your business plan and start-up estimate, assume that you won't become profitable for several months. Set aside an appropriate safety net—at least $25,000 to $50,000—to cover all your operating expenses, payroll, and advertising, and a weekly salary to cover your own living expenses for the first six months. This cushion should also allow for any unforeseen repairs, upgrades, or changes in inventory as your operation and menu evolve.

Determining Your Contribution

Regardless of how profitable your idea may appear to potential investors, you'll need to invest a considerable amount of your own money into your new enterprise. You must take a corresponding level of financial risk to back your passion if you want investors to take you seriously. When your own money is on the line, you'll find yourself even more motivated to succeed, and it's that determination that will inspire confidence in investors.

Using your own money has numerous additional benefits as well. If you choose not to seek help from investors, you don't have to divide control of your business with people who may not share your vision. It can be very tedious, not to mention disheartening, to have to answer to others when you're the one doing all the work to realize a personal dream. Should you want to alter your concept, menu, pricing, or locations, those decisions will be yours and yours alone. You'll be able to take pride in knowing that your food truck's success is a reflection of your own dedication, creativity, and the risks you were willing to take.

BEEP! BEEP!

Be very cautious when using credit cards to finance your start-up inventory and operation. You don't want to incur high interest charges or destroy your credit rating. While credit cards can be convenient short-term solutions with some real benefits, like frequent flyer miles and cash points, I recommend saving them for the occasional (but inevitable) crisis: theft, equipment failure, or truck damage. There will be times when you'll have to pay for immediate repairs and seek reimbursement from your insurance company later, a process that can take several weeks or months. Avoid the trap in which too many small business owners have been caught and always regard credit cards as your last and least-desirable finance option.

But before you invest your retirement savings and your child's college fund, remember that risk also means risk of failure. Should your food truck not succeed, you could jeopardize your savings, your credit, and your assets. Always allow for the worst possible outcome when making any investment. Making a business plan, even if you're financing the project yourself, will help you spend thoughtfully and predictably, and can alleviate waste, confusion, and surprise. (See Chapter 6 for information on writing a business plan.)

Identifying Investors

Don't feel bad if you can't (or don't want to) finance your food truck venture all by yourself. You can seek financing from many different kinds of investors, from partners to friends and family, but there are important things to consider when seeking outside funds to feed some green into your food truck dreams.

Potential Partners

A partner is an investor who actively participates in the formation and/or operation of your food truck, as opposed to an investor or silent partner, who is distinctly less hands-on. A partner may invest money, expertise, some other financial service, or his or her reputation, filling a void and strengthening your overall concept and operation. A partner doesn't just invest money in your success; she invests her skills, experience, and sometimes her name and personality. It's important to choose the right partner for the right reasons. You want someone who won't just bet on you but increase the odds in your favor.

If you want to bring on a partner, consider your biggest weaknesses and seek someone whose skills can fill those voids. Here are some examples of areas where a partner can fill a void for you:

- **Culinary experience:** If you lack culinary experience, consider bringing on an accomplished chef as a partner/consultant to help develop your menu, streamline the inventory, and train your staff.

- **Business/accounting:** If you lack confidence on the business and accounting end of the operation, consider finding a partner with strong bookkeeping or fundraising skills who can manage the books, negotiate with vendors, secure loans and investments, or handle legal matters and paperwork with ease.

- **Name recognition:** You might seek a partner because he or she can lend his or her name and reputation to your venture. With a "celebrity" partner attached to your business plan, you can access investors, earn free publicity, and build a tremendous buzz on the local culinary scene.

You can similarly seek partners with marketing expertise, food truck experience, or restaurant management skills.

It's crucial, however, that whoever your partner is, there's a clear chain of command that you both mutually agree upon and respect. While the partnership is a collaborative relationship, one person must be in charge so that decisions can be made effectively and problems resolved as efficiently as possible. Many businesses fail because partners haven't clearly defined their roles from the very beginning and later clash, bringing the entire operation to a halt when no decision can be made.

> **TRUCK TALES**
>
> Since its launch in 2010, San Diego–based Devilicious has built an enormous following and attracted more than its share of media attention. Classically trained chef Dyann Huffman partnered with Kristina Repp, a seasoned waitress and restaurant manager, to create mobile fare reminiscent of their childhood comfort food favorites. The friends have turned their combined 38 years of culinary experience into a profitable brand that's widely and wildly blogged and buzzed about, even competing on Food Network's *The Great Truck Race*. Interviews with Huffman reveal a distinct division of labor based on each partner's expertise and a shared love for "devilish comfort food," as she describes it. They're the perfect example of an effective partnership: two passionate women, two skill sets, a single vision.

Silent Partners

Outside investors who agree to be silent partners invest cash but have little say in how a food truck is run. Once the business is launched, it's common for investors to break their silence in an effort to protect their returns. It's very important, as with taking on a partner, to clearly define your roles in the business from day one.

Family and Friends

You've probably been cautioned never to do business with family and friends, and for good reasons: it's a recipe for financial and emotional disaster. It's very difficult to hold our loved ones accountable, especially when it comes to something as vulgar as money.

Your family and friends are a wonderful resource for guidance and inspiration but not for capital. If you must seek money from them, be sure to put everything in writing, just as you would structure any other business deal.

What You Need to Show Potential Investors

In order to attract outside investors, you'll need to have a business plan. The materials you prepare for them should be concise: What are you doing? Why are you doing it? How are you going to do it? And will it make money?

Potential investors will expect to see the following:

- A business plan of no more than 10 pages
- Estimated start-up costs
- How much money you need from them
- How soon before they'll see a return on their investment
- How much they can expect to profit
- Your vision of a working relationship with them

How to Structure an Investment

Each investor will have his own preferred method for structuring returns depending on his reasons for investing in your business in the first place. Some investors may want to make a quick buck and seek a short-term compensation deal, while others, perhaps those who love the food business and want to be involved in your operation, will seek a long-term payment plan.

It's important to negotiate a deal that's fair to your investor, fair to you, and puts reasonable pressure and expectations on the business. The terms of your agreement must be clearly outlined in writing and be vetted by your attorney. Don't accept a deal that could potentially overburden your business with unrealistic payments or timelines; this is where a well-researched business plan can save you a lot of grief, confusion, and money. If you suspect that an investor is trying to take advantage of you, he probably is.

A very common way to compensate your investor is to pay her back her initial investment plus interest. There are countless ways to structure these payments, and your investor will have her own preferences depending on how long she wants to stay involved in your business. For example, you may agree to pay back her initial $30,000 stake plus 30 percent interest, for a total of $39,000, over three years. You could plan to pay her 15 percent ($4,500) annually for the first two years and repay the $30,000 principal the third. Or you could agree to pay him $13,000 annually for three years. Whatever you decide, you must be confident that you can satisfy your investor without compromising the business or your own bottom line.

Another way to structure the investment is to offer your investor a percentage of the profits. If his $30,000 investment is worth 30 percent equity in your business, then he receives 30 percent of your profits. He may expect his return in the form of *capital gains* after selling his equity share to you or another partner.

 DEFINITION

Capital gains are the increase in value of a share from the time of the investment to when it's sold. This translates into profit for an investor.

As the business grows, each equity share becomes more valuable, so your investor can sell his stake for more than his initial outlay. Your compensation deal can include a buyout clause, allowing you to regain equity (and control) in your company. You can also structure your partnership so that you acquire more equity in the company incrementally over time without having to invest more cash.

Whatever you decide, it's crucial that you not lose sight of the long-term needs of your business when considering an investment agreement. No amount of start-up capital is worth compromising your company's future with unrealistic payments on an impossible timeline. I'm not asking you to bet against your company's success but rather to bet in its best interest. Always make sure that the terms of your deal are consistent with the most reliable and conservative estimates of your business plan.

Finally, remember that if you have to turn down an investment deal, you'll be able to find another source of capital. Don't get discouraged; in business, it truly is better to be safe than sorry.

Getting a Loan

The food truck industry was already a risky business before the recession, and banks are extremely reluctant to lend money to first-time owners. Those lucky enough to get a loan are usually required to personally guarantee the note, making them responsible for the money regardless of the success or failure of their business.

What You Need to Show the Bank

I'm going to be honest; if you're a first-time food trucker with no other small businesses under your belt, you're going to have a very hard time being approved for a bank loan. You'll probably need to seek private loans, a partnership, or a government-backed loan from the Small Business Administration. Applying for a loan is a critical decision that requires a lot of preparation; make sure you understand all the risks, fees, and procedures before you proceed.

TIP

If you're looking for a partner anyway, seriously consider bringing on someone who owns or has owned a successful food truck. That credential would significantly decrease the financial risk of your venture and boost the bank's confidence in your business plan.

The bank weighs your financial and business records, credit rating, and experience to determine your ability to repay the loan. Your business plan must be thorough and well researched, and include details of your background in the industry in order to convince them that your projected earnings are realistic.

Be prepared to demonstrate not only your experience but also how you intend to use the money you borrow. Discuss what equipment and services you'll buy and how these investments will shape the quality and efficiency of your business. Your explanations should demonstrate to the bank that you know what you're doing and have carefully thought out your spending plan. Banks want to invest in people who are business savvy, fiscally responsible, and qualified in their industry. Someone with a clear strategy is less of a financial risk than an unprepared first-timer just asking for cash.

The bank will also consider your equity in the company; that is, the amount of your own money you have or are prepared to invest. The bank regards this as a security deposit of sorts and an indication of your seriousness. They'll likely review your tax returns and credit history for a general impression of your personal risk. If your credit rating is poor, your risk is high, and you'll have to supply a qualified guarantor, who will repay the loan if you aren't able to. The bank will also demand collateral—assets of significant value that can be seized should you default on your loan.

Ultimately, if you're a first-time food truck owner, you're better off seeking a partner or private investor. Once you've built a successful business, banks are a great resource to help you expand.

Small Business Administration Loans

If you don't qualify for a commercial loan, your bank can help you determine whether you're eligible for assistance from the U.S. Small Business Administration (SBA). If you qualify—and most first-time small businesses do—the SBA can guarantee your loan in full or in part, thus alleviating the bank's risk should you default.

Your bank will help to prequalify you and prepare the necessary paperwork in accordance with SBA guidelines. This will include a business plan, your business and financial records, credit rating, equity, collateral, and experience. Even with an SBA guarantee, you'll still be personally liable for repayment of the loan.

You may also seek venture capital from an SBA Small Business Investment Company (SBIC), which partner with private investors to provide private capital for eligible businesses. For more information on SBA assistance and guidelines, visit sba.gov.

Other Ways to Increase Liquidity

Beyond borrowing money or printing it in your basement, you have other, more creative ways to free up cash and even extend your credit.

Supplier Credit

Many food truck owners seek an unofficial line of credit from their vendors and suppliers—their purveyors, in restaurant jargon. For example, a supplier might agree to defer the payment of your bills, allowing you to use your cash for other things in the short term. Conventional wisdom dictates that new truck owners would find it difficult to persuade their purveyors to grant extended credit terms, but that's not necessarily the case.

You're already anticipating those first moments of interaction with your very first customer. That person will respond not just to the quality of your food and the cleverness of your design, but also to you, to your passion and authenticity and charisma. The first impressions that are so crucial in building lasting relationships with your clientele are also important to your relationships with your suppliers.

Purveyors ultimately want you to succeed because you're a source of revenue for them. There's nothing inappropriate about introducing yourself with a smile, wearing your passion on your sleeve, and asking them to invest in you, the same way you'd ask a bank to invest in your business. Invest in your vendor and supplier relationships the same warmth, vigor, and gratitude you will with your customers, and opportunities will become available to you.

> **TIP**
>
> Consider partnering with an established restaurant brand. Many times these operators are looking for ways to generate revenues but are too busy focusing on their core businesses. They may consider licensing their brand or partnering with you on a truck business. This gives you instant credibility and a following, significantly decreasing the risk of failure.

You should also consider negotiating with suppliers to get free equipment when buying other pieces from them. As you gain the confidence of your purveyors, they'll be open to haggling, bartering, and renegotiating with you. The bottom line is that while you should never expect to receive something for nothing or on a deferred payment plan, you should never be afraid to ask.

Sponsorships

Anyone who has ever seen a sporting event has surely noticed the preponderance of flashy corporate sponsor logos. Almost any film in your local multiplex and 100 percent of the shows on television incorporate slightly less-obvious logos into their production design in exchange for capital from corporate sponsors. This allows those sponsors to build *brand equity* and positively associate their products with popular consumer trends.

> **DEFINITION**
>
> **Brand equity** is the commercial value of a brand based on the consumer perception of it.

Your first food truck probably isn't going to win the sponsorship of a mega-corporation, but it doesn't need to. You can still take advantage of sponsorship opportunities from companies that are more accessible to you. Any company that sells a product or service—and all companies do—is concerned with building brand equity. It's time to get creative and determine what your food truck can do for them.

The easiest place to start is with your purveyors; you're already in dialogue with them. Instead of asking for capital, offer to feature their name, product, or service in exchange for free or discounted products or services. For example, if you want to buy your produce from Farmer John's Organics, offer to proudly state on your menu and signage that you exclusively use their organic fruits and vegetables. Print up a sample menu and sign and show it to them during your first conversation. Visual aids can be extremely persuasive.

> **TRUCK TALES**
>
> In June 2011, mega-retailer Macy's capitalized on the food truck craze and launched Macy's Chefs-a-Go-Go, a nationwide food truck tour that featured celebrity chefs and that received a lot of press coverage. Macy's cleverly offered special giveaways and other truck-side deals to foodies who visited their website and social networking profiles. This gave the company a huge platform to build brand equity and remind consumers that they specialize in kitchenware as well as fashion.

You need to communicate to potential sponsors exactly why they want their product or service to be associated with your truck. Who are you? What's your concept? What's your company's philosophy? Who's your clientele? Write up a proposal and include visual aids whenever possible.

As your business grows and you build your own brand equity, sponsorship will be easier to secure. In fact, once you're profitable, you may want to be a sponsor yourself, providing food to a local sporting event, school fair, or charity. It's a highly effective way to leverage your relationships with other businesses and your community to attract more customers.

The Least You Need to Know

- In addition to the money you'll need to start your food truck, you'll want to give yourself several months' cushion, because food trucks can take that long to be profitable.
- Using some of your own money to finance your truck will make you look like a serious businessperson to investors; however, don't use your last dime, and try not to involve family or friends.
- Getting a bank loan to finance a food truck can be very difficult; consider taking on a partner, silent or otherwise.
- Many purveyors are willing to offer lines of credit or discounted supplies or equipment, and they're also a great source of food truck sponsorship.

Regulations and Licensing

In This Chapter

- Learning the laws that apply to food trucks in your area
- Obtaining licenses and other necessary permits
- Following changing regulations in a growing industry
- Insuring your truck
- Trademarking your name and logo

My business law teacher in high school, Ms. Sibovits, made a very strong impression on me. She taught us about many aspects of the world of business, lessons I'm sure I still unconsciously utilize today.

I recall a few of Mrs. Sibovits's words with complete clarity: "Ignorance is no excuse when dealing with the law." These words are as true today as they were then. When it comes to legal matters, if you break the law, it doesn't matter whether you knew the law existed or not. You're accountable.

In the world of food trucks, what you don't know can definitely hurt you. Without knowledge of local regulations and proper permits, you'll end up spending a lot of money for nothing. Food trucks may have begun as an unregulated—or at least minimally regulated—business, but their recent success has made them targets. As a truck operator you'll be subject to as much and sometimes more regulation than bricks-and-mortar restaurants. In the current environment, regulators are being pressured by restaurants and other businesses to get food trucks out of their neighborhoods. This has put truck operations under a microscope, and local authorities are looking for any reason to ticket, fine, or revoke licenses.

The success and intrigue of the food truck business that led you to purchase this book has also led to a legal standoff that will determine the future of the business. In Chapter 8, I cover how to become a responsible member of the community and know the laws before the regulators show up.

Knowing Your Local Laws

Prior to making a decision to start a food truck business, you must be aware of local laws; your business plan can be greatly affected by what's allowed or required by your local authorities. Laws and regulations apply to every aspect of your operation. You'll have to deal with regulations that apply to all retail operations as well as ordinances specific to the food truck game. You'll need to deal with taxes, licenses, labor laws, and many other standard hospitality business regulations, but you'll also have to worry about the rules of the road, parking, how much propane you can carry, and other components of operating that are very specific to running a food truck.

Most of the laws you'll be dealing with are established by local and state agencies; you'll rarely, if ever, be involved with federal authorities. Your local health department is the governing body that oversees specific codes for serving food in your area. The department of transportation decides where and when you can park your truck. There are even regulations for street food businesses concerning how far away from the curb you should be located or how close to the entrance of a building you can park.

Let's use my friend Gelareh as an example. She was planning to sell fruit smoothies in downtown Claudiaville, Wisconsin. The area she chose for her truck is the hottest place for nightlife, so she planned to sell alcoholic smoothies in the evening. She was excited to get started and had purchased her truck and smoothie equipment. When Gelareh was ready to open her smoothie truck she met with her lawyer, Diane, to apply for the licenses. Diane informed her that local regulations don't permit food trucks to park on Main Street in downtown Claudiaville. Additionally, the liquor licenses for food trucks only allow them to serve before 9 P.M.

Gelareh had to change her entire business plan. Fifty percent of her revenue was supposed to come from her late-night business, and she wasn't sure if she could get the traffic she needed if she couldn't park on Main Street. She messed up big time: Gelareh had already spent $50,000 on her truck!. She ended up selling her truck back to Gilda, a local truck dealer, at a loss. Gelareh was done before she even got started.

That's a sad example of what can happen if you don't know your local laws. The best solution is to consult with an attorney, because the law is all about interpretation. A good lawyer will save you time and money. You can locate a specialist by reaching out to your local bar association.

You can also do your own research by visiting the website or office of your local regulatory body. Someone there will happily assist you, and there are often easy-to-read guides for beginners on their websites. Remember, they want you to succeed.

> **TIP**
>
> In New York City you need a Mobile Food Vending License and a Mobile Food Vending Unit Permit to operate a food truck. The first one is a matter of filling out some paperwork and taking a few classes; the second is a different story. The permits have been capped at 3,100 total since 1979. The only real way to obtain a permit is to purchase one illegally or partner with someone who holds a permit for cash and a portion of the profits. No matter where you live, expect to do some legal maneuvering because permits are in high demand.

Getting Permits and Required Licenses

Licenses are legal documents issued by government agencies giving you permission to do a particular thing or conduct a particular type of business. When it comes to food trucks, you'll need a license from your area's governing body to operate, to sell certain items, even to collect sales tax. If you choose to do any of these things without a permit and/or license, authorities can shut down your business, fine you, and even send you to jail. It's critical that you take the proper steps to obtain the correct paperwork to operate your food truck.

For the most part, obtaining a license isn't something you do once and never have to think about again. You need to renew most licenses annually, and the process could include payments, exams, and in some cases a full reapplication. Work with your attorney and your support staff, if you have any, to establish a system that will let you know when and if you need to renew your permits. You never want to be in a situation where you're operating with an expired license. It's a foolish mistake that will cost you and your business money.

Make permitting and licensing for your business a top priority. By doing so you're not only keeping yourself out of trouble, you're protecting your customers and your employees. Do everything in your power to protect them.

> **TIP**
>
> Always keep your licenses and/or permits on board during operation and locked up in a safe place when you aren't on the road. Losing the actual documents can cause you major issues when you're being inspected and dealing with authorities, not to mention the time and energy you'll expend replacing them.

Following Health Codes

The Food Code is created and published by the Food and Drug Administration (FDA) every four years as an example for health departments nationwide. It includes the best practices for storing, preparing, and handling food as recommended by the federal government. Your truck is subject to local, state, and national food laws outlined in this code. The actual local codes are adapted from the federal one, and vary from state to state and county to county.

The most immediate authority for your truck is your county health department. Generally their code outlines minimum requirements for safety, but local jurisdictions may have stricter regulations. While you plan your business and throughout its operation, it's important to have open communication with your health department to make sure that you're following the code and not making mistakes that could cost you big time. Each county has clear outlines as to how commercial kitchens must be laid out, and it's better to have this information prior to constructing your truck.

Health codes regulate multiple areas of your commissary and food truck, including the following:

Employee hygiene. Cooks and service staff must be clean and well groomed. If they're sick or have exposed cuts your customers can be exposed to potential infection.

Inspections. Food trucks are usually inspected at least twice a year in addition to potential random inspections. A bad grade on an inspection can lead to your truck getting shut down and result in lost business. Don't take chances.

Cleaning. Health codes tell you what cleaners and sanitizers are acceptable for use in your truck. The code also stipulates how often equipment and surfaces must be cleaned.

Storage and handling. You're responsible for all food that's served to your customers. Once you accept delivery of a product it becomes a raw material that will eventually be turned into an item you sell. The code outlines how food should be handled and stored. For example, a potentially dangerous item like raw chicken shouldn't be stored above cooked food because of the potential for cross contamination.

Equipment and supplies. The equipment you use in your truck and commissary must be in line with health code requirements. Examples include sinks that have multiple compartments and color-coded cutting boards for meats, poultry, and vegetables.

BEEP! BEEP!

People have a tendency to get frustrated when dealing with detailed regulations, and they sometimes take their frustrations out on local health inspectors and other regulatory authorities. However, such conflicts will make you a target for violations and make life much more difficult than a random inspection or small fine. Always make sure that you and your staff maintain a positive relationship with authorities and be patient and friendly when dealing with bureaucracy.

Obtaining Health Inspections

Every food truck needs an inspection and permit from the health department to do business. The permit requires you to file an application and pay a fee ranging from a few hundred to a few thousand dollars a year. (The amount is determined by your local government.) Other than the fee and application themselves, the most problematic part of the process is the time you'll have to spend getting them. Health departments can get backed up, leading to weeks of waiting to get an inspector to check your vehicle. Assume the process will take up to four weeks and include the delay in your timeline. As with all legal issues, the requirements for your health inspection will vary from city to city and state to state. Check with your local health department early in the planning stages of your business to be sure you're aware of all the steps you need to take.

In order to get more of a grasp on the process, let's take a look at the licensing procedure for food trucks in one locality, Washington, D.C.:

1. **Obtain Food Protection Manager Identification from the health department.**

   Food truck operators are required to have this identification with them at all times during the operation of their truck. To get it you have to enroll in a food manager certification course for proper training. After you've taken the course you bring your certificate, test scores, a check for $35, and two forms of identification to the D.C. treasurer's office.

2. **Have the health department do a process plan review of your truck.**

   Your process plan lists the food items you'll be serving and how you'll be preparing them. You must submit that plan along with a check for $100, to the health department for approval. Only after you've received approval of this plan should you start building your truck. After you've determined all the equipment you need for your truck, you have to bring the plan back to the health department for secondary approval. In Washington, D.C., the only requirement for truck design is that the truck be no bigger than 18.5 feet long, 10.5 feet tall, and 8 feet wide.

3. **If you're planning to use propane, schedule an appointment through the fire department to get your design approved by the fire marshal.**

   Propane is dangerous and requires an inspection by an expert in the safe handling of hazardous gases.

4. **Submit a vending application to the health department for your vending unit inspection.**

   This is a standard inspection done to all street vendor equipment.

5. **Submit a Depot letter to the health department.**

   A Depot letter from a health department–approved commissary saying that it has the ability to support your operation for food supply/storage, water supply, food preparation, general supply storage, truck parking, repairs, cleaning, and waste disposal. The letter must be approved and remain on file with the health department.

6. **Have your truck inspected by the health department.**

In D.C. inspections are performed at the health department's inspection site on Tuesdays and Wednesdays from 9 A.M. to 12 P.M. (It's possible to get an off-site inspection, but you'll have to wait until a field inspector in your area is available.) If you pass inspection, you'll get a 30-day, temporary permit until your permanent license is ready to be picked up.

The inspection will verify the following:

- Proof of Ownership, proper ID, and driver's license
- Proof of district-issued Food Manager ID Card
- Food purchase records and storage
- Proof of commissary and their license to operate with recent inspection

If your commissary facility doesn't have prior approval, you'll also need to submit the plan for the facility prior to getting your inspection.

7. **Apply for a roadway class A license for the person(s) who will be driving and operating the truck.**

Even when fully licensed, you're subject to additional legal issues in Washington, D.C. As we've already discussed, you can only solicit customers who flag you down, a 35-year-old law put in place for ice-cream trucks that doesn't take into account twenty-first-century inventions like social media. Although the regulation is completely antiquated, the authorities must and will enforce it.

TIP

In addition to a truck permit, some states require individual employees to be licensed by the health department. The types of licenses required differ by municipality but include food handler's permits, food protection certificates, and certificates of qualification. Employees may be required to take a test and may have to submit to a health check for contagious diseases such as tuberculosis and hepatitis.

Are you exhausted? The process of licensing in Washington, D.C., is the rule, not the exception, and if you think it's complicated, you're right. There are a lot of steps and it's probably one of the most tedious parts of starting your truck. Take your time and make sure that you don't miss any parts of the process. Failing to meet any of the requirements can delay your opening for months, which can greatly affect your profitability.

Staying on Top of Evolving Regulations

The thorniest issues in the food truck business today are the enforcement of antiquated regulations and the possible creation of new regulations. Food trucks flourished over the past few years because they existed in a gray area, outside of standard regulation. They aren't exactly food carts or street vendors, but neither are they bricks-and-mortar restaurants, so it wasn't clear which regulations applied to them. As long as the number of trucks remained manageable, authorities allowed them to operate under the radar. They were welcome additions to many communities and rarely took significant business from competing establishments.

TRUCK TALES

Pera Turkish Tacos was awarded the first food truck liquor license in New York City in June 2011. Operating out of a food truck lot located in front of the former landmark restaurant Tavern on the Green, the truck is allowed to sell beer, wine, and cocktails for consumption in their assigned seating area. Will this be a sign of things to come? No one knows, but now you can enjoy an ice-cold beer with your piping hot lamb taco from Pera. Who said drinking and driving was a bad combination?

But when the revolution began, the number of trucks exploded. All of a sudden there were food trucks on every corner in many cities, a situation that forced the authorities to more strictly enforce current laws and create new ones to police a burgeoning industry. Local businesses became hostile toward the trucks because they began taking more custom from rent-paying establishments.

In almost every major metropolitan area, legislation related to the operation of food trucks is being proposed. Some areas want to expand permitting while others are talking about charging rent for good spots. Health inspectors are making spot checks on trucks, and cities like Los Angeles are beginning to give letter grades to trucks based on their health inspections.

In response, trucks have started organizing associations to protect their rights and fight to be heard on the local political scene.

By the time you read this book, regulations will have changed tenfold in most cities and states. So what do you need to know? Whatever the regulations are, you have to be aware of them. You also need to join a trade organization and get involved in the discussion. Speak to local lawmakers, enforcement agencies, and fellow truckers to find out the current situation. Is it friendly or unfriendly, stable or likely to change? You need to make sure you're aware and protected before you invest your hard-earned cash in this business.

In Chicago, New York, Los Angeles, Seattle, Miami, and Atlanta, campaigns are underway to change the food truck regulations. Here are some examples of what's going on around the country:

- **Atlanta:** City Councilman Kwanza Hall is working to do away with restrictions that keep food trucks from operating early, late, and close to bricks-and-mortar businesses.

- **Chicago:** Blogger Matt Maroni gathered over 4,000 signatures to help change the laws there to allow cooking on trucks.

- **Seattle:** Local vendors are pushing hard for specialized zones within the city that are open to the expansion of their gourmet trucks.

The landscape is changing, so know your local laws and become an active member of the community.

Buying the Insurance You Need

When considering your insurance needs, you need to realize that you're insuring both a mobile restaurant and a vehicle. You need insurance that covers your kitchen and business, as well as your truck. Restaurants can face many potential claims every day, but food trucks face additional risks and exposure to different types of claims.

Here are a few risks to consider:

- Automobile accidents

- Food poisoning

- Slip and fall risks around your parked truck

- Kitchen equipment replacement and damage

- Employee injury

I recommend carrying commercial auto and general liability insurance.

General Liability Insurance

Your general liability should have at least a $1 million umbrella policy.

A general liability insurance policy offers specific coverage, like property and bodily injury, in one policy. You need it because your commercial auto insurance won't cover your entire rig. Many truck operators don't get this coverage, but I say it's better to be safe than sorry. A general liability policy will protect you from nondriving related issues such as property damage or bodily injury that doesn't result from driving. You don't want to have a flourishing food business shut down because you didn't have the right coverage.

Commercial Auto Insurance

Because your food truck is customized and much heavier than an automobile, it's going to need much more coverage. Commercial auto policies offer higher limits, allow modified trucks, and permit different types of usages than the insurance you carry for your passenger car.

You spent a lot of time, energy, and, most important, money building this truck; it's critical that you protect it and yourself by insuring it appropriately. You also need to check with local authorities to see if there are insurance requirements for food trucks.

Finding an Agent and Asking the Right Questions

It's important to work with an insurance agent who understands the needs of your business. Many agents deal with traditional restaurants but don't know what's best for a mobile business like yours. Find someone with experience, and make sure to ask the following questions:

- Am I protected if I get into a car accident? If so, for how much?
- Is my kitchen equipment protected from theft or damage?
- Does my insurance permit me to be a mobile business?
- Do I have protection from food poisoning claims?
- What's my coverage if the truck is stolen or vandalized?
- Am I covered if my employees and/or customers are injured? What if they're injured in the commissary or in front of the truck?
- Are my employees covered to drive the truck?

Establishing a Domain Name and Trademark

Once you choose your truck name, the first thing you should do is purchase the Internet domain name through a service like Godaddy.com or Register.com. The food truck business is based online, and if you can get the domain closest to your truck name it's almost the equivalent of having a trademark. Even if someone copies your concept or name, the right domain will make sure the customer finds you before the imposter.

The most valuable thing you'll get from the creation of your food truck is the branding. If you create something notable, it will allow you to expand into a bricks-and-mortar establishment through brand recognition. To maintain the integrity of your brand, you should *trademark* it.

DEFINITION

A **trademark** is a distinctive sign or indicator legally registered by an individual or business or legal entity to identify products and/or services to consumers.

You can do so via a low-cost service such as Legal Zoom (www.legalzoom.com). You should be able to file a basic trademark of your logo and trade name for about $1,500, including fees. This will give you a public record of ownership, create exclusive rights to your trademark, and have the right to file suit if someone breaches your trademark.

The Least You Need to Know

- Do your own research or hire a lawyer to be sure your business is fully compliant with all local laws.
- It can take weeks to acquire all the permits and licenses required for a food truck. Be sure to allow the proper time to take care of all paperwork and inspections.
- Regulations for the food truck industry are in a state of flux. Make sure you stay aware of what's happening in your area and state.
- Insurance for your truck and your entire operation is crucial to have. Don't scrimp; proper insurance can save your business.
- Make sure you purchase your Internet domain name as soon as you choose the name of your food truck. Having it is almost as good as trademarking your business name.

Creating Your Marketing Plan

In This Chapter

- Identifying your core values to design your brand logo
- Communicating with your customers through your website and social networking media
- Making a splash in the local community with opening events
- Reaching out to food bloggers, the food truck operators' best friends
- Building a rapport with your customers to establish a lasting connection to your truck

Just when you thought you were done getting your food truck business set up, you really were just getting started. The truck business is a marathon, not a sprint. Getting your truck on the road is only half the job, the other half is making people love it!

Today's competitive environment makes it impossible to rely on luck. The if-you-build-it-they-will-come mentality doesn't work anymore. Marketing is critical in establishing a successful truck. Food trucks are no longer novelties, and competition in the business is fierce. The trucks that succeed are the ones that have a clear brand identity that saturates every part of the customer's experience. These brands also offer what I refer to as "experiential follow through." They promise something great and then deliver something even better to get customers to keep coming back.

For an example of this type of marketing and experiential follow through, look no further than your local Apple store. Everything from its logo and advertising to store design, employee language, purchasing experience, and the end product speak to

Apple's customer-focused brand. Apple customers love their brand so much that they only buy Apple.

You need to take this same focus and apply it to your food truck business. You want to make your customers' trip to lunch the most exciting part of the day, so much so that the thought of eating at another truck never even enters their minds.

Let's start by establishing your identity through your logo.

Designing Your Brand Logo

When you think of the logos of companies like Coca Cola, Nike, and Google, do you have an emotional response? To me, Coca Cola says classic quality. The Nike Swoosh is hip and athletic. Google is playful, but not too playful. You may have different responses to these logos, but I bet they aren't too far from mine.

Your logo is your chance to create instant public recognition of your brand. It needs to say who you are and what you're like in the simplest and most direct way. So what are you trying to say about your truck with your logo?

Make a list of three to five core values of your brand. For instance, if you're starting an artisanal ice cream truck, your core values could be high-quality ingredients, locally sourced, homemade, with the help of a master ice-cream maker. How would you say this with your logo? Artisanal reminds me of something more classic or from a small town. The same goes for homemade. If you use a master ice-cream maker, you may want to include his or her name in the brand.

TRUCK TALES

Korilla BBQ is a Korean taco truck created by Edward "3D" Song. When he asked himself the question "Who doesn't love Korean BBQ?" he came up with three answers: vegans and vegetarians; people who don't know what Korean BBQ is; and people who don't want to spend $40 or more at a Korean restaurant. That made his decision to start a Korean BBQ truck easy. A Columbia University grad, Edward studied the business, went to cooking school, and teamed up with a great chef, but it was his decision to hire Box Creative digital marketing and design firm that brought everything together and created the ultimate Korean taco brand. The firm took Edward's idea, extracted the core values, and made it a reality. The marriage of Edward's dream and business savvy and the firm's creative talent, is what you need to make your food truck the next Korilla BBQ. Any idea or concept is only as good as its execution, and branding is no exception.

I advocate telling the customer exactly who and what you are in your logo. Consumers are seeing so much information these days; you need to say everything in the few seconds you have their attention. It's best to just spell things out; the words *artisanal ice cream* should actually be included in the logo.

Finding a Graphic Designer

If you don't know any graphic designers, just type "graphic designer" into an Internet search engine. You'll find designers who specialize in logos. I recommend using someone local with whom you can work closely and who can continue to serve your future design needs. To find someone affordable, contact a local university with a graphic design department. Many students will work for you for little or no money to gain samples for their portfolio.

When you have some designs, go to friends and business associates for feedback. Ask them which they like the best and why. Then combine that information with your own instincts to make your final choice. Nobody knows better than you which logo best represents your vision for your truck. So trust your instincts and get cracking!

Creating Your Online Presence

Once you've created your logo, it's time to start building your online presence. Because you're a mobile operation, your website and Twitter account can serve as your home base and the best method for communicating with your customers.

Website

You should think of your website as your storefront, where customers come to visit you. If you're mentioned on a local food blog, for example, it will include a link to your website so readers can click through to find you. And when they do, that's your chance to make a customer. So not only should your website be a source of information but, like your truck wrap (see Chapter 11), it needs to be an advertisement. It should be vibrant and lively but always user friendly. I think music on a site sets the mood for the type of experience the customer has at your truck, so I suggest using it.

TIP

Make sure your website works in all major browsers, Internet Explorer, Firefox, Safari, and Chrome. If you hire a professional Web designer to create your site, she should do this as part of her service.

Here's a list of everything a food truck website should include:

Menus. You should post your food and drink menus in text form. This makes them readable on standard and mobile platforms, as well as easily readable by search engines.

E-mail list sign-up. Customers should be able to submit their name and e-mail address to receive updates about your truck. Building an e-mail database is critical for launching new trucks and promotions.

> **TIP**
>
> Don't forget to include areas for customers to include both their work and home locations when creating an e-mail sign-up on your website. You can organize locations by zip code or neighborhood; either way, the information is invaluable because it enables you to segment your list into areas so that you can target your communications with customers. There's no reason to reach out to people uptown when you're parked downtown.

Twitter link. The site has to have a prominent link so customers can follow you. The more followers you have, the more people will know where you're parked.

Facebook link. Your site needs a link so customers can become fans of your truck on Facebook, and you'll need to link your Facebook and Twitter accounts so all information simultaneously goes to each outlet.

Foursquare link. You want users to "check in" to your Foursquare page.

About us. This is your chance to tell your story. Use this opportunity to create an emotional attachment between you and your customers. Tell them how you got to where you are and why.

Weekly locations. If you have any permanent locations, list them in this section, with times and days. Your locations will likely change often, so you must make sure to keep your customers informed.

Catering. This section should include a *lead generator* form for catering inquiries, along with catering menus.

> **DEFINITION**
>
> A **lead generator** is a form to post on your website that customers can fill out to request specific information about your truck. It's one of the simplest and most effective ways to turn Internet marketing into actual customer connections.

Press. This section should have links to all the latest mentions of your truck in the media, including the Blogosphere. To increase the number of hits you get on search engines like Google and Bing, you should take the time to actually key in the press items as well as include direct links.

Contact us. Provide your e-mail, phone number, and office address, if you have one.

Other cool features include online ordering, a map with a truck locator, and images of your menu items.

You'll want to work with a web design company or an individual to build your site. I suggest spending no more than $5,000 to build your website, though it should be possible to get a quality job done for less than half that amount.

Twitter

Your *Twitter* account will be the lifeblood of driving customers to your truck. The social networking and micro-blogging site is the main way your customers/followers will locate your truck.

DEFINITION

Twitter is a social networking and micro-blogging service that enables users to send and read text-based posts, known as tweets, of up to 140 characters.

To get started, you need to create a Twitter account for your truck. The account name should be as short as possible while making it clear exactly who you are. For example, the Kogi truck's Twitter is @kogibbq; Wafels & Dinges's is @waffletruck.

Building followers takes time, but you can start by inviting your friends and family to sign up for your tweets. Do everything you can to make every customer a follower; you should include a link to your Twitter account on your website, truck, and materials such as napkins and menus.

TIP

The language you use when communicating with customers on Twitter is key. If you're trying to be a hip downtown brand, you need to speak a hip downtown language, slang and all. Instead of saying "the meatball truck will be on Houston St. at 5 p.m." you might say "The meatball truck is rolling into SOHO round 5ish, corner of Houston & West Broadway. Get hungry." Be yourself, speaking the way you would to your friends, and your customers will become both followers and friends.

Your tweets shouldn't only be about your location. Be sure to tweet about funny things that happen on the truck, new menu items, family news—all of these things will help to create interest in the day-to-day happenings of your business. You want to start a dialogue with your customers. If everything goes right, you'll begin to notice tweets from your customers, like "craving a taco from @kogibbq" or "going to get a Belgian waffle with whipped cream from @waffletruck." Not only is it great to hear; it will create action and drive other customers to you because all their followers can see it and click through to check out your truck.

Once you're operating, you should post on Twitter a minimum of three or four times a day. More than that is good, as long as you're saying things that mean something. Customers will tire of your tweets if they're repetitive, so keep them brief and pertinent to your truck. The last thing you want to do is bombard your followers with boring tweets so they end up ignoring you.

Some trucks, such as the Fojol Bros. of Merlindia, create games using their Twitter account to attract customers. Trucks in Washington, D.C., aren't allowed to park unless there's already a line of people waiting for them, so they entice people to line up and do crazy dances before they'll park and start serving. Establishing games, customer rewards, or discounts through Twitter is a great way to further involve your customers in the experience of your truck.

Facebook and Foursquare

Facebook and Foursquare are also important marketing tools for your truck, though not as pertinent as Twitter.

Because you're a business, you need to establish a Facebook *fan page*. You gain Facebook fans through the same techniques that you use to attract Twitter followers. If you link your fan page to your Twitter account, your tweets will automatically repost there.

DEFINITION

A **fan page** is a page on Facebook dedicated to promoting a commercial interest such as a business or celebrity.

Foursquare is a location-based social networking site. People "check in" at different locations using their mobile device, earning points when they do. You should link your Foursquare account to your Facebook and Twitter accounts.

You can use Twitter, Facebook, and Foursquare to create a powerful virtual conversation about your truck, so much so that when people talk it spreads like wildfire. The key to success is making sure everyone's saying good things. If you handle things right, going to your truck will become as much about eating there as it is about creating a social happening to share with your friends, an important step in making your truck a success.

Planning a Launch Event

Now that you've established your virtual storefront and built the most awesome truck ever, it's time to begin planning a launch event. That sounds like fun, doesn't it? This is what you've always dreamed about—you and your staff getting saluted by all your friends and hanging with celebrities, all while chowing down on Grandma's famous meatballs.

Not so quick.

Your launch event is a marketing tool, not a vanity fest. And keep in mind that first impressions are usually the most important.

The goal of the launch of your truck is to make a splash in the local food press and start the buzz among your core clientele. My recommendation is to do two openings: one for press/core clients and the second for the public.

The press event should take place in a scenic location where you can park without a problem. Plan on two hours, providing free food and drinks. Try to hire a local public relations agency for as little money as possible. Their job is to write a press release and invite the most important members of the local press to the opening. Then invite 50 of your closest friends, the ones who love and support you the most; you'll need their encouragement now more than ever. People with complimentary things to say to the press always help at these events.

Your food and service must be absolutely perfect for this event. If you have to bring on extra staff to make sure you have no problems, delays, or excuses, do it. You won't be cooking or serving at this event; you'll be speaking to the press and your guests, telling them all the reasons why your truck is special. You should prepare two or three stories you think would interest the press beforehand—how you source your one-of-a-kind meat from a butcher you've known since you were a kid, or that your truck is the first to ever have a special pizza oven on board. Get creative and be sure to make the most of this opportunity. You'll never get a second chance to make a first impression.

Your public event should be focused on driving sales. After your press event is complete, you want to announce when you will be open to the public. In conjunction with the announcement, you should create a call to action—something that inspires customers to take action when they hear you're going to be opening. Maybe this is live entertainment or complimentary food to your first 100 customers. Whatever it is, it should attract crowds to your truck from day one. Launch this promotion with an event during a time period you know is going to be busy, and cast your new product in the best possible light. This should get your business rolling, generate some cash, and pique people's interest right from the beginning. One of the best pieces of advice I have ever received is to "throw everything you have at an opening." You never want to hold back when introducing your product, so use everything in your arsenal to drive interest and get the buzz going.

> **TIP**
>
> Don't forget to have business cards on hand. From your opening party through the first six months of operations, no one should leave your truck without your business card in hand. In exchange, you should get their e-mail address or phone number. Within 24 hours of their visit to your truck they should receive a thank-you e-mail from you. This type of personal touch will go a long way toward creating goodwill for you and your business.

Reaching Out to Bloggers

Food trucks are different than restaurants, and food bloggers aren't the same as traditional restaurant reviewers. Why? Food bloggers can say anything they want—and they will. Anyone from the most popular food writer to your neighbor can have their very own food blog.

In a way, food blogs are to writing what food trucks are to restaurants. Culturally, they go hand-in-hand. Someone who loves to write and loves food can start a food blog; someone who loves to cook and loves food can start a food truck. Technology and ingenuity have lowered the barrier to entry more than ever before. If the food bloggers love you, it's a blessing for your truck, but if they don't, you'd better watch out. You need to put the percentages in your favor and play nice with them from the beginning.

The first thing you should do is reach out to local bloggers personally. They're anti-establishment, so as much as a PR firm can help, you personally reaching out to local bloggers to represent your truck is always a plus with them. You should be able to find the writer or editor's e-mail address on the main page of most blogs. Next, I would do everything in my power to have them sample your food prior to your launch. Ask for their feedback on the product. If they love it, that's great. If they think it can be improved, then improve it. The key here is that you're getting them vested in your success.

Now invite those bloggers to your private opening event. Even better, get them to invite their readers to it. And if you can, offer their readers a benefit when dining at your truck, like a free cookie or a soda with their order. Anything you can do to get the readers to be part of your army of supporters is great. The people who write and read about food do so because they're passionate about it. It's in your best interest to get them on your team, because they'll tell everyone they know how much they love your product. And it definitely doesn't hurt to shout them out on Twitter. A little love goes a long way.

BEEP! BEEP!

If a blogger writes negative things about you, ignore them. Engaging them in a fight adds attention and validity to their claims. Blogs are trying to gain readership; the less you do to help that cause, the less important you are to them. And never forget, you'd have much bigger problems if people weren't writing about you at all.

Working with the Mainstream Press

You aren't in this business to have just any truck; you want to have *the* truck. The next Kogi! If you've played your cards right, you have a great website, had an awesome opening, and the blogosphere is buzzing almost as much as your Twitter feed. But how do you get the attention of your local news? Magazines? Newspapers?

After you reach out to the bloggers, your next step is to go after the mainstream press. For food trucks, bloggers are the necessity, while mainstream press is a luxury. PR firms can help, but PR firms are only as good as what you give them to work with. You need to come up with the great ideas that will attract attention and make your truck special. The way to get to the mainstream press is to do everything in your power to establish great relationships with writers. Once you have these relationships, focus all your efforts on pitching them one great idea.

Reaching out to writers is as easy as surfing the Internet. All writers have their information online, and most can be reached through the website of their publications. Despite your trepidations, the truth is that writers need things to write about to make a living. They're always looking for good stories to fill the pages of their publications.

What you need to do is to become an insider. You need to invite writers to your truck to become friendly with them. Park outside their publication's building every Wednesday and bring them lunch. Make them aware that you exist and are a quality vendor. It's amazing what people will do for you when you're genuinely nice to them.

Then you have to do your part. You need to come up with your big idea, the thing that makes you and your truck so interesting and special. What about the creation of a special menu item like a $100 ice-cream sundae with gold leaf and the rarest cocoa nibs in the world, or celebrating your 10,000th meatball sold by creating the biggest meatball ever? You could campaign to have your chicken wings declared the best in the state, or maybe you could take a page out of the Nathan's book and hold an annual hot dog–eating contest. The key is to do something bold that accentuates you and your product. After all, there's no point in having a hot dog–eating contest if you sell pizza.

Remain focused on one thing and scream only when people are listening. Whatever idea you choose, stick with it. Make it your signature and don't give up until you've pitched it to every writer in the county. And don't forget that timing is everything. It doesn't make sense to try to get attention for your product during the Super Bowl. That's when the big advertisers are spending every dollar they can to maximize the attention they're getting. Look for opportunities when the news cycle is slow or complementary to your product. For instance, Cinco de Mayo would be a great time to launch a special taco for your taco truck. That's when the press is looking to write about other things related to Mexican American culture.

TIP

Your job with mainstream press is to recognize opportunities and make the most of them.

Treating Every Day As an Event

I'm sure you've realized by now that there's always going to be something to do; some aspect of your truck business to perfect. It's going to take many days and nights of hard work for your truck to become a well-oiled machine. It would be very easy to start getting lazy, just doing the same thing over and over again. But that's not an option.

Your energy and passion needs to be infectious to ignite the fire in your staff and customers. You need to make every day on your truck an event. Every day has to be special. You and your staff have to be motivated to become better than the day before every single day. Whose job is it to make that a reality? You and only you.

In order to make every day an event you need to add little things to the truck experience that change every time a customer visits. Maybe Tuesday is fried chicken day, the only day you serve your special recipe. Wednesday you offer free lunch to the first 20 people who reply on Twitter, and at the end of the week you have a DJ play outside your truck to celebrate the coming weekend.

To make this a reality, you need to apply yourself to create great programming. Take the time to sit with your staff and think of ways to make every day special. Get a calendar and don't put it down until you schedule something different for each day. Create customized promotions that will set your truck apart from the competition, and dedicate yourself to executing them every week.

Making Social Media Your Friend

After you've decided on your programming and promotions, you need to utilize your website and social networking tools to promote these happenings to your customer base. If not, you're the tree that falls in the woods: It made a noise, but no one heard it. You need to activate all your promotions through these tools. They'll be the impetus for creating chatter and dialogue on your Twitter feed and Facebook page. And this chatter is what leads to customers eating at your truck.

Bloggers should receive news of your promotions in advance of their release on your Twitter. This is because press outlets will provide you more exposure for the promotion, but will only publish it if the info hasn't been released elsewhere. If they choose to release it on their blog, I advocate making people sign up to follow you on Twitter in order to redeem specials and promotions. By doing this you will gain direct access to the blog's readers and become less dependent on their coverage over time. Even if the blog passes on including the information, you've still established good will by offering it to them. The bottom line is that you must be strategic when utilizing your social networking tools, website, press, and e-mail database to disseminate information on your promotions, thereby maximizing your return on investment.

BEEP! BEEP!

Only speak when you have something to say. Social networking, e-mail lists, websites, and press contacts are great, but only if they're used with respect. Be mindful of how often you're sending out messages and what you're saying when you do. If you don't use them with care, people will tune you out. Then your assets aren't worth anything.

Creating Strong Product and Personal Relationships

The world seems to get more impersonal every day. Products are mass produced and less artisanal. The revolution in the food truck business is a reaction to these factors. Your job as a food truck operator is to break through; make everything about your business personal. Know every customer's personal preferences and ask about their lives. Get them invested in your success by sharing your passion. Your product needs to be as personal as your relationships. The way it's prepared needs to mean something to you. The ingredients you use must be ones you personally choose. Most of all, your feed has to taste great, every single time.

Why am I saying this in a chapter on marketing? It's because all the marketing in the world won't get you anywhere if you aren't giving your customers a great product and experience. Remember the importance of experiential follow through in creating a grand brand: promise your customers something great to get them to the truck and deliver something even better to keep them coming back.

The Least You Need to Know

- Your logo is who you and your truck are.
- Social networking has been key to the growth of the food truck revolution, and it's absolutely necessary to your truck's success.
- Connecting to local food bloggers is your first priority. When they've been taken care of, you can think about reaching out to the mainstream press.
- Building personal relationships with your customers and knowing their preferences are a recipe for success.

Setting Up Your Office

All small business owners need an office, and food truckers are no exception. Your business may be on wheels, but it's important to establish a fixed space in which you'll organize all your administrative paperwork and records. With little expense, you can set up an office that serves the needs of your business, keeps your data safe and organized, and helps you run your business efficiently from one central and convenient location.

In this chapter, I show you where to set up your office, what to put in it, and how to personalize a system that keeps you in control of your important information. I explain how to determine your communication needs and design a payroll system that works for you. Finally, I show you where to seek help if you get lost along the way.

Deciding Where to Put Your Office

As a new small business owner, you're going to have a lot of important documents and digital information to organize, including financial and business records, supplier receipts, inventory lists, expense and cash flow projections, and tax forms, just to name a few. Keeping all of this in order is crucial to running a successful business.

You don't want to split your administrative data between your laptop and the passenger seat floor of the truck; you need to establish a secure and organized space from which to conduct business while your truck is parked for the night.

When deciding where to set up your office, you must first ask yourself who will be using it most. If you're a one-man show, you're probably the one responsible for all the administrative and accounting duties, including payroll, bookkeeping, ordering supplies, and paying your purveyors. In this case, you can set up a small office in your own home.

Choose a space that's quiet, private, and large enough for you to sit and work comfortably for several hours at a time. You'll need a desk, a computer, and plenty of storage space for your records. Your office doesn't need to be fancy, but it should feel professional, organized, comfortable, and, if possible, inspirational. If you have kids, be sure to set boundaries with them so that they know not to enter your office without your permission or tamper with any of your business-related documents.

TIP

Don't store your business or financial records on the family computer. Purchase a separate computer or subscribe to a cloud service; and back up your files regularly to protect your important information. Storing your information on a home computer makes it too vulnerable. Remember, should the IRS audit you they can look into your past for years, so good record keeping is critical to protecting your business.

If you have a partner, your home might not be the best place for your business office. It should be conveniently located for both of you and large enough for both of you to sit comfortably and work side-by-side. If either of you already own a related business, you may want to work out of that office. Wherever you choose to set up shop, make sure that you and your partner are equally satisfied with the decision.

Here's a quick list of the basic necessities you'll need for your office:

- **Computer or laptop.** Keep things simple. You'll only need one that supports a basic word processor, a spreadsheet application such as Excel, and bookkeeping software like QuickBooks, if you choose to handle the accounting yourself. You should spend no more than $1,500 dollars on this computer.

- **Internet.** You'll need a high-speed Internet connection to quickly communicate with your staff and vendors, send out the week's schedule, and manage your food truck's website and social networking applications.

- **External hard drive.** You'll need at least 50 to 100GB of memory to back up your important data. You can purchase a high-quality and compact backup drive for less than $150.

- **Telephone.** You'll find information on company communications later in this chapter.

TIP

If you're using your cell phone for your business, make sure your voicemail reflects it. Your image as a respectable and established business is important to those who choose to work with you. Your voicemail should say the name of your company, an alternate method of connection such as e-mail, and your web address.

- **Calculator.** Get an old-fashioned one with a paper roll that provides a hard-copy of your math.

- **Envelopes and stamps.** Even though you'll be using electronic communication as much as possible, you'll need a supply of legal envelopes and postage stamps.

- **Printer.** Save yourself space and money by investing in a two-in-one fax and printer. It's a good idea to get a unit that also scans *and* makes copies; that will save you many trips to the copy shop.

- **Ink and paper.** Stock up on printer paper and ink; you'll be printing menus, checks, memos, fax confirmations, spreadsheets, and reports for your own records every week.

- **File cabinet or storage tub.** You don't need anything massive, but you can expect to accumulate many hundreds of pages of records that you need to file. Be sure to label each drawer or plastic tub so that you can easily retrieve documents when you need them.

TIP

A cloud storage service allows you to store your important files and documents on the Internet and can be a good option for your truck business. It can save you space, protect your documents, and cost very little. Plus, you can access the documents anywhere as long as you have an Internet connection.

- **Legal forms.** Keep a supply of W-4 and I-9 tax forms, employee manuals and contracts, and copies of all your own business contracts and insurance policies.

- **Safe.** Keep your cash protected in a small, discreet safe until your next opportunity to visit the bank. Don't keep money in the safe longer than necessary and *never* leave it in the truck overnight. Take care to limit the number of people who have access to the combination.

- **Basic office goods.** Stock up on pens, pencils, legal pads, staples, paper clips, folders, rubber bands, and highlighters. Make sure you have a hole-puncher and a few strong three-ring binders to help keep things organized.

Creating a Communications Hub

As the administrative headquarters of your food truck business, your office must be equipped with the appropriate communication technologies. Vendors, clients, employees, investors, accountants, lawyers, and (hopefully) members of the media need to be able to contact and exchange information with you quickly, easily, and in a variety of ways.

The elaborateness of your communications setup will depend on the complexity of your concept and your expectations for expansion; if you plan to have a fleet of trucks, you'll need more infrastructure to monitor the trucks' locations, supply needs, and other necessary components of a larger operation.

Telephone

Running a business requires that you spend many hours on the phone every week. While you will likely be conducting business via your personal cell phone for much of that time, I advocate having an official landline in your office.

Any standard telephone should be more than sufficient for your needs. Be sure to subscribe to call waiting and voicemail services for both lines and record a very professional outgoing message. You may want to consider a telephone unit with built-in speakers and conference call capabilities so that you can conduct meetings over the phone with one or multiple vendors, lawyers, investors, or partners.

Internet Services

Internet access is crucial for any modern office operation, and a web presence, as discussed in Chapter 9, is a critical tool for expanding awareness of your truck and products. Your vendors, partners, accountant, lawyer, and anyone else with whom you conduct business will expect to be able to contact you via e-mail, which is often more efficient than picking up the telephone or mailing a letter.

Many of your purveyors will allow you to place orders with them via e-mail or through their websites. You'll find that it makes for a much cleaner operation; receipts are automatically e-mailed to you, and you'll spend considerably less time on the phone. E-mail also offers an alternative way for customers to contact you with feedback, questions, requests, and catering orders. You'll find that when you provide the option of contacting you via e-mail, more customers will reach out to you than if you only offer a telephone number.

Proactively accumulate customer e-mail addresses so that you can send out special promotional offers, truck alerts, and general advertising materials. You can offer your customers an incentive for registering with you, such as a free drink or a raffle ticket. The more e-mails you can accumulate and the better they are organized, the more effectively you'll be able to market the happenings surrounding your truck business.

TIP

Computer tablets, like Apple's iPad, are incredibly powerful computers in a compact, portable design. You may find it worthwhile to invest in one of these and synchronize it with your main office computer or laptop. That way you'll be able to access all your business information, instantly record customer e-mail addresses, update your inventory spreadsheets, and even place orders from your truck or anywhere on the go.

Fax

Fax machines remain an essential staple for any business. Many vendors still prefer that you place and confirm orders with them via fax, and you can expect to send and receive legal forms by fax as well. If you plan on sending out your catering menu (and you should) to potential and interested customers, fax or e-mail are the preferred method of delivery.

Handling Payroll and Records

Calculating and distributing payroll can be very time-consuming for most businesses. Your food truck probably won't have more than four or five employees, so outsourcing payroll to an expensive service company isn't necessary. You can do it yourself—and do it efficiently, too, if you follow the procedures laid out in this section.

First, you need to decide on a pay period: the number of days after which a paycheck will be issued. For most businesses, the pay period is either one or two weeks.

There are benefits and drawbacks to both the one- and two-week models. If you pay your employees every week, your payroll expense will remain consistent from week to week, but you'll spend twice the time and energy calculating hours, running numbers, and issuing checks than you would if you paid them every other week. A two-week pay period will save you time and energy, but your expense will jump from nothing to quite a large amount every other week, so you'll have to make sure you have the funds to cover payroll when it comes due.

To calculate and distribute your payroll, follow these simple steps:

1. **Open a payroll account.** You need to have a separate bank account that *only* covers payroll checks. Link it to your main business account so you can transfer money into it online, which will save you countless trips to the bank.

2. **Calculate the total hours worked for the pay period.** You have a small staff so it shouldn't take you more than 10 minutes to calculate and double-check. Have your employees sign in and out on a printed schedule every day they work. Confirm their check-in and check-out times as they do this and initial their names. If you're on top of this during the week, you'll be able to reliably tally their total hours for payroll with ease.

3. **Tally the gross pay for the week.** Multiply total hours by hourly wage to calculate each employee's gross pay.

4. **Subtract taxes and FICA.** Be sure every new hire fills out all the necessary legal paperwork, including a W-4 tax form. Use that information to subtract the appropriate withholding tax, along with Social Security contributions. A payroll company can help you with these calculations if necessary.

5. **Transfer the gross pay to the payroll account.** Once you write a check and transfer money into the payroll account, you must consider that money spent, regardless of how long it takes an employee to cash his or her check. Your employees will receive net pay unless they are being compensated as an independent contractor. You are responsible for paying the balance, tax payments, and FICA to the government in an interval determined by your accountant.

6. **Print and issue checks.** Each check should indicate the gross pay and total number of hours worked, with all tax and Social Security deductions itemized. Distribute checks at a set time on payday and require a signed confirmation from each employee as he receives his check. Never fall behind on payroll; always have the paychecks ready at the scheduled time on the scheduled day. You can, of course, pay your employees in cash if you wish, but paying by check has the benefit of leaving a paper trail and verifiable proof that you issued payroll.

Keeping Records

It's crucial that you properly store certain documents, receipts, and information for your business records. You're required by law to keep some of these records. Others will help protect you if you are audited or if someone disputes a charge or bill.

Keep indefinitely all of your financial statements, accounting records, cash and credit card receipts, balance sheets, and contracts of any kind. You should keep tax records, invoices, bank statements, health inspection reports, and payroll records for no less than 10 years.

TIP

Remember that the more records you save, the safer you'll be in the long run. Keep in mind when you're choosing your office location that you'll easily fill a small filing cabinet over the next few years. While backing up your digital files onto an external hard drive is important, it isn't enough. You'll need hard copies of your records in the event of a tax audit or lawsuit.

Getting Outside Help

Knowing the ins and outs of local laws and regulations is crucial for any entrepreneur. It's very common and advisable for new and seasoned business owners alike to seek guidance from lawyers and accountants as they decide on a business structure, seek permits, and design their business plans. Investing in the expertise of these specialists is something you should be prepared to do if you're starting out with little or no experience in building a business.

You'll want to find a lawyer or accountant who has experience and a proven track record in the food industry in your city. If you know people who own restaurants or food trucks in your area, ask them to recommend someone with whom they have worked. If you're approaching one of these specialists directly, ask them for references and follow up on them. You want advisers who have helped business owners save money, navigate bureaucracy, and make sound decisions about their businesses.

A qualified lawyer can help you understand local laws and regulations and assist you in obtaining all the necessary permits for your food truck. He can draw up or review contracts, including partnership agreements, and register your business as a sole proprietorship, partnership, or corporation. An experienced lawyer can also provide you with valuable contacts in the industry.

If you're having difficulty understanding some of the financial concepts involved in developing your business plan and managing the accounting records for your truck, consider hiring an accountant to help guide you through the process. He can help determine whether your concept will be profitable and suggest the best way to structure your company. Once you've launched your business, you can retain the accountant to continue managing your weekly and monthly finances to whatever extent necessary.

Lawyers and accountants can become very pricey. Many charge an hourly rate of $200 to $300 that can quickly add up to monstrous fees. It's important that you speak to them up front about the charges prior to engaging their services. I would recommend that you ask them about setting a fee for the work being done rather than their working on an hourly basis. That way you can budget appropriately and they'll be committed to finishing the job, no matter how long it takes.

The bottom line when working with accountants and lawyers is to choose people you feel comfortable with and trust. These professionals will be handling your most sensitive documents and financial matters. You want to find people who provide great advice and security in these important matters.

The Least You Need to Know

- No matter how small your food truck company is, you'll need an off-truck place to manage and conduct business.

- Communications are of the utmost importance. Make sure vendors, customers, and others are always able to reach you.

- Whether you hand out paychecks weekly or every other week, you need to set up a system that handles payroll easily and seamlessly.

- The possibility of IRS audits and possible lawsuits make it imperative that you keep your business records, including hard copies, in a safe and handy place.

Getting Road Ready

Execution is everything in the food truck business. You only have a small space, so you need to maximize efficiency. And efficiency, speed, quality, and low waste are what lead to profitability in the food truck game. How do you become efficient? Through proper kitchen layout, great design, flawless systems, and many other things I cover in this part of the book.

But even if you have great systems, you still need the right people to execute them. Locating the best employees for your truck could be the most important step in the entire process. I help you get your staff "on the boat," as well as get the best performance out of them.

Last but definitely not least, I talk about what you need to do to make sure your truck is safe. Food safety through proper preparation is vital to protect your customers, employees, and business. The slightest sign of food-borne illness might put your business on life support.

Setting Up the "House"

In most hospitality businesses, there's a front and a back of house. The front of house refers to all areas that deal with customers and service (waiters and waitresses). The back of house refers to the areas customers never see, such as the kitchen and supply room. In general, these areas require vastly different skill sets and personality types. Some people are great at slicing tomatoes but not so good at talking to customers; they're clearly back of house people. Others look beautiful and are great at service but can't even fry an egg—front of house people. Neither of those kinds of people will work for your food truck. You won't have the luxury.

Understanding Your Unique Situation

When it comes to employees for your truck, you need individuals who have an understanding of both your front and back of house. You won't be able to indulge the extravagance of hiring a great cook with a terrible personality. If he's in the truck yelling at the other cooks, your customers will see and hear him and that will negatively affect your customers' experience. And if that surly chef has to take over the window while you go get supplies, you're in big trouble. You have one truck, and one house. There's no such thing as hiding in the back.

Everyone who works for you needs to serve multiple functions. Your employees must be able to work the grill *and* the window. More important, you need to apply the one-house philosophy to all aspects of your truck. Your exterior and interior design and how you deal with customers must be put together so that all elements work together to add to the total experience.

In a restaurant or hotel, for example, staff can collect the garbage in an area away from customer view and take it out a service entrance. You don't have that option on your truck. You must discreetly collect garbage and quickly remove it from the truck. A day's worth of garbage in a small truck can become an issue very quickly, chasing away customers with its odor and creating health concerns from cross-contamination.

In this chapter, I discuss how you set up your house, which is a very important step in the process of creating your food truck. Let's not waste any time getting to it.

Designing the Exterior of Your Truck

The exterior design of your food truck is critical to your success. It serves two purposes: marketing and functionality.

The outside of your truck is the ultimate advertisement for what you're selling. Just as the outside of a restaurant sets the tone for a customer's dining experience, the exterior of your truck does the same thing for your customers. The difference from a bricks-and-mortar restaurant is that your exterior is constantly on the move. The more you drive, the more you advertise. Your truck design must immediately attract the attention of the consumer. And after you grab their attention, you need to convey some important details immediately:

- Your name

- What kind of food you serve

- Your Twitter handle

Within five seconds of seeing your truck, customers need to recognize that they want what you're selling and know how to get it.

There's no point of having the most beautifully designed truck if nobody knows what you do or where to find you. That's why there are so many trucks with bold and exciting exterior designs. It isn't because food truckers are the most artistic people in the world; their flair is a matter of necessity. Your truck is a mobile billboard, and you need to utilize it to make a statement and attract customers.

> **TIP**
>
> The back, right, and left panels of your truck must all include your logo, the type of product you're serving, and your Twitter account, website address, and phone number. Your job is to find a design that does this in a tasteful manner. Your truck's name should be sized at 100 percent, the type of food you serve sized at 75 percent, and your contact information at 30 to 50 percent, depending on what looks best.

You have two options for exterior decoration: paint or vinyl wrap. I consider the pros and cons of each option in the following sections.

Painting

Painting your truck is the cheapest way to go, but is generally less effective. To get maximum marketing value from painting you would need to find someone extremely talented. A talented artist is probably going to be pricey, which defeats the whole purpose of using the cheaper design method.

If you do choose to paint your truck, use contrasting colors for your base and logo. If your truck is black, for instance, use a bright color like fluorescent pink or green for the logo. The best way to add your logo to a painted truck is to either use a stencil or have the logo printed as a sticker at your local print shop. Whichever method you choose, make sure the logo is bold. You don't want to get lost in the crowd.

Painting your truck should cost less than $2,500.

Vinyl Wrap

Truck wraps are the most cost-effective way to maximize the exposure of your brand with the design of your truck.

The company you choose to create the wrap should have an in-house designer who can assist you. If not, reach out to fellow truckers whose designs you admire and ask who they used. An experienced designer will understand which areas of the truck will be exposed and where seams are located in order to fully maximize the wrap. Working with a graphic designer who has done this kind of work before, you'll be able to create any imaginable design. The fee for the design is usually around $500.

The designer must use high-resolution or vector images to create your truck wrap, with the printing done using a very high-dpi printer. Your customers will see your truck both from far away and close up, so the design must be recognizable from a distance and look like a custom paint job up close. Ask to see a proof prior to the printing of your design so you'll know exactly what it will look like when it's applied to your truck. Review the proof very carefully; you'll have to live with any mistakes you don't catch at this point. Make sure you have the opportunity to sign off on the design before your wrap is installed.

Not all vinyl wraps are of equal quality. You can get wraps for as little as $1,500, but the vinyl is likely to be thin with no protective laminate coating. These cheaper wraps will begin to peel rather quickly and are much more time-consuming to remove.

A thick, high-quality wrap with a protective laminate costs anywhere from $4,500 to $5,000. Laminate enhances the appearance of your vehicle while protecting your truck from fading and scratches.

Protect your investment by choosing a thick 3M wrap with laminate. Your truck will look brand new year after year if you go for the high-quality version. Customers will be attracted to the pristine look of your rig, so the better wrap should lead to more sales. And if you choose to sell or trade-in your truck one day, a better-quality wrap will lead to a higher resale or trade-in value. This is because cheaper wraps are harder to remove and can cause damage to the vehicle.

> **TIP**
>
> According to *Outdoor Advertising Magazine*, mobile billboards have a 97 percent recall rate, and 99 percent of survey respondents said they thought mobile advertising was more effective than traditional outdoor advertising. The Traffic Audit Bureau says that during a single month a truck can give between 1 and 4 million impressions to potential consumers. Trust me when I say that your vehicle wrap is your most valuable advertising outlet. Don't let that opportunity go to waste.

Window

There's no standard window size for food trucks, but I recommend as large a window as possible. The larger your window, the more involved your customers will feel in the life of the truck, and the more people you can serve at a time. It's always best to have a window on each side so you have more parking possibilities, though if you have two windows you'll probably need to go with smaller versions than if you had just one. That's a decision you'll have to make based on your own preference and what works best for your concept.

Awning

After you deal with your window size, you'll need to decide what type of awning you want.

Most trucks come with a stainless steel panel that you secure in the up position when your truck is operating. It acts as an awning when you're open and a security cover when you're not. For the most part you won't really have much for people to steal on your truck. The cooking equipment is heavy and will be bolted down, and your materials are refilled on a daily basis. I feel the cover is unnecessary and suggest replacing it with an aesthetically pleasing awning that you can extend when you park. You can purchase these types of awnings at your local home supply store or from an awning specialist for $1,500 to $2,000. The awning should cover the length of your truck's window and be incorporated into your design.

Drink Fridge

Your drink fridge or cooler should be accessible to customers from the outside of your truck so they can reach in and make their choice. This alleviates the need for internal storage and removes one step from the serving process. Make sure the storage container is deep enough to store and cool a sufficient number of beverages for multiple hours of service. Additionally, with the beverages outside, it is important that you make sure all beverages are paid for.

Exterior Menu Holder

You should place a plastic menu holder outside the truck. Having printed menus handy limits the number of customer questions during the ordering process, especially at peak times. Encouraging customers to take copies of the menus with them also acts as a form of advertising for potential customers and encourages take-out orders. Place the menu holder in a spot that's easily accessible even during busy times.

Menu Board

Your menu board should be located on the outside of your truck to the left of your window. It should be made out of plastic poster board and be large enough to be read from at least 10 feet away. Refer to the menu design information in Chapter 3 when designing the layout and content of your board. The most important point to remember is that item you want to sell the most of should be in the top right corner.

After you've designed the menu, you'll need to bring it to a printer who specializes in printing on plastic, which will hold up for a long time when mounted very securely on the outside of your truck. That board needs to withstand weather and travel while still maintaining its shine and splendor. It's one of your main sales tools, so make sure it's a beautiful representation of your product.

The Point of Sale System

So long to the days of Grandma sitting behind the cash register monitoring the day's take. Nowadays point of sale (POS) systems (your digital cash registers) manage inventory, process credit cards, calculate food cost percentages, and handle ordering. Many of them even monitor your business every minute you're operating by generating real time reports.

Old-fashioned cash registers or manual sales monitoring techniques are subject to human error, leading to inefficiencies, potential theft, and loss of cash. A POS system is essential to running a healthy modern hospitality business. Yes, they cost a little more in the beginning, but they pay for themselves quickly by saving you money and giving you peace of mind. A quality POS system not only gives you insights into what your customers are ordering, it tells you on what days and times they're ordering it, and if they made any substitutions.

POS systems are preloaded with basic reporting options that can assist in monitoring your truck's performance. If you want a report that provides hourly sales breakdowns by item and compares them on a month-to-month basis so you can monitor growth, your POS system can do it. Here's an overview of the types of performance reports a POS system can help you with:

- **Basic reports.** Average spend per person, how much of each item is selling, and percentage of people buying sides and beverages with their orders.

- **Trends.** Monitor the trends within your business; are falafel sales decreasing and gyro sales increasing? Maybe it has something to do with people wanting to eat proteins and not fried foods. You'd better know, because it's affecting your business, and your POS can tell you.

- **Cost centers.** The system will create them for different workers and meals. Maybe you do more business when Jason is working the window and Isaac is on the grill. You can use this info to maximize your revenues.

These reports should be more than enough to cover a small operation, but you can also work with your POS company to create customized reports specifically for your business.

A simple POS system for a truck should cost around $5,000, including a terminal with a printer for the kitchen and all necessary installation and setup. In addition you should budget for service and maintenance fees, which for an operation of this size should be less than $50 to $100 per month. To save money, try purchasing a used system from restaurants that are going out of business or through websites such as Craigslist.

TIP

Companies like Micros, Aloha, and Squirrel dominate the POS system market. They offer technologically advanced systems and are adding capabilities daily. These systems have endless possibilities and options for customization, most of which aren't necessary for your purposes.

Tablet Systems

The introduction of tablet computers offers a much better solution for mobile hospitality businesses. Many companies are making iPad-based POS systems that are much more affordable and offer many of the same features as the more advanced ones. You can get a tablet system for between $500 and $2,500 plus a subscription fee of $30 to $50 per month. Try for a system setup for $1,500 with a minimal subscription fee inclusive of the cost of an iPad, iPhone, iTouch, or similar tablet computer. These usually come with cash drawers and printers, and generally take up much less space than traditional systems.

TIP

Because social media is so important to your business, you'll definitely need some type of onboard computer. The best option for food truck operators right now is a smart phone such as an iPhone, BlackBerry, or Motorola Droid. These phones have applications that allow you to post on Twitter, Facebook, and Foursquare directly. You can also use one of these phones as the direct number for your truck. Other options include a laptop with WiFi capabilities or a tablet computer such as an iPad.

Credit Cards

I don't recommend accepting credit cards on your truck. Card companies charge fees that range from 2 to 5 percent of each transaction, which can add up very quickly and amount to hundreds or thousands of dollars a month. In the food truck business you have very low margins of profitability, and credit card fees will cut those margins in half. The average purchase on your truck will probably be under $20, so the fact that you don't accept credit cards shouldn't deter customers. Even for larger catering orders it's easier and more profitable to accept a check. If you decide to accept credit cards, I suggest not taking them for orders under $20, and I'd pass along the credit card fees to the customer for catering orders. (Be sure to check your local laws to make sure credit card minimums are legal in your area.)

If you do choose to accept credit cards, you'll have to set up a merchant account with your bank so that you can accept payment from both credit and debit cards. You can handle your credit card processing through your POS system. You'll also need to contact a credit card processing organization such as First Data and sign up for an account with them. There are many different kinds of plans, so be sure to comparison shop at least three processing companies to get the best rate based on your expected volume of sales.

BEEP! BEEP!

Don't just look at the transaction fees when choosing a credit card processing company. Some companies lure customers with low rates and hide charges, like administration fees, in the back end that make them more expensive than the normal rates. And most of these processor agreements automatically renew unless you specifically say not to, so be sure to remove that clause from your contract.

Setting Up the Kitchen

The next step in setting up your house is organizing the design of your kitchen for efficiency. By this I mean making sure you have enough space to prep and plate your food quickly while maintaining the quality of your product. This requires military-style organization and precision.

Organization

The first step is making sure that everything within your on-truck kitchen is located in the right place. The storage of your serving materials must be in the same area or right next to where you're doing the plating. You don't want to waste time walking to the back of the truck to get buns and containers every time a burger comes off the grill.

This same rule applies to the way you organize your refrigerated items. If you're making cheeseburgers, you want the cheese in the closest refrigerator to the grill. That's common sense, but not everyone thinks about it.

> **BEEP! BEEP!**
>
> If you haven't noticed it yet, there are so many moving parts in the food truck business that it's easy to make silly mistakes. If you don't fix these issues immediately they'll snowball, making day-to-day operations unbearable. Pay attention to details.

Here's a checklist of things to consider when organizing your kitchen for prep and plating:

- Figure out which areas of the kitchen will be used most and least based on your menu mix.

- Ensure that you have enough refrigeration for a full day's service. If you need to sell 100 hamburgers a day to make money, you'd better have enough refrigeration to accommodate ingredients for those 100 hamburgers every day.

- Make sure the prep area and the storage of prepared materials is close enough to where you're doing the cooking to be quickly restocked during service.

- Make sure there's a clear line of sight and speech between the sales window and the kitchen; the person running the window also acts as your *expeditor*.

- Make sure the cooks have easy access to the plates and take-out containers.

> **DEFINITION**
>
> The **expeditor** is the person on the truck in charge of organizing the orders. Once an order is taken, the expeditor monitors its progress by coordinating with the kitchen. Then he or she checks the order to ensure that it's prepared properly prior to delivery to the customer.

Job Assignments

The bottom line is that everyone on the rig should be able to get his job done without hindering anyone else's ability to get her job done. The best way to figure that out is by creating detailed descriptions of every task that needs to be completed by each worker on your truck. Then you can sit down with your initial kitchen design and begin to flesh out the process that each employee must go through to complete his or her job. As you analyze the processes, you'll be able to identify potential bottlenecks and begin to place things in the best possible locations. If you take the time to do this, you'll limit the number of issues you'll run into during your first months of operation.

Don't forget that you need to take into account local regulations. Cities like Chicago have laws that don't allow for cooking on the truck. Windy City food trucks are only allowed to sell preprepared or packaged items; even chopping of vegetables is prohibited. Check with your local health department to determine exactly what's legal and what isn't in terms of your kitchen. It could have major impact on how you choose to prepare your food and how you lay out your kitchen. You might have been planning to make sandwiches to order on your truck in Chicago, but now you know that all of your sandwiches have to be packaged in your commissary.

> **TRUCK TALES**
>
> Chicago's original food truck, Chicago All Fired Up, made its way onto the Windy City's streets through some legal maneuvering. Years ago owner Troy Marcus Johnson convinced the health inspector to approve his truck as a restaurant. Since then he's been selling Baby Back Ribs and Jerk Chicken from his truck and cooking them on board. Who knows how he got past the long arm of the law, but it's great for Chicagoans looking for late-night eats.

Creating an Efficient Workflow

In order to establish an efficient workflow, you need to utilize the assembly line. Assign each worker on the truck a particular job in the process of getting out orders with ease. The employees can assist one another, but only if they've already fully completed their assigned tasks in the process.

Here's how it works:

1. The employee in charge of the window takes the customer's order, provides him or her with a receipt or order number, and then passes along the order to the kitchen, manually or automatically through the POS.

2. The kitchen receives the order and one or two employees begin preparing the food. (In some cases the cooking process has already begun before the order is taken because the items take longer to fully prepare than you want the customer to wait.) The cooks monitor the order and are in constant communication with the window worker/expeditor, who can update the customer on order delivery.

3. When the food is prepared, the cook plates it for serving and hands it to the expeditor.

4. The expeditor checks the order and gives it to the customer.

Each truck's system will likely vary slightly from the preceding process, but overall the process is very similar. The key is to maintain the flow and not create any bottlenecks in the line. If one worker in the process is taking longer than the other members of the team, the assembly line comes to a halt. Everyone needs to be equally skilled in their part of the process or the system doesn't work. Skilled employees, combined with fanatic organization and attention to detail, will make your line efficient and consistent.

The Least You Need to Know

- The outside of your truck is the ultimate advertisement for it.
- A truck wrap is more expensive in the short term but is ultimately more economical than painting it.

- Your menu board is one of your biggest selling tools, so make sure it's durable, looks great, and is visible from a minimum of 10 feet away.
- A point of sale system acts as a cash register, provides reports, and can process credit cards.
- You need to establish a proper workflow so that the assembly line can deliver food efficiently.

Hiring and Managing Staff

In This Chapter

- Deciding what positions are crucial to the success of your food truck
- Assembling your team
- Setting standards for food preparation and customer service
- Scheduling work hours and company policies
- Motivating your staff

"If you have the wrong people, it doesn't matter whether you discover the right direction; you still won't have a great company. Great vision without great people is irrelevant," says Jim Collins in *Good to Great* (HarperCollins, 2001), one of the greatest business books ever written. In the book he researches the greatest companies of our time—those that have shown consistent growth over a long period of time.

Choosing the right people to prepare and represent your food is just as important as choosing the right ingredients. A strong team can make your truck a success, while an undertrained or unmotivated staff can sabotage your entire vision. In this chapter, I show you how to choose and train the right people and how to create a work environment that keeps them motivated.

How Many and What Positions?

Food trucks are typically intimate operations, with an average of three to four people on board: one running the window, one or two other(s) in the kitchen, and one outside of the truck organizing the line, monitoring the neighborhood, and handling the marketing. The idea is to consolidate as many responsibilities as possible into just a couple of positions.

It's impossible to know how many people you need or in what capacity until you've clearly defined your menu and concept. The nature and complexity of your offerings largely dictates what responsibilities need to be filled.

For example, a soup truck can usually operate with just two people. The main person takes the orders, handles payment, and serves the soup—not an unreasonable amount of work for one person. The second employee would assist during the busy hours, refill soup pots and supplies, clean, and assist as needed. If the truck operator were to expand her menu to include Panini sandwiches, for example, she would need to hire an additional kitchen worker to prepare the sandwiches and run the Panini press.

TIP

You should never have more than five people working on your truck and, unless you're operating an ice-cream truck, it would be difficult to handle a truck with just one. For maximum return on investment you should strive to run your truck with a three-man crew.

To determine the number of employees your food truck requires, begin by analyzing your menu for the following characteristics:

- **Prep time.** How long does it take to prepare all the ingredients for service? How many people are required to prep the kitchen before you open? In a soup truck example, the majority of labor and cooking time occurs before the operator opens each day, so she can have one employee help her once the truck is open and two working to prep the soups prior to service.

- **Cook time.** Do you cook your food to order or do you merely assemble a plate for your customers? A burger cooked to order requires significantly more time and effort than a meatball sandwich, for which most of the work is done before you open.

- **Complexity.** How complex are your dishes? Do they each require great skill and attention, or can multiple orders be prepared simultaneously? It's much easier to grill several burgers at one time than to properly cook the same number of fish entrées at once. The more focus a dish requires, the fewer orders the kitchen can fill at one time.

- **Variety.** The greater the variety of made-to-order dishes on your menu, the harder it will be to fill multiple orders simultaneously and the longer it will take to fill an order that includes two or more wildly different dishes.

As you analyze your menu, you should begin to get a sense of what processes and responsibilities will require most of your time and labor. For example, if you specialize in fresh pastas, plan to spend a significant amount of time preparing the dough and making sauces. Create a list of the major responsibilities that make up the bulk of your operation. Break down each step from taking the order to serving it, and assign an employee to each role in the process so you can begin to know how many people you'll need.

Also consider your own role in the kitchen or at the window. Which of the responsibilities on your list are you going to take on yourself? While you'll want to do as much as possible, you shouldn't take on too much. Micromanaging is a classic mistake of first-time truck operators. You need to delegate work to your crew so you have enough room to step back and supervise, manage, and interact with your customers.

If you have a partner, you need to consider which role, if any, would make best use of his strengths. One of the best reasons for taking on a partner is because that person brings a special set of skills or expertise to the operation. If your partner has a strong culinary background, then his role is clear from the beginning: he should oversee the preparation of the food and determine whether he needs an extra pair of hands in the kitchen.

Once you know what you'll be doing on the truck, consolidate the remaining responsibilities on your list into one or two positions. If you're still unsure how many people you'll need to get the job done, go with your best guess. You'll know very quickly once you start operating if you need to downsize or expand your staff needs. If you communicate well with your employees you'll be able to implement changes easily.

Getting the Right People On Board

It's time to assemble a qualified team to help make your food truck dream a reality. Depending on the demands of your menu and concept, you'll need experienced, enthusiastic professionals to fill one or two positions.

> **TIP**
>
> Notice I didn't include chef on the list of staff positions to consider. At this point in the game, you should have a fully conceived menu, and most chefs won't want to produce someone else's recipes. If you don't have any culinary inclination or just feel uncomfortable designing a menu on your own, consider a partnership with a chef who can create a menu to fit your concept. A food truck has no need for a chef for any other reason than to develop the recipes and for marketing. Your cooks should be more than capable of handling the work with adequate training.

The primary positions you need to fill are as follows:

- Prep cook
- Cook
- Cashier/greeter

The following sections detail the job duties of each of these positions.

Prep Cook

The quality of a kitchen's prep work is a big part of the quality of its finished product. Depending on the type of truck, your prep cook might do all the cooking. Prep cooks ready every ingredient for service, from trimming meat to deboning fish to chopping veggies. They make sure the kitchen is fully stocked and that every component of the menu is on hand, clean, fresh, and ready to be cooked or served. They're often responsible for preparing soups, sauces, and baked goods as well.

A good prep cook should have a solid working knowledge of every piece of equipment in your kitchen and understand the proper way to handle all the ingredients on your menu. She must be highly organized, punctual, and responsible. She should be able to take orders and criticism, and endure long hours on her feet, doing repetitive work. Most important, she should take pride in her work and feel motivated to do her job well.

A well-trained and dedicated prep cook can save you countless hours of tedious labor while giving you the peace of mind of knowing that your product is in safe and loving hands. She can also double as an on-truck cook during service, should you require her to do so.

> **TIP**
>
> Ninety percent of the people you hire to launch your truck won't be with you six months later. This isn't a reflection on you; it's the nature of the business. The truck is your dream and you must do everything in your power to protect it, which includes firing someone who isn't right for the job. Constantly be on the lookout for good people and have a file of backups.

On-Truck Cook

The on-truck cook executes the entire menu. Other than the prep cook, the quality of your product is solely dependent on the skill and execution of this individual.

As with prep cooks, you want to find an on-truck cook who is experienced but still receptive to learning and taking direction. Laboring long hours in a truck kitchen can be thankless and exhausting work, so he must be responsible and dedicated, and demonstrate a positive attitude toward his work. You should ideally find two people who can work either as a prep or an on-truck cook.

Cashier/Greeter

I highly recommend that you take this position yourself. It's your truck and you should be the face of it. It's also your money, and at least until you find someone trustworthy, you should be handling it. If you aren't going to be greeting customers and taking orders yourself, you must find a cashier/greeter whose personality and enthusiasm will represent your business in the best way possible. This person should not only care about the product but able to sell it.

Your cashier/greeter must be familiar enough with the menu to answer any question about the food and to gently *up-sell* your customers.

> **DEFINITION**
>
> An **up-sell** is a casual suggestion to your customers to purchase appetizers, side dishes, drinks, and desserts. Up-selling to your guests can greatly increase your revenue and average check. It's a great way to bring attention to areas of the menu you'd like to push, such as high-profit items.

The Hiring Process

When you're ready to begin the interview process, place an ad in the newspaper or online. I recommend using Craigslist.com, which offers free and paid advertising space for employers to reach out to jobseekers. It's an invaluable resource for attracting food service workers.

BEEP! BEEP!

Never hire the first person you interview; always meet multiple candidates and ask for references. Be aware of red flags—applicants who are late for their interview or have a history of jumping from job to job. In the end, rely on your instinct to tell you whether someone is a good fit for your business. Make sure you like them: you'll be in tight quarters with these people, so you'll be better off if you enjoy their company.

Here are a few questions you can ask applicants on their first interview:

- Why did you leave your last job?
- Why do you want to work on our food truck?
- What are your major strengths and weaknesses?
- Why do feel you would be a good fit here?
- What are your personal and professional goals? How do you believe they will affect your employment?
- What is your passion?

For prep and on-truck cooks, you definitely want to include one or two auditions in the kitchen after the initial interview. You'll want to observe their skill, conduct, efficiency, and attitude, and see if you can work comfortably and amiably beside them in small quarters.

Beware of arrogant cooks in the food truck kitchen. You want to work with people who are eager and open to learning, receptive to criticism, and respect your authority. There's no room in a food truck for people with inflated egos and their own vision of your business. You're better off with someone who's reserved, fastidious, and respectful. Your food truck should be run like an army, and there's no room for dissension among the ranks.

For your cashier/greeter applicants, you'll want to observe them interacting with customers. Ask them to learn the menu and give them a trial period during which you compare their customer service skills and salesmanship with that of your other candidates.

> **TIP**
>
> Choose employees who, in addition to their normal duties, are qualified to drive the truck. Make sure they have a license and obtain a report on their driving history from the department of motor vehicles.

Training and Educating Your Staff

After you've hired an experienced, enthusiastic team for your food truck, you need to educate them on your menu, concept, and expectations for the business. Don't assume that just because someone has a strong background in cooking or customer service he or she won't need guidance and a clear outline of your expectations.

Setting the Right Tone

It's crucial for the morale of your team and the overall success of the business that you establish from the very beginning an open dialogue between you and your staff, in which they can safely express any concern, suggestion, or grievance. Remember that you set the tone for the workplace; if you seem to see and expect the best in people, they'll usually prove you right. If you choose to see the worst, your employees will prove you right on that, too.

Clearly communicate to each of your team members exactly what you expect from them and by what criteria you'll be judging their performance.

Training

Taking the time to conduct training sessions and staff meetings not only keeps your employees on top of their game but also shows them that they're valuable parts of the team.

Train your on-truck or prep cook one-on-one. Never throw a cook into the kitchen without giving him the opportunity to learn and practice the recipes. The auditions you hold as a part of the hiring process should double as training sessions. Teach your cook the recipes and ask him to replicate them. You'll quickly sense the skill level of your potential employee.

Consider holding regular staff tastings to familiarize everyone with specials and to review the menu. Product knowledge is crucial for your *front-of-the-truck* staff.

DEFINITION

Front-of-the-truck is a variation of front of the house, restaurant jargon for all the staff members who are on the floor and interact with customers.

Teaching the Importance of Customer Service

Set very specific customer service standards for your front-of-the-truck staff. Customers should be regarded as *guests* at all times. Your staff should strive to not just serve food but to provide an experience to each guest from the moment they're greeted in line to when they walk away.

BEEP! BEEP!

Studies demonstrate that your guests will remember poor customer service *more than the food*. No matter how great your burgers are, customers won't come back if they feel your staff was rude or dismissive. Good customer service, on the other hand, can outshine an average meal and make the overall experience positive and memorable. It's by providing a high level of customer service that you connect with your clients and build a dedicated following.

Here are the complete steps of service, including some rules for interacting with your guests. You can copy this list and display it in the truck, or include it in your employee manual:

- Greet every guest as they approach the truck. Smile and ask them how they're doing. Offer to answer any questions they may have and offer samples, if possible.

- Never have a conflict with other employees in front of the guests, who should never be aware of any problems on the truck.

- Learn the names of your repeat guests.

- Never be distant or too formal. Treat your guests as if they're old friends. Always act excited to see each guest, whether it's her first or thirtieth visit. This will make guests more receptive to up selling, as customers will see you as a friend, not a salesman with ulterior motives.

- Never argue with a guest. If someone is upset, try to accommodate him in every way possible. If you can't, get a manager/owner to deal with the problem. Always smile and remain calm.

- Try to anticipate the needs of every guest. Give extra napkins with a messy item or extra utensils if guests plan to share with friends, without their having to ask for them.

- Don't try to save a penny and end up losing a dollar. In other words, if your customer drops her food or spills his drink, give her a new one.

- Know the menu inside out. Be prepared to answer questions about allergies, spiciness, and portion size. This knowledge will allow you to make useful suggestions, helping your guests to pair entrées and sides and increasing their check totals.

- Accommodate modifications to the menu whenever possible. Yes, it's annoying when customers try to create their own dish, but they'll remember that you went out of your way to please them. Knowing the menu well will help you make recommendations to people whose requests you can't accommodate.

- Thank every guest for his or her business, and always say good-bye.

- Never point out the tip jar or mention tips in any way.

Customer response can be rather surprising when these principles are put into action. People respond well to kindness and gratitude, and will remember that they had an enjoyable interaction with you and your staff. The key is consistency. You must treat every guest the same way. It only takes one negative experience to lose a customer for life.

Scheduling

The most efficient way to schedule employees is to create a simple spreadsheet. Post a printed schedule in the truck and the commissary, and e-mail a copy to your staff at least three or four days before the start of each work week. Making schedules can be really tough for any business, especially when you have multiple part-time employees fighting for shifts or requesting time off. Luckily, your food truck doesn't need a huge staff; making the schedule should be fairly straightforward if you hired wisely and chose people who are making this job a priority.

In general there are three shifts for workers on a food truck:

- **Prep:** Prepares the food at the commissary;

- **Breakfast/lunch:** Prepares and serves meals on the truck during the breakfast and/or lunch shift

- **Dinner:** Prepares and serves evening meals on the truck

> **TIP**
>
> Be sure to get your schedule posted by the deadline you set for yourself so your staff can plan their personal time efficiently. If you can't be punctual, how can you expect them to be?

Your spreadsheet should list the days you're open, with a row for each position you're scheduling. On slower days, you may be able to cut back on a set of hands in the kitchen or front of house. After you've been open for a couple of weeks, you'll have a better grasp of which days require more help and on which you can do without, though business will always be changing based on spot availability.

Your staff should generally be able to predict the days on which they'll be working, and their total hours for each week should remain reasonably constant. If you're not consistent, their pay will fluctuate from week to week and they won't be able to predict their income. It's important to provide your staff with as much stability as possible so they can focus on doing the best job rather than looking for other work. Regard your staff's scheduling needs as you would your own and never forget that everyone is there to make money.

Here's a sample food truck schedule:

	Mon	Tues	Wed	Thurs	Fri	Sat	Total Hrs
	6/1	6/2	6/3	6/4	6/5	6/6	
B.O.T. (Back of the Truck & Commissary)							
Henry	Off	Off	10 A.M.–6 P.M.	10 A.M.–6 P.M.	10 A.M.–6 P.M.	12 P.M.–6 P.M.	30
F.O.T. (Front of the Truck)							
Sarah	11 A.M.–6 P.M.	11 A.M.–6 P.M.	11 A.M.–6 P.M.	Off	Off	12 P.M.–6 P.M.	27
Alice	Off	Off	Off	11 A.M.–6 P.M.	11 A.M.–6 P.M.	Off	14

Establish a firm attendance policy from the get-go. Require your employees to notify you at least two hours in advance if they're going to be late or absent. Be clear that it's their responsibility to reach you or another supervisor; leaving a voicemail or text message, or having a co-worker explain your absence, isn't acceptable. Request a doctor's note for consecutive absences. If an employee is tardy and/or absent multiple times, disciplinary action may be warranted. Be sure to outline your attendance policies in your employee manual (see the following section).

Setting Policies

Even though you might be a team of only five or fewer, it's important to set official policies and standards for your food truck. Actually, the fact that yours is such a small operation can give the impression that it's okay to treat it less seriously than other businesses. You have to seize the reins from the very beginning and demand respect for your company and authority.

A great way to do this is to create an employee manual that provides information about the company and the standards, rules, and expectations you have for your staff. It should explain the concept behind the truck, the history and inspiration of the menu, and a little background on yourself so that your staff knows who you are and what inspired you. This information can be especially useful to your front-of-truck people when answering guests' questions. All employees should be required to read and sign the manual, stating that they understand the policies and the consequences of violating them.

Your manual doesn't have to be fancy, but it should be thorough and look professional. The policies and signed statement need to be very clearly worded; you never know when a disgruntled ex-employee will take you to court to dispute the clarity or existence of the policy that got him or her fired. The manual is a way to not only educate your staff and get them excited about your business, but to legally protect you and your company.

Your manual should include but not be limited to the following:

- **Mission statement.** Introduce yourself and explain the history and concept behind your company. Your mission statement should set the tone not just for the product and experience you want to give your customers but for the work environment you want to foster for your staff.

- **Performance and behavior standards.** Discuss your expectations for professionalism and lay out a code of conduct.

- **Confidentiality.** Agree to guard whatever personal and financial information you, as the employer, must collect from them. Your staff, in turn, is asked to respect any private information to which they're exposed.

- **Drugs and alcohol.** State your policy against on-premise drug and alcohol consumption and identify the repercussions for violating said policy. Illegal activity of any kind cannot be tolerated on the premises.

- **Emergencies.** Identify emergency procedures, including an evacuation plan, and collect emergency contact information for each employee.

- **Sexual harassment.** State your policy that sexual harassment won't be tolerated and warrants immediate termination.

- **Safety precautions.** Provide safety information about driving your truck and operating in your kitchen.

- **Smoking.** Identify an acceptable distance from your truck where employees are allowed to smoke.

- **Menu.** Include detailed descriptions of each item on the menu, including all the ingredients and identifying the most common food allergies.

- **Customer service.** Feel free to include the customer service outline from earlier in this chapter.

- **Food safety and health department guidelines.** It's crucial that your employees understand and follow all department of health (DOH) food safety guidelines.

- **Uniform, hygiene, and appearance.** Outline your expectations for your staff's physical appearance and attire.

- **Attendance and lateness policy.** State your protocol for reporting lateness and absences, what documentation you may require, and the consequences for repeated lateness and absence.

TIP

Establish a set policy and protocol for requesting time off. Require the request in writing before that week's schedule is made. Try to be flexible, but don't tolerate last-minute requests. If you establish a healthy flow of communication with your staff, scheduling conflicts can be anticipated and solved.

- **Disciplinary protocol.** Lay out the steps that will be taken to enforce company policies.

- **Employee agreement form.** Your employees must sign this form, which states that they understand and accept all the policies, guidelines, and procedures in the manual.

Be sure to read the manual aloud with your staff and answer any questions they may have. They will respect you for setting firm policies and should feel valued, because most of the policies exist to protect them. Make it clear that these guidelines are designed to provide a safe and comfortable working environment. Keep a copy of the manual posted in the truck so that you and they can refer to it when necessary.

Motivating and Retaining Your Staff

Once you've assembled a great team and put firm policies in place, you want to keep them motivated and encourage a spirit of camaraderie. We've all had bosses who used fear to control us and make us feel small. You can foster warm, familial bonds between you and your staff and still maintain your authority. In fact, it's the only right way to manage a business.

If you use kindness and reason, instead of threats and shouting, to persuade and motivate your staff, your team will *want* to work for you. Most people haven't been exposed to this management style, and I'll tell you from my own experience, that's the only way to build loyalty to your company. At the end of the day, it doesn't matter if the money isn't great; if your employees enjoy being at work, they'll stick around. Not only that but they'll come on time, avoid calling in sick, and bring their A game 100 percent of the time. An employee who's excited about his job will bring his friends to eat at your truck and spread the word about you to his family, neighbors, and acquaintances.

The number one way to create a safe and peaceful working environment is to encourage open communication. Your staff should feel comfortable voicing their concerns, grievances, fears, and suggestions. They should never think they have to hide a problem from you or from anyone else on staff. One way to establish a strong flow of communication is to hold daily or weekly staff meetings before or after each shift. Open the floor to whoever wants to say something and applaud those who do. Remember that your employees may be aware of problems you aren't; instead of taking these reports as criticism, you should welcome them for the betterment of your business.

This style of communication requires humility. You need your staff to respect your authority, but being humble in no way diminishes that. Your staff will respect you more for respecting them and seeing them as individuals. You can reinforce this by openly praising them for a job well done. Nothing—I repeat, *nothing*—will uplift and motivate your staff more than a little praise. It takes nothing away from you and can mean the world to them.

When you need to be negative, offer constructive criticism. Never throw your employees' shortcomings back in their faces. If you're communicating well and offering praise when warranted, they'll have incentive enough to learn from their mistakes without you embarrassing them. They'll appreciate the discreet way in which you point out room for improvement and work hard to prove to you that your gentle but firm style is effective.

You might want to take it a step further and express an interest in their personal lives. Don't be intrusive, but inquire about their activities outside of work. Ask about their vacations, hobbies, dates, and performances. Not only will they be more at ease around you, but you'll feel more comfortable leading your staff knowing that they trust and value your opinion.

A great way to encourage team spirit is to host company outings outside of work. Take your staff to a theme park or a sports event. Make sure no one ever feels left out; that can happen easily with workers who are less outgoing or assertive. You're all stuck in a small space together so you might as well like each other and get along.

TRUCK TALES

In 2007, 23-year-old Tiger Wu founded Veggie Ninja, a vegetarian food truck in Reseda, California. Uncomfortable about managing a staff that was mostly older than him, Tiger encouraged them to express themselves by bringing their talents and personalities to their work. Together, they formed a singing group and later incorporated a karaoke machine into the side of the truck so patrons could perform while they waited in line. Tiger demonstrated that managing one's staff with kindness translates into big success.

At the same time, you can't tolerate any behavior that's blatantly aggressive, disrespectful, or illegal. If company policies are violated, don't get angry; simply apply the disciplinary protocol outlined in your employee manual. For many businesses, it goes something like this:

- **First violation:** Verbal warning

- **Second violation:** Written warning

- **Third violation:** Suspension or termination

Of course, some infractions may warrant immediate suspension or termination, such as sexual harassment, drug abuse, or theft. These are instances where you'll need to use your best judgment, keeping in mind that you never want the company to be in any way complicit in the illegal activities of an employee. Don't lose your temper; remain cool and deal with the situation rationally.

If you can incorporate just a few of these principles into your management style, you'll be operating well above the industry standard for positive work environments. Remember that there's no conflict between being kind and being respected, or between humility and leadership. Furthermore, your staff's collective warmth will infect your customers and attract many more.

The Least You Need to Know

- Your menu and concept define the number of employees you need on your truck, but in general more than four or five people will make for an uncomfortable workplace.

- Try to hire two people who can change off as prep and on-truck cooks, and consider handling the greeting/cashier duties yourself.

- Take the time to educate even experienced staff members on the rules of service for your truck, and create a manual that clearly sets forth your expectations and requirements for your employees.

- Good communication and praise when warranted will do more to motivate your staff than almost anything else.

Inventory and Maintenance

In This Chapter

- Handling purchasing
- Keeping inventory counts
- Dealing with theft and waste
- Maintaining your truck

Every action you take when planning your business is a seed. If you plant crab apples, don't plan on harvesting a golden delicious. That's especially true when it comes to a project like your food truck. Because it's a relatively small business, all the decisions you make will immediately affect every other area. If you change how you run the window, for example, your kitchen operations will immediately be altered. It's particularly important to take this interconnectedness of your operations into account when you start thinking about purchasing, managing your inventory, and even maintaining your truck. You could be running the most popular truck in the country, but if you're spending too much on food, aren't managing your inventory properly, or aren't taking care of your physical plant, you won't be able to establish long-term success.

In this chapter, I discuss purchasing food and supplies, managing inventory, and maintaining your truck. Purchasing and maintenance aren't the sexiest part of the food truck game, but they're just as important as the food you're serving.

Purchasing and Managing Supplies

Prior to placing any orders for supplies it's of the utmost importance that you have a clear understanding of your concept, staffing, and expected preparation time. By identifying where and when you'll be cooking and prepping your food, you'll have a better sense of the types of products you'll need to buy.

If you're selling hamburgers, for instance, you can purchase regular ground beef, prepackaged and formed hamburgers, or grind the beef yourself from certain cuts. The easiest option is the prepackaged and formed hamburgers, but that decision leads to secondary questions: Will it allow you to produce the best-tasting and highest-quality product? Will your butcher make you a proprietary mix of meats for your burgers? What's the most cost-effective way to get the product you want? That's what purchasing is all about.

> **TRUCK TALES**
>
> Pat LaFrieda is a New York butcher who was credited with reinventing the hamburger. When recession hit the city in the late 2000's, LaFrieda's restaurant customers were looking to take the best cuts, like Dry Aged New York Strips, to turn them into high-end comfort food such as a signature burger. LaFrieda, now known as the mad scientist of burgers, gave them what they wanted and established a national trend in the process. He created proprietary blends of beef for restaurants like Shake Shack, Minetta Tavern, Spotted Pig, and 5 Napkin Burger that have sprouted national chains and been copied by butchers around the country. Thank you, Pat, for giving us the gourmet burger. Our stomachs salute you.

Understanding the Role of the Purchasing Agent

For most hospitality businesses the purchasing agent is the unheralded champion of profitability. Think of this person as the great offensive linemen on a football team; he protects the quarterback and is invaluable to the success of the team, but he'll never win the MVP award and is rarely talked about in the press.

After you've decided on your menu and put your systems are in place, the work of your purchasing agent—probably *you*—has just started. You know you'll need canned corn or barbeque sauce, but you most likely haven't figured out the brand or size of the order. Now is the time to work all this out.

Researching Your Product Options

To decide your type and quantity, you need to do a lot of research. The first step is to find the products you think are best for your recipes at local grocery stores. Then follow that up by speaking with commercial distributors to see who can supply you with those products at a reasonable price. Most major metropolitan areas have dozens of distributors who supply dry goods, meat, dairy, and other products to restaurants. Contact them, sample their products, and speak to sales reps to find the products that you think are best for you.

> **TIP**
>
> Don't waste a lot of money going out and buying samples of different products for your truck, especially if you're on a tight budget. Distributors want your business and will send you free samples of their products. They need you as much as you need them.

Make a list of all the items you'll need to execute your menu on a weekly basis, including the beverages you're selling to accompany your food. Create this list before you start researching suppliers and interviewing sales reps. Break things down into the same categories that distributors use: fish, meat, poultry, dairy, dry goods, baked goods, and so on. Use spreadsheet software such as Microsoft Excel so you can easily edit and update the list.

Be very specific about the items you're looking to purchase. It may be hard in the beginning, but as you learn more about the products don't leave any details to chance. Don't just write down Cheddar cheese; write Millers White Cheddar Cheese Shredded 15-pound case. If you aren't specific you'll end up getting something you don't want, which will affect both your bottom line and your end product.

Determining Preparation Time

Consumers want the best product available, not a frozen hamburger or fish filet. You can definitely save yourself time, energy, and money by using frozen or preprepared products, but you'll probably lose money over the long run in lost customers. The key is quality: getting the best quality you can at the best price.

The food on your truck should be fresh and cooked as close as possible to when it's going to be served. I also advocate using fresh herbs over dried or prechopped items because they greatly improve the flavor of your final product.

It's time for another list: breaking down all the tasks involved in your truck's daily operations. It will help you identify which items have the highest impact on your bottom line and which tasks will most greatly affect the quality of your product.

Let's say you serve a chopped salad on your truck. It will cost you $10 an hour to have a prep cook chop the vegetables by hand, and you need 30 pounds of salad per day. It takes four workers to chop five pounds of vegetables in an hour. That costs you $240 a day. It is possible that your local vegetable supplier has pre-chopped tomatoes, onions, and cucumbers that cost you half what it does to chop them in-house. Using the prechopped veggies will save you time and money, while giving your clients a high-quality product. To maintain the fresh flavors, however, you decide to chop fresh herbs and add them to the salad. By breaking down the process you are able to identify which prep you should do in-house and what you can outsource, while still maintaining the quality level of your product.

The most important thing you need to consider when using preprepared items is taste. Taste everything you serve to your customers, especially the things that are prepared by outside suppliers. You have less control over them and therefore need to monitor the end product more carefully. Your customers will know if you change an ingredient.

TRUCK TALES

One of the most famous restaurants in New York, Peter Luger Steakhouse, used to serve the most delicious onion rolls. I'd been eating there for years, and suddenly they started using a different bakery. From the minute I saw the rolls I knew they weren't the same. They didn't have the homemade goodness they did before, and that took a little of the magic of a meal at Peter Luger away for me. It's important to realize that all the little decisions you make will effect how your customers enjoy their visits to your truck.

Locating Suppliers

After you've identified what you need to buy, it's time to choose who you're going to purchase it from.

BEEP! BEEP!

Establish a budget prior to reaching out to suppliers. You know your guidelines for profitability. Don't let your eyes become bigger than your wallet, and don't let a supplier sell you anything you don't need.

The best way to find purveyors is to speak with other truck, restaurant, and commissary owners. Your peers will know the best people for you to work with and will be happy to share them with you. Locate a truck or restaurant that uses products similar to the ones you're looking to serve. Ask them why they chose one supplier over another, and take notes on who's better at what.

Choose at least three purveyors you can call on in every category, giving you backup if someone is out of an item. Having multiple suppliers also enables you to comparison shop. Don't take anyone's word for it when it comes to finding the best price. The best one for them may not be the best for you.

Set up accounts with each supplier. Call the purveyor's office directly and fill out the paperwork to have a sales representative assigned to your business. All your dealings with the purveyor will go through this representative, so set up a meeting with him or her as soon as possible to establish a personal relationship and outline your needs.

TIP

Ask the sales rep to have her boss come along to the first meeting you have. Many times the boss has the only true negotiating power, so having a direct relationship with her will be helpful. It also gives you a second contact if you ever have issues with the supplier.

Also, get your sales representative's cell and home phone number. Your relationship is all about service, and you don't want to be stuck not being able to get a delivery to restock your truck on a weekend.

You should be very clear about the needs of your business with the sales rep. Explain how you plan to operate and give her a breakdown of how you'll execute and serve your menu. Also provide her with a copy of the inventory list you created. You may be surprised at the breadth of the items distributors carry. They'll often be able to help you with more items than you originally thought.

When you review your inventory list with your suppliers, explain what you're looking for in terms of cut, flavor, packaging, and volume. Suppliers may or may not be able to service your needs, but you should always make your desires known. Tell them you'll work with whichever organization can come closest to your preferences, and that you plan to place orders on a regular basis, with your money going to whomever can service your needs best. It's a clear and simple way to show them that you're serious and expect prompt and professional service.

Your suppliers should be eager to work with you and understand your business. They should bring you new ideas and products to help improve your business's bottom line and your food's quality. Your purveyors must understand the goals of your business, along with your cost expectations and delivery requirements. A great supplier will give you information about local food and business trends that will be invaluable to maintaining a thriving food truck.

Comparison Shopping

Once suppliers get back to you with their pricing, terms of service, delivery schedule, and credit terms, it's time for you to start making decisions. It shouldn't be necessary to get into a contractual agreement with specific order volumes and time periods at this point because you need to establish your business first. With that said, you still need to work out some logistical details, particularly your payment terms.

Will you pay on delivery or in 30, 60, or 90 days? The longer you take to make the payment, the more money it will cost you. It's your job to balance your cash needs against your pricing needs and then make a decision that's best for your business. Additionally, you need to let the supplier know when you need your deliveries and how often. Find out the process for placing orders and how much lead time the supplier needs to make a delivery.

BEEP! BEEP!

Always check the items you receive against what you actually paid for. If the products you ordered and paid for aren't the ones you received, you've got an issue. This is a regular problem in the hospitality business. Additionally, the person who does the ordering should also be the person doing the receiving. And if they aren't, the two of them should be in close contact with one another. If you paid for chopped shallots and received chopped onions, there'll be a vast difference in the taste of your final product and, potentially, your bottom line.

Negotiating

Pricing is the next most important issue when dealing with suppliers. You won't get the best price unless you're able to negotiate. You need to identify the best product for your use and then push back with the supplier to get the best price. Don't just take the price you've been given; look for an opportunity to get a better deal.

The key to negotiating is establishing volume. You want to purchase as much as you can from as few suppliers as possible. Your purveyor wants to sell as much volume as he can, so the more you're able to purchase from him or her, the better price you'll get.

See if you can enter into an agreement for a fixed price on certain items that you buy regularly. The cost of commodities is in constant flux these days, and such arrangements can add up to significant cost savings. With these types of agreements, your business agrees to purchase a particular item only from one supplier in exchange for fixed pricing and volume-based discounts. Many suppliers love to score consistent business like this and will do whatever they can to accommodate you, including discounts, special orders, and flexible delivery terms.

Inventory

Managing the inventory of your truck and commissary is critically important to your success. If you purchase too much of a perishable item it can go bad and literally "spoil" your profitability.

Your inventory is defined as the stock of supplies you have in your truck and commissary at any given time. Inventory is all potential revenue; you get nothing back from it until you sell it to customers. Therefore, you need to have a minimal amount of money tied up in it so it won't negatively affect your business's performance.

Obviously, you don't want to run out of menu items on a regular basis, but you also don't want to have a year's supply of tomato paste tying up your cash flow. You need that cash to run a healthy business.

> **TIP**
>
> Salespeople love to try to get you to buy in bulk with pricing incentives. Make sure you look at these offers closely, so that you can tell whether the cost savings are worth tying up your cash. You have limited storage space, so before you purchase a product make sure you have somewhere to put it. Sometimes suppliers offer bill and hold, storing the product for you until you need it; if they do, take advantage of it

You can manage and track your inventory in any number of ways. The most important thing is to have a system in place, and to keep it as simple as possible. I recommend the *par system* for food trucks because it's so easy.

> **DEFINITION**
>
> The **par system** refers to the level of stock you need to service your truck over a set period of time. If you use two cases of carrots a day, for example, then that's your daily par.

Choose a particular employee to count food every day or every shift, updating a daily par sheet with the amount of prepped and nonprepped inventory you have. Compare your inventory with specified par levels and place orders when necessary. For example, if you need 3 pounds of carrots every day, the amount of carrots you enter on the par sheet is 3 pounds. At the beginning and end of the day, review the par sheet, check inventory, and then place orders for the following day to make sure you're always at par levels.

Inventory Counts

You need to count your inventory for your monthly profit and loss statements (see Chapter 15). Whether you prepare the statements yourself or have your accountant do them, your counts determine the cash value of the inventory you have on hand. That means you have to count the items and then multiply them by the unit price you paid for them. For example, if you purchased 30 pounds of chicken for $200 and have

15 pounds left, the inventory is valued at $100. The total of everything you have on hand gives you your month's ending and beginning inventory values, an important aspect of monitoring the profitability of your truck.

You'll also want to utilize purchase orders to monitor purchases and requests for purchases. Have your prep cook check the par on vegetables so you can put in an order for additional quantities if necessary. That puts one more check and balance into the system. You should monitor your par sheets, purchase orders, and inventory regularly until you establish trust with your employees.

Preventing Theft

There'll always be some theft in your kitchen; how much depends on what you consider theft. An employee eating a carrot or cooking a piece of chicken for lunch is different from taking a case of soda home. You need to clearly communicate what's acceptable in your kitchen. I suggest focusing on theft deterrence and then matching it with random checks of inventory.

Here are some ways that you can deter theft:

- **Accountability.** Put someone in charge of a particular item or duty, and make sure that person is aware of what the punishment for theft will be. By doing so you're establishing responsibility. If something happens, you now have someone to hold accountable—a partner who should care about that item as much as you do. That employee is going to do everything in his power to protect his position.

- **Security cameras.** Whether they work or not, people usually won't steal if they think they're being watched. The best option on a food truck is an Internet-based camera in a hidden location. (Make employees aware that they are being taped, but don't reveal the location of the camera.)

- **Locks.** Put locks on everything you can. People are less likely to steal if doing so requires effort. And make keys a big deal: employees only get keys if they earn them. The fewer people with keys, the easier it is to find the thief.

- **Be present.** It's your business, and the more people see you around, the more they think you're there. It's much easier to steal from someone you don't think is around or will notice.

Minimizing Waste

Waste is the food you throw out because you can't serve it to customers for reasons such as spoilage. Waste is like giving away money. It comes from laziness and poor planning, and it influences your labor, food, and even transportation costs. Once you've been in operation for a month, analyze all aspects of your business to see where you can eliminate waste. The easiest way to limit it is to be watchful and methodical. Provide incentives that encourage your employees to limit waste in the kitchen and other areas by creating contests with rewards.

> **TIP**
>
> Being cheap and shortsighted can cost you as much as being wasteful. People often try to save money in the short term by purchasing inferior packaging or lower-quality food, which ends up costing them more over the long haul. Make the best decision for your business, not the cheap one.

You can take steps to prevent spoilage. Make it unacceptable in your kitchen from day one. You must become very knowledgeable about the shelf life of the items you're selling. That means you need to know how long you can serve food items before they go bad, as well as how they should look and smell upon arrival. You have no one to blame other than yourself if you accept an item for delivery that isn't fresh.

Investing in the proper means to store, handle, and extend the shelf life of food also helps prevent spoilage. Covering, labeling, and in some cases vacuum sealing food can vastly extend its usable shelf life. Finally, make sure your storage facilities are clean. It will not only help extend the life of perishable food, it will prevent food-borne illness.

Truck Maintenance

You're spending thousands of dollars on your food truck, so it's important that you maintain it in the best possible condition. That means maintaining the automobile part of the truck as well as the kitchen.

Have a mechanic you trust who's familiar with servicing commercial vehicles look over your truck twice a year to check the engine, oil, brakes, etc. Doing so will not only improve the long-term value of your truck, it will ensure that you won't lose days of business because it's in the shop. And don't be cheap; good work costs money. Try to arrange a payment or maintenance plan with your mechanic. It would be a shame to have spent all that money and then not keep the truck in good shape.

TIP

Some commissaries offer maintenance onsite as well as roadside assistance. Look into these options. Maintenance on the truck is crucial to a food truck business. A truck down is time lost on the road and money lost as well.

Here are some ways to identify a good mechanic:

- **Ask your friends, family, and colleagues for recommendations.** Someone who has given them good service is likely to do the same for you.

- **NAPA, ASP, or Parts Plus Certification.** This ensures that the mechanic has gone through the certification of these organizations.

- **Cleanliness.** Look around the shop to see how it's maintained. It's a garage, so don't expect it to look like a hospital; but how organized and neat it is goes a long way toward foretelling the kind of service you'll receive from the mechanic.

- **Manufacturer certification.** Mechanics certified by car makers like Ford, GM, or Mercedes are familiar with the latest technology and are serious about their craft.

- **Food truck experience.** Food and catering trucks are specialized vehicles. It would be helpful if your mechanic has experience working on them.

The Least You Need to Know

- Because you'll probably be acting as your own purchasing agent, you'll need to familiarize yourself with types of foods and other on-truck necessities before you start talking with distributors and suppliers.

- Be prepared to negotiate with purveyors to extend your purchasing power.

- Set up a simple system to manage and track your inventory, to watch for theft, and to avoid waste as much as possible.

- Part of keeping your truck maintained includes a trip to the garage twice a year for servicing by an experienced mechanic.

Food Preparation and Safety

In This Chapter

- Overseeing the cleanliness of your kitchen
- Training staff to handle food safely
- Avoiding cross-contamination and food-borne illnesses
- Being prepared for emergencies

As a business owner, you're responsible for the safety of your employees, patrons, purveyors, and neighbors. And as a food truck owner you have the additional burden of assuring the safety and cleanliness of your kitchen, food products, and truck. This can be a challenge even for the most seasoned food truckers. As a first-timer, always remember that knowledge, planning, and persistent upkeep are key.

In this chapter, I examine some of the basics of food preparation safety, food storage, and maintaining a clean work environment. I show you what to do, what to avoid, and what might happen if you don't pay attention.

It's impossible to overstate the importance of safety in the design and operation of your business, so take your time and take notes. I recommend keeping extra copies of this chapter on your truck and wherever else you prepare food for your business so you can reference the information easily.

It's easy to take safety for granted because enforcing it properly requires attention to detail. Don't fall into that trap. Nothing is more important than maintaining a safe environment for you, your employees, and your customers.

Working with Your Chef

If you're the executive chef on your food truck, you'll be responsible for overseeing all the preparation and storage of your food and maintaining the cleanliness of your kitchen. If you've hired or are partnering with a chef, you're *still* responsible for making sure your staff adhere to all the necessary safety and hygienic standards I talk about in this chapter.

> **TIP**
>
> When it comes to food safety, inspections that you perform yourself are as important as those performed by health inspectors. Performing regular random walkthroughs of your truck and commissary is a necessity. Your local health department should have self-inspection forms on their website that you can download and use. By doing self-inspections, you'll know your business better than the health inspector and can protect your business and your clientele.

Not all chefs are created equal. While we automatically expect professional chefs to be obsessively clean and knowledgeable about food safety, many fall far short of the mark in this regard. Thousands of people get food poisoning from restaurants and food trucks every year; that means hundreds of chefs are neglecting this critical aspect of their duties and hundreds of owners aren't paying attention to what's happening in their own kitchens.

When hiring or partnering with an executive chef, make sure to ask him about food safety and cleanliness. Here are some things to look for:

What health department grades/scores has he received in the past? Ask him to provide this information or do the research on this on your own. Most cities post the details of inspections on their websites, so you can see exactly what your chef did wrong.

Does she have a cavalier attitude toward safety and cleanliness or does she seem to truly appreciate the importance of it? A good chef will care about safety not just out of fear of getting in trouble but because she takes pride in her operation. Does the cleanliness of your chef's kitchen seem to be a source of pride for her?

Can your chef demonstrate a solid knowledge and understanding of local health department guidelines? He should know these by heart and be able to spot a violation without having to refer back to the guidelines.

Does your chef demonstrate outstanding personal hygiene? Are her nails clean, her hair groomed, her clothing clean and pressed? Often the care your chef puts into her own appearance will reflect the care she puts into maintaining a clean work environment.

Is your chef someone who can submit to authority and endure scrutiny? Chefs are notoriously hot-headed, an unpleasant stereotype that I've found to be largely true. You're his boss (or partner) and he needs to recognize and respect your authority. He should have a thick skin and be able to take criticism, especially when it comes to adhering to food safety guidelines.

At the end of the day, you're responsible for everything that happens on your truck and all of the food that comes out of it. If a patron gets sick from your product or if your truck is cited for a health code violation, the blame falls on your shoulders. If you aren't leading the kitchen yourself, you must still maintain a very hands-on approach to making sure your executive chef is adhering to all food safety standards.

Too many restaurant and food truck owners turn a blind eye to their employees' neglect of safety standards in their facilities. Their excuse invariably is that they didn't think it was their responsibility: because they hired an executive chef to deal with all that stuff, it's her problem. Wrong! It's her problem, and now it's your problem, too. City health inspectors don't care who is in charge of making sure everything is clean. Nor do patrons who become ill from tainted food. The blame will always fall on you, the owner, and it should: you're in charge and food safety is ultimately and without excuse *your* responsibility.

> **TIP**
>
> Food can be contaminated anywhere along the supply chain. It's important to purchase food only from approved suppliers and personally inspect all incoming deliveries. Learn to identify signs of spoilage in fruit, vegetables, fish, meat, and poultry. You can't afford to let someone else's mistakes ruin your business.

Learn the health code guidelines and inspect the kitchen yourself. If you find a problem, discuss it with your chef immediately. If he or she tries to make excuses, you may not have chosen the right person for the job. Make it clear to your chef and your staff that laziness and negligence regarding health won't be tolerated. Remember that nothing—I repeat, *nothing*—is more important in the food industry than safety and cleanliness.

Food safety classes are offered across the country. Require your head kitchen cook and prep cook to take the classes. Cashiers also can take a less intense class.

Keeping Your Kitchen Clean and Safe

Keeping your kitchen free of common dangers and health code violations is a constant battle that requires knowledge, dedicated attention, and diligence. The most common threats, which can be avoided when proper food safety standards are in place, include bacterial contamination of food, food spoilage, and pest infestation (which brings a whole list of additional health concerns).

You must be proactive in your approach to food safety and cleanliness. Don't think you can get away with doing the bare minimum and hope for the best. The consequences of one food poisoning incident, one bacterial infection, or one significant health code violation can be very expensive and potentially irreparable to the reputation of your business. You must take pride in how you maintain your equipment, facilities, and, especially, your food.

Health code guidelines are different in every city. It's crucial that you know your local laws and standards, as your city's health department will evaluate your truck and publish a report. In some cities, like Los Angeles and New York, health officials issue letter grades—A, B, or C—that restaurants and food trucks are required to post in their windows. I've seen the way even a B grade can embarrass and negatively affect the business of a great restaurant, even when it's the result of seemingly trivial violations. Of course when it comes to health, no risk is ever trivial. Visit the webpage of your city or state's health department for a detailed list of regulations so you know exactly what to expect when inspectors come knocking on your door. And they will.

In the following sections, I explain the basics of food safety, including how to ensure cleanliness and the easiest steps to prevent cross-contamination.

Battling Illness

In *The Art of War*, Sun Tzu wrote, "Know thy enemy," and in the war against foodborne illness, it's useful to know which bacteria pose the greatest threat to your customers and how to prevent the growth and spread of each one. The three major bacteria that you must be prepared to fight are as follows:

- **Salmonella.** Found predominantly in raw poultry and eggs, salmonella's symptoms include cramping, diarrhea, fever, and intestinal pain. In individuals with weakened immune systems, like children, the elderly, and HIV patients, salmonella can result in life-threatening complications. To prevent infection, thoroughly cook all poultry products and disinfect any surface that comes into contact with raw poultry or eggs.

- **Campylobacter.** Also found in raw poultry, campylobacter causes fever, diarrhea, cramping, and dysentery-like symptoms. As with salmonella, campylobacter can be life threatening for individuals with compromised immune systems. To prevent infection, thoroughly cook all poultry and disinfect any surface, utensil, or food product that comes into contact with raw poultry (see the next section on avoiding cross-contamination).

- **E. coli.** Found in the intestinal tract of cattle, E. coli is extremely dangerous, causing diarrhea, vomiting, and even kidney failure. E. coli is almost always traced back to beef products, most commonly ground beef. E. coli can be killed by cooking beef to well done. You must be extremely cautious with raw beef so that it doesn't come into contact with any foods that won't be thoroughly cooked.

TRUCK TALES

The Poppa & Goose Food Truck along with its sister truck, Goosebeary's, formerly located in Massachusetts, were shut down in November 2001 because of multiple cases of food poisoning. Six people were sent to the hospital. The associated restaurant that acted as the truck's commissary was also shut down due to unsanitary conditions. This incident not only affected the victims and the businesses: it created fear among customers and gave food trucks a negative reputation in that area. Protect the food truck community and keep your truck safe!

Bacteria grow and thrive between 40°F and 140°F. Most health code regulators require food to be stored above or below that range. No food, whether or not it's particularly susceptible to food-borne illness, should be kept within this temperature range for more than two hours. A piece of raw poultry that's lightly contaminated by campylobacter and salmonella will become exponentially more infected if stored between 40°F and 140°F for even an hour.

Here are some essential steps to ensuring the safety of your food:

Cook all foods to the proper temperature. That means poultry is cooked all the way through and beef products (especially ground beef) are cooked enough to prevent E. coli from spreading. Once the food is cooked, make sure it's immediately stored well above or below the 40°F to 140°F range.

Never defrost frozen products to room temperature. Move frozen foods to the refrigerator or place them under cold running water to thaw. Because bacteria thrive between 40°F and 140°F, leaving any product at room temperature—even if it's frozen—is a serious health code violation.

If you aren't serving cooked foods immediately, chill them below 40°F as quickly as possible. Divide the food into small containers and soak them in ice baths. Some bacteria are heat resistant, so cooked foods are just as susceptible to breeding food-borne illnesses as raw ones if they aren't stored at the proper temperatures.

Don't reheat foods multiple times. This can actually worsen the presence of certain bacteria. After a few weeks on the truck, you'll get a sense of how much product you'll need to reheat on any given day. Until then, discard any leftovers that have been reheated once. With experience, the amount of waste will diminish.

Use thermometers. It's important to monitor the temperatures of stored foods, both hot and cold, and to determine the temperature of cooked meats and fish to make sure they're heated thoroughly.

Establish a rotational system for your inventory so you always use your oldest product first. This strategy will not only protect your customers from spoiled ingredients but also save you money, because you'll throw away less food.

Implement and enforce a mandatory hand-washing policy for all of your employees. They should wash their hands after using the restroom, handling trash or raw foods, smoking, coughing or sneezing, eating or drinking, or touching their hair, faces, open wounds, or any bodily fluids. Your staff should use plastic or latex gloves when handling any food products and you should have hand sanitizer on the truck for their use, as well as for your customers and yourself.

Preventing Cross-Contamination

Cross-contamination occurs when foods and surfaces that might be contaminated with bacteria come into contact with foods and surfaces that otherwise wouldn't be a potential threat. If you use a pair of tongs to move raw chicken and then use them to toss a mixed salad without disinfecting them first, for example, your salad is now likely infected with salmonella and poses just as great a danger to your customers as a piece of the raw chicken.

Because cross-contamination is, by definition, accidental, you really need to take steps to ensure the safety of your customers. The following suggestions are industry standard for protecting your food and equipment.

- Have separate designated cutting boards for poultry, meat, fish, raw foods, and cooked foods. Make sure they're labeled or color-coded so they're never used incorrectly.

- Use plastic, stone, or rubber cutting boards only; wood boards are porous and can absorb blood and bacteria in a way that can withstand disinfection. Be sure that all cutting boards and cooking surfaces are cleaned after each use with a strong "kitchen approved" disinfectant.

- Keep poultry, ground beef, shellfish, and other potentially dangerous foods in a separate refrigerator and, if possible, have a separate space designated for prepping them. Never store raw meats, poultry, or fish on the same refrigerator shelf as cooked meats, poultry, or fish.

- Clean and sterilize all pots, pans, utensils, surfaces, and equipment after each use. Be sure to brush your grill between cooking meat, poultry, and fish.

Food Safety on the Truck and Off

You have two main environments to police for food safety, your truck and your commissary. It's important that you have a trained individual present in both spaces at all times, monitoring the work being done. The local health department will spot check and approve your truck setup and commissary, but it's up to you to enforce the rules and procedures on a daily basis. There are no exceptions when it comes to food safety. Just because you're on the truck and busy with all aspects of your business doesn't mean you have an excuse. There's no room for error when the health and safety of your customers is on the line.

Here are some specific issues to think about regarding on-truck food safety:

- There's less space and less access to power, which makes it more likely for food to fall into dangerous temperature zones or cross-contaminate.

- Trucks have a limited supply of water; if you run out during service it becomes much more difficult to clean utensils, surfaces, and hands. This can make for a dangerous situation. Reserve water for hand washing and cleaning surfaces on the truck. Have extra utensils for service, and wash dishes back at the commissary. Your water supply is your lifeline, so make sure that you always have the maximum you can carry on the rig.

- Many food truck operators are inexperienced and don't know the rules. Make sure you learn about food safety before diving into operations.

Cleaning Supplies

Maintaining a clean kitchen is the single most important factor in preventing food-borne illness. It's also the job no one likes to do. It's your responsibility as owner and manager of your business to make sure that your truck is thoroughly and routinely cleaned. Diligent cleaning not only prevents contamination but keeps you aware of your inventory so that no food ever sits forgotten in the back of the refrigerator. If you clean consistently, you won't have to wonder whether your product is fresh; you'll know that it is.

To do a proper job of cleaning your truck, you'll need to invest in the right supplies. Here are some of the bare necessities for any kitchen:

- All-purpose cleaner

- Degreaser

- Dish detergent

- Floor cleaner

- Hand soap

- Hand sanitizer

- Multipurpose sanitizer

- Oven cleaner

- Soaking fluid for pots and pans

BEEP! BEEP!

All cleaning agents contain dangerous chemicals. You and your staff must be aware of the possibility of chemical residue on food prep surfaces and rinse them off thoroughly so that no ingredients ever come into contact with any cleaning product. Be sure to store your cleaning supplies far from your food, especially fresh produce, which can absorb toxic fumes from bottled chemicals.

Enforce a very strict cleaning schedule on every shift. If you allow dirt and grease to accumulate, you're not only in violation of your local health standards but you're putting your customers' lives at risk and inviting pests to nest in your kitchen. It may be helpful to type up a list of what needs to be done and post it on the wall, or simply keep a checklist for your personal use. Do whatever works for you, so long as you see the job all the way through and inspect it afterward.

Do a walk-through of your kitchen and note everything that needs to be cleaned and how often. Some things require an occasional more thorough scrubbing in addition to daily maintenance. If you're inexperienced and don't know when certain equipment would typically need to be cleaned, consult your executive chef or the owner's manual for each appliance. Don't, however, leave it up to your staff to decide when to clean. It's always up to you to enforce a strict cleaning schedule.

Your cleaning schedule for each shift should include:

- Empty the trash multiple times
- Mop the floor multiple times
- Wipe down the line and prep areas (constantly, as needed)
- Sanitize cutting boards after each use
- Clean and sanitize all surfaces
- Clean the fryer and change oil
- Change water in the sanitizer systems
- Wipe down walls and hood vents
- Empty waste tank
- Fill water tank
- Rinse floor mats

Once-a-week chores:

- Deep clean the oven

- Scrub the inside of the refrigerators

- Clean behind the hot line (if possible)

- Conduct a full inventory as you do so.

For weekly chores, choose the day of the week when your inventory is lowest; it will speed up the process and help you gauge how much food you need to order from your purveyors.

> **TIP**
>
> Use different color-coded towels for different types of jobs. Use one color for wiping down food-prep surfaces and another for handling dangerous chemicals, for example.

One a month, do these chores:

- Deep clean the walls, floor, and ceiling of the truck

- Recalibrate your oven thermometer

- Restock your first-aid supplies

- Empty, clean, and restock your dry pantry.

Your chores for every six months should include:

- Clean the hood above your stove

- Clean the pilot lights on all of your gas appliances

- Test your fire extinguisher to make sure it works

- Spray your truck for bugs (do this every three to six months, depending on your location).

Keeping your truck clean should be a matter of pride for you. Remember that the safety and cleanliness of your kitchen is a reflection of your leadership and will all be reflected in the final product you sell to your customers. Don't wait for a bad report from the health department or for a customer to get sick. Take the necessary precautions from day one and relax knowing that you've created a safe, clean, and profitable environment for you and your staff.

Emergencies

Every city and state has its own laws and regulations regarding fire exits and emergency readiness. You'll have to research local policies to determine what kind of hardware to put on your doors and what sort of emergency equipment or supplies you may be required to keep on your truck. There are, however, a few items that every food truck must have on board:

- Fire extinguisher

- First-aid kit: Band-Aids, antiseptic, burn gel or cream, gauze, first-aid tape, eyewash, antibiotic ointments, aspirin, and antihistamine.

- Clearly labeled emergency door handle that opens the door from the inside whether or not it's locked

- Emergency procedures, which should be typed up and posted where everyone can see them, outlining what your staff is expected to do in case of fire, injury, severe burn, collision, or if a customer is choking. A copy of this information should be in the employee manual you hand out when each member of your staff is hired.

BEEP! BEEP!

Never offer any medication from the truck first-aid kit or your personal supply to a customer. If he or she has an allergic reaction, you and your company can be held legally responsible.

The Least You Need to Know

- Safety should always be your first consideration in your business, on the truck or off.
- Food-borne illness is a real concern, especially for mobile food businesses. Having enough water and implementing the proper operating procedures will protect your business and your customers.
- As the owner, cleanliness and food safety are ultimately your responsibility—even if you hire an executive chef.
- Cooking foods to the necessary temperature, keeping raw and cooked foods separated, and adhering to a strict cleaning routine will keep your food safe, your truck clean, and your staff and customers healthy.

Growing Your Business

Once your truck is operating, you'll want to protect and grow it into a profitable enterprise. You need clear systems in place for reporting results—daily, weekly, and monthly financial reports that will allow you to monitor the health of your business and make proactive decisions to keep it moving in the right direction.

Controlling your costs and monitoring spending is important, and so is building your clientele. You need to listen to your customers' feedback and make sure they're having an incredible experience every time they visit your truck. And if you do make a mistake, you have to fix it immediately. I show you how great service recovery will make you customers for life.

Growth also means exploring opportunities. Food truck festivals, food truck lots, and television shows featuring food trucks are just some of the incredible opportunities available to help you earn money and build your brand. And if you're doing great business, you might be thinking of expanding. What's standing between you and a fleet of trucks? I'll make sure you know before you graduate from Food Truck University.

Protecting Your Business

In This Chapter

- Setting up breakeven, sales, and expense reports
- Watching your cash flow
- Performing operations reviews

Once your food truck is open for business, you may find yourself asking if you're running it or it's running you. To be successful, you need to be proactive, not reactive. And to be proactive, you need to set up an accurate system to evaluate your success.

The only way to determine how well you're doing is to examine the numbers. That's not to say that common sense, intuition, and your business experience aren't valuable tools to gauge the success of your enterprise. But at the end of the day, it's vital you know the brutal truth, and numbers never lie. Don't fool yourself with press clippings, long lines of customers, or gross revenues. The bottom line profitability of your truck is all that matters long term. If you aren't profitable, your business is unsustainable.

In this chapter, I show you how to create reports that will help you track your progress. I explain how to create daily sales and expense reviews, as well as how to determine if your business can be more profitable. Finally, I give you tips on reviewing and replenishing your inventory in order to maximize profitability and minimize waste.

Financial Reviews

The details of your financial reports and the factors determining your performance are fundamental to your making good decisions about your truck. Most important, you need to know how much money you're profiting, not how much money you're generating. If you're making thousands of dollars in income but it's costing you even more to generate that income, you have a problem. Knowing what happens to every dollar that's generated by your truck will tell you whether you're succeeding or in need of improvement.

Acting like a detective and doing a forensic analysis of your business unveils any inefficiencies that exist. Even the most successful businesses in the world have inefficiencies, and you need to find yours to protect yourself. By putting a review system in place to monitor these figures on a daily, weekly, and monthly basis, you'll be able to maintain an accurate perspective of how your business is performing and make the necessary adjustments.

Playing by the Numbers

Numbers reveal the hard truth about the success and profitability of your business. You have to have a system for reviewing and analyzing your sales and expenses. Doing this on a daily basis will allow you to spot trends, both positive and negative, and detect waste. Use your experience and common sense to look for irregularities in the reports and figure out whether they're business or reporting issues.

TIP

Accountants and bookkeepers aren't on the front lines of your business. They take information that you communicate to them and put it into an acceptable format. Often these numbers just don't tell the full story. Take the numbers and combine them with what you're seeing on the streets to make the best business decisions.

Be diligent, even if the truth hurts. You don't want to be surprised by your financial situation, and ignoring negative information only makes matters worse. Use the sales and expense reports you generate as tools. They reveal what's working and what isn't. Use this insight to make meaningful and informed changes to avoid negative situations.

Calculating Your Breakeven Report

In order for your business to be profitable, you have to reach and then exceed your breakeven—the figure you must make in gross sales in order to cover your expenses for the week, month, or year. Establishing a weekly and monthly breakeven for your business is the primary step in determining the health of your truck.

Create a list of all your *fixed* and *variable costs.* Add up your fixed costs and divide them by the amount of time for which you're determining the breakeven. If you're trying to figure out your weekly breakeven, divide the total number by 52; for the monthly breakeven, divide the total amount by 12.

> **DEFINITION**
>
> Your **fixed costs** are business expenses that aren't dependent upon the level of goods or services produced by your truck. They stay the same no matter how good or bad business is, and include things like insurance and commissary costs, for example. Your **variable costs** are expenses that change in proportion to the activity of your truck: if you sell more food, the amount you spend on the ingredients will be higher.

To determine your weekly or monthly variable costs, generate a sales forecast for an average week or month on your truck. You can do it by reviewing historical data after a few months of business. If you're trying to do it prior to having that information you'll have to make a conservative educated guess. Add up the costs for food, beverages, and staffing to generate your weekly or monthly variable costs. Because of inventory rollover—the current value from the beginning and ending of a specific time period—it's easiest to deal with food cost on a monthly basis. Counting your entire stock of food on a weekly or daily basis won't give you accurate data.

Now combine your fixed and variable costs. The total will be your weekly or monthly breakeven. This is the amount of money you need to generate on a regular basis to cover your expenses. Anything beyond your breakeven is profit.

Reviewing Daily Sales and Expenses

Your daily sales and expense reports break down all the money you're earning and spending each day, including your labor and food costs, fuel, tickets, and all other expenses you incur. The sales reports should be broken down by individual menu item. You need to know how many of each product you're selling daily to determine which items are making and losing money, and how you should order for the following day's operation. You should also have a tally of how many customers you served on your daily report.

By keeping detailed records every day, you'll accumulate a history of your business. You can track and compare your sales and expenses on a day-to-day, month-to-month, and year-to-year basis. Being able to refer to what you made on the same day of the previous year allows you to determine trends. The patterns that emerge will help you anticipate these trends with moderate accuracy so you can adjust your staffing, inventory, and other variable costs accordingly.

> **TIP**
>
> If you've invested in a point-of-sale (POS) system (see Chapter 11), it should include a feature that prints a variety of reports. These reports will allow you to better harness the power of historical information and implement changes to your truck that will help you succeed. Have your POS provider program your system to generate the reports you think can best assist you in managing your operations.

An accurate, detailed, and organized history of your revenue generation and expenses will prove useful for several reasons. Here are a few:

Determine if your business is growing over time, and if not, why. This will be reflected in sales trends, profitability, and cover counts.

Avoid overstaffing. A daily report will help you accurately forecast demand. Being able to predict which days you can do without that extra pair of hands saves money.

Determine the quality of your cashiers' salesmanship. You may notice that your Friday sales are consistently lower when one employee works the window. Either the person working the window on the other days is great or the one working on Friday is sub-par. Either way, you'd better find out.

Determine the profitability of specials. By tracking the sales of your specials and the number of customers that they draw, you'll know which specials are most effective and worth repeating.

Monitor the consistency of your product. Is a lot of food thrown out, burned, spilled, or wasted on the days that a particular chef is working? If you find a pattern of food having to be remade, you may need to retrain or replace him or her.

Evaluate promotions and how they affect sales compared to the previous year.
What effect does a particular marketing campaign or loyalty program have on your
gross and net revenues on a year-to-year basis?

Discover signs of theft. If your cover counts remain constant but your sales are
fluctuating, you may have an issue. Someone might be giving away food or stealing.

> **TIP**
>
> Always include the weather in your daily reports. Inclement weather can have a
> huge effect on your truck's business. You may have done half the business you
> did on this date last year, but if it's raining today that doesn't necessarily mean
> your business is trending down. Don't draw inaccurate conclusions based on
> flawed information; make sure you know all the facts before making changes.

Generating an Income Statement

Also known as a profit and loss statement, an income statement is a monthly report
that reviews your sales, expenses, and profits. It's basically a summary of all your daily
financial reports over a 30-day period and can be as simple or as complicated as you
like. Naturally, the more detailed your report, the better you'll be able to diagnose
problems. With that said, for a small business like a food truck, I recommend keeping
things as simple as possible.

Itemize all your expenses, including a breakdown of payroll, inventory, and sales, so
that you can see exactly where your money's going each month. Include the figures
for the same month of the previous year and your projected figures.

There's no right or wrong way to format your income statement. Again, if you've
invested in a POS system, it should come preprogrammed to generate a monthly
statement for you. Otherwise, simply plug your figures into a spreadsheet. This is
for your own use, so make sure it's clear enough for you to read and understand. The
document should be broken down into three sections: revenues, expenses, and profits.
Separate your food and beverage sales from one another and the food and beverage
costs from the rest of the expenses.

TIP

If you don't feel confident dealing with your daily or monthly figures yourself, consider working with in an accountant. You'll still need to keep a detailed and accurate record of your revenues and expenses, but you won't have to analyze the data yourself. Your accountant will take the information combined with bank statements, generate the necessary financial reports, and then give you advice. You can also have an accountant help you set up your systems and then manage them on your own. That's a good way to save money but still run a professional and efficient operation.

Performing a Cash Flow Analysis

Your cash flow is the rate at which money enters and leaves your business. All businesses strive to maintain a delicate balance between the rate of spending and revenue generation. As you accumulate an accurate financial history of your business through daily and monthly statements you'll develop a sense for predicting the rates at which you can expect to earn and spend money. It's a very important skill set, as you must always be cognizant of how much debt you carry in relation to the income you're generating. You need to know when the bills are due and always have enough cash on hand to cover your expenses.

To determine your cash flow, use as many "real" numbers as possible, including your current bills for food, labor, and other expenses. Then use the forecast you created earlier to anticipate your sales for the coming weeks. As a truck owner you must not only be aware of how much money you have at any given time but also how much you owe. Determining your cash flow involves taking the cash you have in the bank, adding next week's expected revenue, and figuring out what expenses need to be paid at the same time. Perform this calculation for the next four to six weeks and you'll determine your expected cash flow.

Here are some tips to help you balance your cash flow:

Reduce your staff to lower payroll costs. If your cash flow figures aren't sustainable, you need to cut costs. Use your daily reports and monthly income statement to choose at least one or two days on which you can reduce staff by one team member.

Reduce inventory. Use your daily reports to determine which menu items are the least profitable (see the next section for help doing this). Downsize your inventory by limiting the menu or opting for less expensive ingredients. Never sacrifice quality, but aim to operate with minimum inventory until you build up your cash flow.

Opt for longer pay periods with your purveyors. Many suppliers will offer a small discount in exchange for paying within 7 to 10 days instead of the customary 30. Consider the benefit of foregoing the discount in exchange for holding on to your cash.

Never open tabs for customers. People, however well intentioned, are unpredictable. You're in the business of serving meals, not collecting debts. Always require payment up front in exchange for your products. If you do open a tab for anyone, don't count on receiving payment when predicting your cash flow.

> **TIP**
>
> When making cash flow predictions, always round up for expenses and round down for sales. That will give you a worst-case prediction. You should always plan for the worst, not the best. If you take the worst-case approach, you'll never have to worry about covering your expenses.

Require a down payment for large catering events and parties. This cash can buy you some time by covering your immediate expenses and underwriting the costs of executing the event. As long as you don't misallocate the funds, nothing is better than using other people's cash to earn more money for your business.

Evaluating Operations

In addition to daily cash flow, income and expense reports, and monthly profit and loss statements, it's important to run more detailed reviews of your operations to help find solutions to problems that aren't revealed in the financial reports. You can do this by evaluating your menu and inventory item by item. These reviews will quickly illuminate what's making you money and what's causing inefficiencies in your operation.

Reviewing Your Menu Mix

An itemized analysis of everything on your menu will indicate which items are selling, which aren't, and the profitability of each. A menu mix report is a valuable tool, and it can be as simple to construct as a computer spreadsheet. Include the following columns of information laid out in a horizontal format:

- **Menu item:** The name of each item on your menu

- **Weekly sales totals:** The total number of that item sold that week.

- **Percentage of total sales by item:** If 10 out of the 100 entrées sold are burgers, they have a 10 percent popularity percentage.

- **Cost of item:** Include the food cost only.

- **Retail price:** What the item sells for on your truck.

- **Item profit:** Subtract the item cost from the retail price to determine the profit.

- **Total cost:** Multiply the cost of the item by how many were sold this week.

- **Total revenue:** Multiply the retail price of the item by the total number sold.

- **Total profit generated per item:** Subtract the total cost from the total revenue generated. Now you know how much this item contributed to your bottom line.

- **Total menu costs:** The sum of all your food costs.

- **Total menu revenue:** The sum of all your food revenue.

- **Total profit:** Subtract the total menu revenue from the total menu costs.

After you've completed your spreadsheet, take some time to analyze the information. You should be able to answer some very important questions about your menu, including which items are the most and least popular and which have the highest and lowest profit margins. Often you'll find that a dish with a low profit margin is one of the most popular and vice versa. Think of ways to make items with the highest profit margin more popular: making them a special, changing the name of the dish, or making your staff aware of the item's profitability so they'll push it more to your customers.

Your menu mix report will also reveal important trends. You may notice, for example, that your customers prefer lighter dishes in the summer. Use that information to your advantage; change your menu seasonally to offer more of what your customers are looking for. Remember that they're voting with their dollars every time they order from your menu and, as with any vote, there will be winners and losers.

BEEP! BEEP!

As Gordon Gekko said in the movie *Wall Street,* "Don't get emotional about stock." Your menu items represent potential revenue. If something isn't selling, you're sacrificing potential revenue and increasing your waste. Don't keep an item on your menu because you like it or it's your grandmother's recipe. Keep what sells, cut the rest, and don't look back.

If certain items on your menu are selling poorly, consider making one or more of the following adjustments:

- **Price.** You may be charging too much for these items. See Chapter 3 on how to price your menu to your market.

- **Visibility.** Is the item easy to find on your menu? Consider ways of highlighting your high-profit items to ensure that your customers notice them.

- **Imagery.** Does the language on your menu convey deliciousness, or does it sound bland, boring, or even intimidating? Consider renaming these items or rephrasing their descriptions.

- **Product knowledge.** Your staff needs to be completely familiar with everything on the menu, especially the high-profit items and those that may seem intimidating or unusual to customers. They must be able to describe the items confidently, and up-sell the higher-margin ones through enticing language.

- **Incentives.** Consider offering an inducement to the employees working the window to encourage them to sell a quota of high-profit items. It's a great way to motivate staff and push the items that add to the bottom line. With that said, make sure what they're pushing will also make the customers happy. There's no point in pushing an item if it doesn't induce them to return to your truck. Repeat business is your number one priority.

Reviewing Purchasing and Inventory

Inventory can be incredibly complicated, and there's no perfect formula for handling it. No two food trucks, even with similar menus, will choose the same ingredients or purchase goods the same way. You need to find out what works best for you and your business in the most cost-effective way possible. It's a matter of trial and error, making incremental adjustments over time.

While purchasing and inventory are radically different for each food truck, there's one universal tool that can help you maintain a broad perspective of the cost-effectiveness of your purchasing habits. A cost of goods sold (COGS) report measures the true food cost percentage for your menu and inventory as a whole. It isn't very useful as a diagnostic tool, because it just provides a general figure, but it's the easiest way to keep your finger on the pulse of your total food budget.

To determine your COGS:

1. Determine the total cost of your starting inventory.

2. Determine the total sum of inventory purchases you've made during the time period for which you're calculating.

3. Determine the total value of your ending inventory.

4. Subtract your ending inventory from the sum of your starting inventory and additional purchases.

5. Divide the sum from Step 4 by your total sales.

The figure that you end up with is your COGS percentage.

There are no hard-and-fast rules about where your COGS percentage should be, but I recommend keeping it at or below 30 percent. For a quick service business like a food truck you'd ideally want your food cost to be even lower, but with the trend toward gourmet trucks, a lower figure may be difficult to achieve.

Controlling your food cost is vital to the health of your business, but you need to find a balance. What you're really doing is determining the point at which price meets value and quality. Your customers will notice minor changes in portion size or the types of ingredients you use, so you need to be diligent in the managing of your food cost while making sure you don't negatively affect the experience you're trying to offer.

The bottom line is really the last word when it comes to operating your business. Generating these reports and using them to make proactive decisions will govern the long-term success of your truck. Don't hide from the numbers. Deal with the fiscal realities and empower yourself to grow and protect your business.

The Least You Need to Know

- To maintain a healthy business, you or your accountant need to review your food truck numbers on a weekly, monthly, and yearly basis.

- Keep careful note of the way cash flows in and out so you can step in to make changes as necessary.

- When predicting cash flow, always round your expenses up and your sales down to avoid overstating your situation.

- A menu mix review tells you which items work and don't work on your truck and helps you make appropriate changes to increase profitability.

Building Your Clientele

In This Chapter

- The best ways to get valuable feedback
- Dealing with positive—and negative—reviews
- Figuring out what your customers want
- Expanding your customer base

As a seasoned marketer, when I discuss customer behavior I tend to repeat the old saw, "You can bring a horse to water, but you can't make him drink." Marketing, promotions, and advertising creates buzz about your truck and gets people to show up, but it doesn't turn them into customers.

What will build your clientele long term is the product and the experience people have when they visit your truck. It's your job to under-promise and over-deliver on your customer's expectations. They should leave your truck blown away by the incredible food and service they received. That's the way to not only create customers who will spend money there regularly, but also get the best advertisement money can't buy. The word of mouth spread by a satisfied customer is pure gold when it comes to establishing a new truck.

Developing your clientele isn't about being in the newspaper or sending out Tweets. It's about delivering your customer's desires and surpassing their expectations. Most people know exactly what to do to make someone feel valued or special, but they don't go out of their way to actually do it. This chapter is about establishing a strategy to build and maintain your clientele by putting systems in place and doing that special thing that your customer remembers, thereby creating loyalty and repeat business, which are the lifeblood of any entrepreneurial venture.

Feedback: Listen to the People Who Feed You

Have you ever watched a person or business make all the wrong decisions? We all seem to have the ability to see what's wrong with someone or something else, but when it comes to our own issues we just don't get it. The same thing is true when it comes to our own businesses. And in the case of a food truck, you don't have years to come to the realization that you need help. Your business will flourish or fail based upon your ability to quickly accept and implement feedback.

There's no one better able to give you feedback than your customers and employees. These people are eating, drinking, and/or working at your truck all the time, and they know exactly what they like and don't like. The key is for you to make it comfortable for them to share this information with you. Why? Because you want to be the best, and you become the best by listening.

> **TIP**
>
> In his book *Setting the Table: The Transforming Power of Hospitality in Business* (HarperCollins, 2006), famed restaurateur and service expert Danny Meyer says, "While the customer is not always right he/she must always feel heard." Meyer says his business strategy is built on both good service, defined as technical delivery of the product, and "enlightened hospitality," which is how the delivery of that product makes its recipient feel. These are words to run your truck by.

Naturally, all the feedback you receive won't be useful. Some of it won't make sense or be practical based on your business structure. After all, you know the intricacies of your business better than anyone else. The key is to approach all feedback with the most open mind possible. Always think to yourself, *what can I do to best deal with this particular point?* Sometimes the answer will be nothing, but more often than not you can make your truck more efficient or enjoyable because you chose to hear what that employee or customer had to say.

Now that you know its value, the question becomes how to get honest and valuable feedback without negatively affecting your customers' experience. The most effective ways I've found are truck conversation, feedback cards, and online dialogue.

Truck Conversations

Truck conversations consist of communicating with your clientele to garner as much information as you can. In more simple terms, ask questions. I talked in Chapter 2 about how important it is for you to be a personality, to interact with your clients. This is just another reason why it's so critical to your success. You can interact with your customers in a variety of ways; I detail a few ways here:

Observe and converse. Observe your clients. When you see that they're enjoying themselves, say hello and introduce yourself. Let them know that you value having them as your customers and ask them what's been good about their experience with your truck. And if you notice someone who doesn't look pleased, introduce yourself as well. Do everything in your power to fix the problem and *listen* to what made their experience negative. Thank them for their feedback whether or not you plan to use it. Then get cracking to make sure your truck is the best it can be.

Infuse positivity. It's amazing how you can turn an okay experience into a great one with a bit of positivity and enthusiasm. Say something like, "Isn't that the best meatball you ever had in your life?" This kind of comment makes customers feel special and opens them up to thinking the way you do: like attracts like.

Open-ended questions. Don't ask customers anything that can be answered by a simple yes or no. Ask questions that require a more extensive answer to get to their personal preferences.

Listen attentively. Don't look at your phone or other customers or allow yourself to be distracted in any way. Fully engage the person giving you feedback and respect the time he's spending for your benefit. By giving the customer your full attention he'll know it means something to you and take it more seriously.

Names and faces. Make an effort to recognize your customers and try to speak to them by name. Recognition will make them feel special and more comfortable with you. Building a relationship with your customers will lead to a regular dialogue, and dialogue leads to honest feedback.

Feedback Cards

Feedback cards are another great way to garner information. I recommend using a postcard-size card and with no more than five easy-to-answer questions that customers can respond to by rating an item—service or food quality—from 1 through 10.

Their experience at your truck is going to be brief; customers won't have a lot of time to reply. At the bottom of the card, have a couple of lines for suggested improvements. You can do this playfully by saying something like "Help us help you" or "How can we better satisfy your cravings?" Customers should feel like they're speaking to someone who cares and that their feedback is valued.

Leave a box, with a pen inside, right next to the window of your truck, to make it easy for customers to drop in the cards upon completion. The best time to offer the cards is while the customer is waiting for his food or with the package when you make a delivery. Expect only 50 percent of your customers to fill them out, and don't get discouraged by negative results. Use the feedback to get better.

Online Dialogue

Another way to get customer feedback is through the online dialogue you and your customers are having about your truck. People will place reviews of your truck on websites like Yelp, Google, and Urban Spoon. These reviews will be invaluable to you in monitoring your progress as a business. You need to be aware of what your customers are saying about you and then register on the sites so you can respond. Always respond positively to reviews, good or bad. Thank customers for taking the time to review your business, making sure they know their voice has been heard. Invite them to e-mail you at your business address, and if they follow up, invite them in for a special visit or event at the truck. Going the extra step is what makes the difference between a good truck and a great one.

Expect additional chatter through social media applications like Facebook and Twitter. When customers post good or bad comments, you should always reply. A simple thank you, with a contact address for further customer service, is meaningful and will make the customer feel heard. Even more valuable than the customer service element will be the information you garner by monitoring feedback and applying it to your day-to-day operation.

Responding to Criticism and Praise

Criticism and praise are part of any hospitality business. Some customers will think you're the best truck in history, others will leave dissatisfied, and many will land somewhere in between. The key to your business is to do everything in your power to make sure the majority of customers leave happy. This will lead to their becoming your regulars. Be the best at what you do, and you shouldn't have any problems.

TRUCK TALES

In 2007 famed restaurateur Jeffrey Chodorow's new restaurant Kobe Club got a terrible review from *New York Times* food critic Frank Bruni. Chodorow decided to take out a full-page ad in the paper contesting the review and vowing to start a blog aimed at "reviewing the reviewers." Because of this response Chodorow continued to receive bad food press for years and brought the bad review to the attention of thousands more readers. What's the moral of this story? If someone chooses to negatively review you and you believe you didn't deserve it, prove him or her wrong through your actions. Make your truck a success, and all the criticism in the world won't make any difference.

How do you respond when someone tells you that you're great or, more unpleasant, when they say you stink? Even more crucial, what should you do when a critic writes something negative about you on a food blog or in the local newspaper?

Take all reviews, praise, and criticism, with an open mind. If someone writes something positive about your business, thank them, put your head down, and keep doing a good job. If someone writes something negative, evaluate, put your head down, and make any adjustments that you believe are necessary. When people are reviewing or critiquing you, it means you're doing something right. You have people's attention and, especially in the Internet age, they're going to express their opinions.

The best way to get a positive review is to run an awesome truck. Great food, intuitive service, and a well-kept truck lead to great reviews. But even then you can't ensure that everyone will love it. If you're lucky enough to receive a good or even great review, don't let it go to your head. Satisfaction is a disease, the beginning of the end for any business. Never let your guard down and always aspire to be better tomorrow than you were the day before.

TRUCK TALES

The Street Vendor Project began the Vendy Awards in 2004 to raise money for the organization and protection of the rights of street vendors. The annual event attracts thousands of visitors to Governors Island to vote on the best food trucks and street vendors in New York and New Jersey. Awards include Rookie of the Year, the People's Taste, and the best dessert truck, among others. A Vendy award is a badge of honor among street vendors and offers incredible exposure in the food press.

Gathering and Listening to Employee Feedback

Who knows your business better than your customers? Your employees. They see all aspects—front, back, middle, and side—of your operation. Speak with them as much as possible to get feedback on what's going well and what could use improvement. Make time to formally sit one-on-one with every staff member at least once a month. And speak with them as often as possible informally as well. Allowing communication to flow freely leads to surprising solutions and ideas from the most unlikely sources.

Here are some tips to assist in establishing an open environment:

Create a manager's log where all issues and problems are noted during operations. This record of any and all issues ensures that you'll remember to resolve them and can protect you if more serious issues arise.

Schedule a weekly staff meeting to discuss important plans and allow employees to vent. Meetings can be invaluable to an organization. Employees will do a better job if they feel free to express their concerns and feel vested in the decision-making process.

Allow for anonymous suggestions. Some employees don't feel comfortable speaking up, so create a suggestion box for people to share their thoughts anonymously.

Understanding Your Customers

Your customers are complex beings, not too different from yourself. Once you've identified who they are, it's important that you make an effort to understand what drives them. Why do they eat at your truck? What is it about your product that attracts them? What can you do to make the experience better for them? What would make them visit you more often or spend more money each time they do?

By taking the time to understand your customers, your business will be more effective at servicing their needs.

Observing and Listening

There's no better way to understand your customers than to observe their behaviors and listen to what they say. People are creatures of habit, and watching what they do will give you an eye into what motivates them. Their conversations and comments can give you even more insight into what they're thinking and feeling.

If a customer says "I love your food so much, but I can't eat here every day because I'll get fat," that might mean you should be including healthier options on your menu. Or if someone shows up with napkins every time they eat at your truck it could mean your food is too messy, or that you need to supply a better napkin. Whatever it is, you'll gain tremendous insight into your customers by listening and observing.

Here are some additional things to consider:

What do your customers have in common that drives them to your brand? Does everyone who eats at your truck love football? Or are they all talking about that new show on HBO? Figuring out their similarities will help you cater to your customers more accurately.

Review your menu mix. Figure out what your customers are eating and not eating. Once you have that information, you can speak to some of them to get deeper insights into why they choose one item over another. Maybe they love your meatball hero, but the portion is too large, so they choose the burger instead.

TRUCK TALES

To help launch HBO's hit series *Game of Thrones,* the company created a food truck serving food themed around it. The network hired top chef Tom Colicchio and served food modeled after different regions in the show, made from rabbit, duck, squab, and venison. The truck parked in different locations in Manhattan and Los Angeles and rotated menus by Chef Colicchio daily.

What is the perceived price-value relationship of your truck by your customers? Do they think your truck is a good deal or too highly priced? Are they looking for a lunch or dinner special? Maybe your portions need to be larger or smaller.

Anticipating Their Desires

Reactivity is a recipe for disaster. Food trucks—and businesses in general—must be proactive to be successful. Once you understand your customers, you'll be able to look at the larger environment and anticipate what they might want. If you're selling hamburgers and you read in a food magazine that sliders are the next big food trend, maybe you should add them to your menu. Or if you're a juice truck and you realize all your friends are drinking coconut water, maybe you should be offering that item as well. Keep your eyes open for opportunities, and then think of the best ways to capitalize on them.

What's important is that you be aware. Just because your truck is successful today doesn't mean it'll still be a hit tomorrow. Doing research, visiting trade shows, and shopping your competition's trucks will keep you ahead of the game.

BEEP! BEEP!

Just because your competition lowers their prices or begins offering an alternative item doesn't mean you should do the same. Take the time to analyze every situation. Make a list of the positives and negatives of any decision and then make educated guesses. The effects of your choices are cumulative, meaning they increase as you make more of them. Take the time to make the best decisions for your truck's future.

Exceeding Expectations

When customers come to your truck, they're expecting a certain level of food, service, and treatment. The better you're doing as a business, the higher your customers' expectations will be. It's your job to exceed their expectations every time. To do that you must make every guest's experience personal.

When I walk into my local coffee shop in the morning, the guy at the counter makes my cup the way I like it without me even asking. It makes me feel like a king. You can do that for your customers, too, by listening to each one's likes and dislikes and committing them to memory. Do everything in your power to ensure that your customers get what they want when they visit you. Some truck owners do it by keeping lists of their best customers' preferences. Each time one of them comes up to the truck, the operator knows what he usually orders. Simply saying, "You want your usual side of spicy sauce?" is a great way to exceed a customer's expectations. The best operators do this every time, and this attention to detail is clearly displayed by their growing profits.

Great customer service is the exception, not the rule. You would think with so many hospitality businesses out there most would be great, but the truth is that the majority are mediocre.

Here are some simple things that can help you be the best:

Go the extra mile for your customers. Amuse their kids, give them an extra side of fries, or get them that soda they always talk about. Do anything you can to make them leave your truck happy.

Give them something to talk about. Customers love to tell their friends how they're treated like VIPs at a truck. Give them an off-the-menu special taco you keep on the side; they'll tell everyone how amazing it is. Or tell them about an upcoming food truck festival before the news is released to the public. Make them feel like insiders.

If a customer has been waiting in line for a while, offer them a free item for their next visit. Also, use social media to engage your customers. For example, use a password to get a special discount or item on any given day.

> **TIP**
>
> Roy Choi, the Kogi chef, runs nightly specials on all his trucks. Some of the more famous ones include Barbeque Sliders and the Venice Beach Vegan Taco. Specials drive the check average up, keep people interested, and get rid of excess inventory before it spoils.

Find out what they love and then use the information. If your best customer loves baseball, get him a hat from the local team. Or if one of your customers always talks about a special type of hot sauce, show him you listen and get him a bottle.

Show your thanks. E-mail or send thank-you cards to your best customers. It's amazing how much a personal note means to people.

Offer preview tastings. Include your customers in your process: let them try the different items you're testing before you add them to your menu. It makes them feel vested in your truck and will provide you great feedback.

Making Amends: Service Recovery

The service recovery paradox is that a service or product failure can offer the chance for a business to receive higher customer satisfaction than if the problem had never occurred.

I promise you, no matter how good you are, you and your employees will make mistakes. The secret to the hospitality business is how you recover from them. Every negative customer service situation is your chance to make a customer for life by quickly and effectively fixing things.

Let's say juice falls off the counter of your truck and spills on a woman's T-shirt. Service recovery would dictate that you quickly make her another juice for free and buy her a new T-shirt. I guarantee she'll never buy juice from another truck.

Service recovery is the way to turn angry people into loyal customers who will tout your virtues to their friends.

Strategies for Earning Customer Loyalty

Events and frequent dining cards are the best ways to encourage customer loyalty on a food truck.

Events. Once you're no longer the new kid on the block, it's important to have special events that encourage people to return to your truck and give them something to talk about. After you've been operating for six months to a year, try to have a special event once every three months. If you have a taco truck, you can host a gathering at a local park with music and all-you-can-eat tacos. Such events will not only garner press coverage, they will also differentiate you from competing taco trucks.

Frequent dining cards. Frequent dining cards are a great way to get customers to return to your truck regularly. Customers love to know that their tenth lunch will be free. It's the perfect motivator, and if you've ever had a card like this you know that there's a certain satisfaction in getting it punched. Customers will be carrying that card around, and every time they go for their wallet, there you are.

You'll have to make sure your employees actively encourage customers to use them. The cards need to be an integral part of the check-out process, and you must honor the commitments you make. Nothing would be worse than promising a customer something and then letting them down.

Your frequent dining card should be about the size of a business card. It should have your logo on one side and boxes or stars on the other. The boxes or stars will denote how many times they have to eat before they get their reward. Each time they dine, the card should be punched with a hole puncher or stamped with a custom stamp. Coming up with a unique name for your rewards program such as "dining all star" or "meatball maven" is a good way to keep people interested.

Gathering Contact Information

As I discussed earlier in the book, it's critical to gather your customers' contact information. The more information you're able to garner from your clientele, the less dependent you'll be on external sources of advertisement and marketing.

Before the launch of your truck, you need to have systems in place to gather and segment e-mail addresses and Twitter followers. The best way to do it is by including your website address and social media application connections on all materials related to your truck. After you've driven traffic to your site, you need to capture the information. Front and center on your website, you should have an e-mail submission form and Twitter follower button.

I highly recommend providing incentives to the customers to submit their contact information by offering a monthly sweepstakes for a gift certificate or other reward that involves your truck. In the marketing business, these are referred to as calls to action. You should never activate any of your marketing campaigns without a call to action—something that causes the customer to act. Providing incentives for the customer to take action allows you to clearly measure the effectiveness of your campaign and get your client to sample your truck.

TIP

Companies like Wufoo.com will help you organize the information customers submit on your website by putting it into an Excel file. Once the information is in Excel, it is much easier to break down by location and other relevant points. Unleashing the power of this information will make you a more effective marketer.

You can also gather your customers' information through direct contact with them. One way to get this information is to have a container where people can drop their business cards to enter a contest of some sort. The other way is to just ask. If you're at the window, tell customers that you want to keep them informed of promotions and your truck location. Most of the time they'll be honored to be asked to be part of something meaningful by the owner; people like to feel special, so make them feel great and build your business in the process.

The Least You Need to Know

- Giving your customers what they want—and more than they expect—is key to building your business.
- Truck conversation, feedback cards, and online dialogues are three helpful ways to get the feedback you need from customers.
- Solving a customer's problem quickly and efficiently can be better than never having had something go wrong in the first place.
- Frequent dining cards appeal to customers and encourage them to visit your truck often.

Expanding Your Marketing Efforts

In This Chapter

- Using layered marketing to promote your truck
- Expanding your reach with social media
- Working with a professional or doing your own PR
- Advertising within your community

The biggest myth about food businesses is that once you're open the customers just show up, as if by magic. People love to speculate about how much money a truck owner or restaurateur must be making when they see a big line or all the tables filled. They'll pat you on the back, smile, and say "Business must be pretty good," as they calculate your truck profits in their heads. But that's like thinking that football is easy because you see the players dancing in the end zone after they score a touchdown. The truth is that food trucks don't have lines all the time, and football players spend countless hours training before they score a touchdown.

The food truck business is a marathon, not a sprint. Like football, it's about teamwork, planning, and how many great days, aka victories, you can put together in a row. In this business you aren't a champion until you're consistently profitable over a long period of time.

In previous chapters I talked about how to set up, launch, and start your truck, but once you're operating, how do you keep the lights on and the money flowing in? It takes great marketing combined with a consistent product. Sounds simple, but what happens after you aren't the new kid on the block anymore? Once everyone has tried your tacos and four brand-new taco trucks arrive in the neighborhood? What do you do then to differentiate your product and attract customers?

In the past that was a mystery. Some trucks advertised, some gave out frequent buyer cards, and others discounted. But the truth is there is a formula. None of these methods work alone, but when combined, magic happens.

The Compounding Cycle

The key to unlocking the power behind your food truck brand is using a *layered marketing* approach. I call it the Compounding Cycle. It combines public relations, advertising, social media, experiential follow through, and personal relationships to reinforce a singular message to the target market. I call it compounding because it's similar to compounding interest: the marketing message and momentum get exponentially more powerful with each repeat of the cycle.

DEFINITION

Layered marketing is a method in which multiple marketing techniques are utilized in one campaign to reinforce the brand's message and intentions, thereby generating tangible results.

Determining Your Message

The first and most important step in the process is determining your message. And there's no point in drilling a message into the minds of consumers unless it's the correct one.

Let's say you're selling meatballs. Is your message that you have the best, the highest quality, the cheapest, or that you'll deliver your meatballs the fastest? All of those are potential marketing messages. The question is, which one will work? And how do you determine the answer before you spend thousands of dollars on a campaign?

Figure out who your consumer is and what motivates him when he makes a buying decision. If your truck is parked on a college campus the price and taste of your product will usually be more important than the nutrition. But if you're in a hip downtown business district, nutrition and quickness may be your customers' main concerns. Identify, to the best of your ability, what motivates your clientele and then tailor your marketing message to those factors. You're looking for the point where motivation meets marketing.

TRUCK TALES

In the 1970s and 1980s, Domino's Pizza built their brand on speed. Domino's promised they would deliver your food in 30 minutes or less; if not, you got your pizza free. Domino's realized that when their customers were hungry they wanted their food quick. They focused on that motivating factor and built a billion-dollar business on it.

The Campaign

Once you've determined your marketing message, you need to design an effective campaign around it. That means packaging the message into flyers, e-mails, social media messages, and consumer experiences that encapsulate it. The goal is to make the information in your materials as easy to consume as possible, motivating your customers to make a buying decision. Unless you're an artist yourself, creating your marketing materials will involve hiring a graphic designer to take your words and present them alongside your truck brand.

For instance, if you're selling the highest-quality beef hot dogs at the best possible price, your slogan might be "Artisanal quality at artist prices. Who says an artist has to starve?" Then you'll integrate your slogan into every aspect of your business. No one should make a purchase from you without being aware of that slogan.

The Steps

Once you have your message and your slogan, the Compounding Cycle really takes effect. You must constantly repeat the program outlined here to reinforce the message and grow your customer base:

1. Distribute the promotional materials for your event or promotion via e-mail, social media outlets, your website, and other methods of direct contact with your customers.

2. Reinforce your marketing message through trusted sources: television news, newspapers, magazines, and other reputable communication outlets. Most consumers believe what these sources tell them because they don't seem to have ulterior motives. The value of press coverage from a trusted food blog or association with a notable personality can lead to much more business than an e-mail blast or Twitter message on its own.

3. Make your promotion come to life with experiential follow through (see Chapter 9).

4. After any successful promotion, you must thank your customers. They're your lifeblood and, like your mother, father, girlfriend, or husband, they want to feel appreciated. Make sure you send an e-mail, Tweet, or post a sign on your truck thanking your customers. And your thank you should be personal. The extra effort you make with a phone call, e-mail, or handwritten note will come back to you tenfold.

The Compounding Cycle is about generating repeat business by forming consumer habits related to your brand.

Let's assume you're planning to offer a special green hot dog for St. Patrick's Day. Create digital and print flyers and distribute them through your communication outlets in as close a time frame as possible to when your customer will be making his buying decision. You don't want to send out a St. Patrick's Day food truck promotion two weeks ahead of time. No one decides what they'll eat for lunch that far in advance. It makes more sense to distribute flyers two to three days before the holiday and then send an e-mail message the morning of St. Patrick's Day.

The best way to ensure press coverage is to make friends with local writers or employ an effective public relations firm. Another way to get a trusted source on your side is to purchase advertising. That magazine or newspaper ad space purchase might include editorial coverage or the sponsorship of an event as part of the package. Getting a magazine to co-promote your truck will greatly enhance the message you're sending to customers.

TIP

When partnering with media outlets or notable personalities, make sure they represent the image you want for your brand. Many times businesses partner just to create buzz but wind up creating the wrong kind of buzz, which could end up with your brand being less trusted than it was before.

Let's say 1,000 people show up for green hot dogs and you only have 300 to sell. That's bad experiential follow through. Good experiential follow through involves being prepared by gauging the demand, setting up a system to get out the green hot dogs quickly, having entertainment to distract the waiting customers, and making sure the green hot dogs taste better than any hot dog you've ever served before. Now you have the opportunity to turn this into an annual St. Patrick's Day promotion. People will talk about the promotion and look forward to it every year.

> **TIP**
>
> Never over-promise. It's always important to under-promise and over-deliver in the hospitality business. Your marketing efforts should be enough to motivate a buying decision, but not too much beyond that. If you promise the best meatball in the world or your money back, you're setting yourself up for failure. It's inevitable that someone's going to be disappointed. Manage expectations so that you can comfortably surpass them and your customers leave thrilled, not disappointed.

The best advertising in the world comes through word of mouth. You can't buy it, you have to earn it. Repeating the Compounding Cycle hundreds or even thousands of times is the only thing that leads to long-term success in the hospitality business. Some people will tell you otherwise, but they either don't know what they're talking about or they're lying. Great hospitality businesses are a combination of meaningful marketing that speaks to the customer and great experiential follow through. Rinse and repeat.

Social Media

In Chapter 9, I gave you a basic breakdown of how you should utilize social media to start your truck business. Here I elaborate by giving you some examples of successful food truck social media campaigns.

Doubletree CAREavan

Doubletree is a famous hotel brand owned by Hilton. They're known for giving out chocolate chip cookies—almost 21 million a year. For the 25th anniversary of the brand, Hilton created the CAREavan, a food truck that's mission was a "10 week, 10,000 mile, 50-city journey to deliver hundreds of thousands of smiles to weary workers, tired travelers, and local charities across the country through the pleasant surprise of a chocolate chip cookie treat."

Social media played a massive role in the execution of the campaign and its eventual success. The Doubletree Facebook page featured an application that tracked the location of the truck in real time, as well as videos, tweets, and an entry form for a CAREavan contest to win free hotel rooms. The Doubletree Facebook page vastly increased the number of "likes" they received after the campaign was launched.

Doubletree used Foursquare to update the location of the truck and teamed with Topguest to offer Hilton rewards for checking in. On Twitter, they offered a contest in which followers had the chance to win a delivery of 250 cookies for using the hashtag *#sweetbreak* when posting. Finally, they used YouTube to capture "Cookie Confessionals"—people talking about why they love cookies.

The campaign was multilayered and blanketed the Internet with a very clear message: Doubletree is welcoming, hospitable, and accessible. They got all of that out of combining social media with a simple cookie.

Made for Mexicue

Seasonal items are a great way to encourage visits from your clientele. One summer, New York truck Mexicue started a "Summer Market Special" contest in which customers submitted recipes for an item to be featured on the truck. The promotion became so successful that the boys decided to continue the promotion every season. Using a Facebook app, Mexicue announces a different seasonal ingredient every couple of months. The truck accepts recipe submissions and posts them for Facebook users to vote on. The winner receives a gift card to the truck, and Mexicue features the winning recipe on its menu the following season. The campaign is a great way to engage customers in the brand.

Chil'lantro BBQ

Chil'lantro BBQ is Austin, Texas's version of the venerable Korean taco truck. The owner, Jae Kim, is an avid fan of Twitter, Facebook, Yelp, and Foursquare for communicating with customers and marketing the happenings of his truck. His most successful social media campaign happened during the South by Southwest festival. Kim teamed up with mobile payment system Go Payment, an iPhone credit card processing company, to offer tacos at a greatly reduced price to customers who signed up to follow the truck on Twitter and paid for the tacos with their credit card. It turned out to be a huge motivating factor for the customers at the festival; many were technologically savvy and weren't carrying much cash.

What made this an awesome campaign was the way Kim matched his desire for more Twitter followers with the target market's desire for cheap eats and fondness for paying through credit. Jae Kim listened to his customers and was rewarded in the process.

BEEP! BEEP!

Beware of becoming overly dependent on social media. There's no replacement for a sound business plan, personal relationships, and great planning. Social media is part of a good marketing plan, but it isn't a good marketing plan on its own.

Publicity

Using public relations properly will lead to a positive perception of your food truck in the blogosphere, local community, and media.

to do proper press outreach for your truck, you'll need to prepare a press should include information on the key players, photographs, and a general of your truck, menus, and possibly a special promotional item related to ess. I've seen press kits delivered by butlers and include chocolates shaped o of the business. You should do whatever it takes for the media to have a nection with your product. Place your information in a clean folder made uality stock with your logo on it. Make sure your business card is promi- on the front of or inside the folder.

TIP

In the digital age, many press kits are PDF files rather than hard copy because they're easily e-mailed to press outlets. That's fine for a truck to use for secondary press outreach. During the first press push, it's better to print something and mail it. Writers tend to delete e-mails, but they'll be more hesitant to throw away something that was clearly created with care.

When it comes to publicity, there are two ways to go: handle it internally or hire an outside company. It all depends on your budget. I suggest hiring a professional for your first three to six months of operation at no more than $2,500 per month, and then go it alone. If you can't afford to hire a publicist, don't worry; you can make it on your own. The main advantage of putting publicity in the hands of an expert in the beginning is that it will allow you to focus on refining your operations during those critical first months.

Handling public relations yourself can be very effective, as long as you live by one rule: avoid being negative. As I've said before, like attracts like, and negativity will only attract more negativity. Never say anything bad about your competition, the authorities, or anyone else for that matter. As far as you're concerned, everyone is spectacular and you're happy to be part of this great industry.

The upside of doing your own publicity is that no one knows your business better than you. You created the project and no one will talk about it with more passion than you. The downside is that you won't have the benefit of working with a professional who has experience and an outside perspective. Interview several PR firms even if you don't plan on hiring one; it's a great way to generate ideas and make connections. Don't worry about wasting someone's time. As long as you're relentlessly positive and cordial, something good will come out of the meetings.

Community Outreach

Your publicity will form the public's perception of your truck and you. My advice is to make a positive contribution to your community. There's no better way to generate positive PR than doing good and sharing. By positively contributing to your surrounding neighborhoods, you'll generate goodwill for you and your business.

Your food truck should be involved in as many charity events as possible to build relationships in the community while enhancing your brand image. Use these opportunities to let people try your grub, sampling what you've worked so hard to create. The people you're helping will become word-of-mouth advertisers, espousing the virtues of you and your business. You should spend a minimum of a few hundred dollars a month on sampling your product through charity functions. If you become super successful, I recommend using up to 10 percent of your income on assisting the community. I promise you it isn't something you'll regret over the long haul.

It's one thing to donate your assets and those of your employees; contributing your own personal time to the community will be even more meaningful. Volunteer for the local chamber of commerce, food truck association, or other groups. An even better option would be to join a group your customers admire or that has a high-profile image within your community. As a leader in the food truck or hospitality community, you'll have a forum in which to promote your views and protect your business.

> **TIP**
>
> PR firms generally work on a monthly retainer, though some will work on an event basis as well, meaning you don't have to pay them when you have nothing in particular for them to promote. For a start-up business like a food truck, paying on an event basis is a great way to work with a PR professional without making a major commitment.

Advertising

Advertising isn't generally useful for food trucks because of the cost. It's very difficult, especially for a small business, to gauge the performance of an advertising campaign.

If you do choose to advertise, you need to be focused. Taking ad space in *The New York Times* doesn't make sense for a food truck. You'd have to sell thousands of falafels or hot dogs to pay for just one advertisement. However, if there's a food festival going on in downtown Manhattan and that's where you park, you could advertise on the ticket or program. The cost will be relatively reasonable and the exposure is targeted to people who love food and will be near your truck.

> **TIP**
>
> Sponsorship is a great way for food trucks to advertise. Local athletic teams and charity events will give you maximum return and generate community goodwill at a comparatively low cost. There can also be opportunities for you to sell your product by parking at the games or events.

When you're a new food truck operator, your primary objective should be to create awareness within your target market. Your advertisements should include all the relevant information about your truck and a call to action. Before running an ad, make sure it covers the five most important aspects of your business:

- Name
- Type of product
- Why it's special
- Website address
- Twitter hash tag

Customers can't take action if they don't know what they're looking for. Mystery makes for great books, not great advertising.

The Least You Need to Know

- Use layered marketing—combining public relations, advertising, social media, experiential follow through, and personal relationships—to effectively market the message of your brand.
- Promotional campaigns involving Facebook, Twitter, and other social media work very well for food trucks.
- The idea behind publicity is to promote a positive perception of you and your truck. You can hire a professional, but don't forget that no one knows your business better than you do.
- Advertising can be very expensive. Be focused to get the most bang for your buck.

Food Truck Events and Opportunities

In This Chapter

- Taking part in food truck festivals
- Joining the community on neighborhood lots
- Getting involved in Food Truck TV
- Forecasting the next big thing in food trucks

It's mid-August 2011 in New York City's South Street Seaport. The sun is shining and beats are pulsing from a DJ booth overlooking the water. South Street is usually a destination for tourists, but today it's twice as busy as usual and filled with what seem like actual New Yorkers. Why are they spending their summer day in the city rather than at the beach? The answer: food trucks. More than 30 food trucks have descended on the seaport for a festival. The event, organized by the New York Food Truck Association and covered by *The New York Times* and food blogs like Eater.com and New York Magazine's Grub Street, has created a frenzy, with Manhattanites ready to line up for a taste of what everyone is talking about.

Did that fire you up? I know it got my juices flowing and taste buds watering. Walking the festival that day, I noticed that some trucks, like Taim Mobile, Rickshaw Dumpling, and Korilla BBQ, were jam packed with people, though others were pretty barren. So I sat down at a table for an hour to observe. Why were some crowded and others not? My conclusion is that it came down to branding and marketing. The trucks that were doing well were putting on a show. They were living their brand, enjoying the process, and engaging the customers. Not only that: the truck operators who seemed to be enjoying themselves were clearly putting out a better product.

Trucks like Korilla and Taim have the whole package—branding, personality, process, colors, music, and food all working together to create a better food truck experience, the kind of experience that produces memories. And, as you know by now, memories create cravings.

Festivals

Food truck festivals are becoming modern-day food courts, featuring the best gourmet grub you can find in one location. No longer are trucks just showing up in high-traffic areas; they're now planning events and happenings that create their own high-traffic locations. Thousands of people attended the festival in New York City, translating into extra income for the food trucks involved.

A food truck festival is similar to a music festival that's centered on eating. As food trucks have become a phenomenon, they've run into parking problems and difficulties in supporting the growing number of trucks on the road. There used to be plenty of business on the street, but these days trucks need to figure out new ways to build their businesses and new places to sell their products. The food truck festival is a fabulous result of American ingenuity that has sprouted from these issues. The truck community and/or event organizers with connections to the world of food have created and promoted these events as a secondary revenue option. They usually involve 10 to 50 trucks in an open-air location combined with live entertainment, other vendors, and, sometimes, contests for the best truck or the best of a specific item. Prime locations for these festivals include harbors, parks, beaches, and urban squares.

TRUCK TALES

Downtown L.A. Artwalk hosts the mother of all food truck events, produced by Philip Dane's Truckit Fest. On the second Thursday of every month, 22 food trucks line up alongside 50 pop-up vendors and multiple art galleries. Lobsta Truck, Tom Bom, Hot Shot Hot Dogs, Tornados Potatoes, Sloppy Gourmet, and Baby's Bad Ass Burgers are among the trucks that regularly attend the event.

Festivals are organized, marketed, and promoted weeks or months in advance of the actual date. The event often sells passes that allow customers to sample one item from each truck for a set price. A festival can attract tens of thousands of foodies and can generate big revenues for the organizers and the trucks involved. Trucks also get tremendous publicity through public relations outreach and inclusion in distributed marketing materials. The ability to expose your product to thousands of potential clients can be both a blessing and a curse; your product will be under a microscope. The key to maximizing the exposure is to provide the best product and service and showcase the culture of your brand.

Getting Noticed

You can't afford to be quiet when there are dozens of other trucks surrounding you. You want to ensure that you make money at the festival and, more important, generate repeat business for the future. Go out of your way to make a statement. Here are some ways to do that:

Offer samples of a signature item. Make sure your samples are just enough to entice customers. Samples will draw a lot of people to your truck, and at these festivals the action around your truck is what draws in more people. Keep people crowding your truck and, soon enough, you'll have a line around the block.

Music. Play great music at your truck through a speaker system, live performer, or DJ. It will generate attention and is a great way to display the energy of your brand.

Signage. Make sure your signs are big and bold, especially at a festival. Make a larger than usual brightly colored menu board to help you stand out from the crowd and focus on the items you want to sell.

Specialty items. Create a one-of-a-kind taco or meatball that will only be available at the festival. Spend the week before promoting it to your loyal clientele and then offer it as an add-on to your more traditional items at the event. It's a great way to increase the customer spend during a food festival.

Combo meals. Create a combination of entrée, side, and drink for a special festival price. It works for McDonald's and Burger King; it can work for you.

TIP

Festivals are incredible places to gather contact information for your e-mail and Twitter lists. Most of the people attending the festival are avid food truck fans and foodies. They represent your most dedicated client base, so make sure you get their information and thank them immediately for their support.

Getting Involved

You can find out about festivals through food blogs, city websites, your local chamber of commerce, and food truck trade organizations. When you find out about one that you're interesting in joining, e-mail or call the organizers to find out how trucks become involved. Don't seem too eager; an event producer will sense desperation and take a hard line on your deal for involvement. If you can swing it, find a friend in the industry who's involved and try to get him to recommend you to the festival organizers.

To make festivals as beneficial as possible to you and your business, you need to generate a lot of buzz about your truck. That buzz and a strong following will make you more valuable to festival organizers. Before long organizers will start calling you to capitalize on your popularity, and you'll be able to decide which festival best suits your needs. It's only a dream until it comes true.

> **TIP**
>
> Review the list of trucks involved in any festival before signing on. If you're a pizza truck and several pizza trucks are already committed, you may want to reconsider your involvement. Make sure all the elements are in place for you to be a success before you agree to participate.
>
> Also, you should see what their marketing avenues are. Check their social media pages and see how many people are following them or "like" them. To be successful, the event must be promoted well.

Covering Costs

Most of the trucks involved in festivals have to pay an entrance fee and sometimes a percentage of total sales as well. In some cases organizers will invite better-known trucks, like Kogi, to be involved for free, and these trucks might even be guaranteed a minimum amount of sales. When you're first starting out that won't be the case for you, and you might actually end up losing money from a festival. Entrance fees can be up to $2,500 for the day, and you might end up not generating enough revenue to cover them.

BEEP! BEEP!

When you agree to attend a festival, make sure there's a weather contingency. You don't want to spend money entering the festival and preparing your food only to hear that the event is being cancelled because of rain. Make a deal with the event organizers that you'll pay a lower entrance fee if it rains, and make sure they have a rain date planned.

Food Truck Lots

The mini-backlash against food trucks has created a need for safe and friendly environments for trucks to ply their trade. When bricks-and-mortar businesses and the authorities are coming after you, there's comfort in being part of the herd. Food truck lots are popping up all over New York, Los Angeles, and other urban centers throughout the United States.

A food truck lot is a piece of real estate, like a parking lot or an empty lot, that acts as an outdoor food court. Trucks pay $25 to $60 per day for access to the property. For that they're provided with a daily spot, access to customers and, in some cases, infrastructure support and restrooms. For many trucks a lot creates the opportunity for steady income and a welcome sanctuary from daily parking tickets and other issues.

The key for any food truck lot is to attract large amounts of steady traffic. That will be a shared responsibility between the lot organizers and the truck operators. All parties need to work together to create awareness within the local community. I highly recommend not depending on the organizer; work with the other trucks to create hype. Canvass the area with promotional flyers, send out coordinated e-mail blasts and Tweets, and do local public relations outreach. Another very effective method is to reach out directly to surrounding businesses, and offer their employees an incentive to come check out your truck. You would be surprised at what you can get with a free soda or side of fries.

Food truck lots aren't typically located in developed neighborhoods. Real estate values are too high, and food truck lots don't generate enough profit. Instead, truck operators should seek out neighborhoods where there aren't already a lot of restaurants. These neighborhoods play to their strengths as mobile business operators who can choose to be in a location only when the traffic is present.

Lots are also placed in cities where food trucks may rarely travel, too. As in a large city such as Los Angeles, it may be difficult for those living in surrounding cities to get to LA for a food truck. Find lots in areas where your customers are and where there is a want/need for food truck love.

For example, Rockrose, a major New York development company, recently launched a food truck lot in Long Island City (LIC), an up-and-coming area in Queens that's close to Manhattan. LIC is home to many major businesses, including Citigroup, but is empty in the evenings, which has made it a difficult place for restaurants to develop. Rockrose is in the process of building multiple apartment buildings and had a vacant lot that wasn't scheduled for construction for a couple of years. To attract attention to the neighborhood and more infrastructure for potential residents, they decided to open a temporary food truck lot. And boy, is it the perfect spot for one. The food trucks gain access to a bustling yet underserviced lunch business and drive off to greener pastures in the evening. This is the perfect opportunity for a truck operator to create stable income in the neighborhood and develop a following for a potential bricks-and-mortar location when it gentrifies.

On the West Coast, the Southern California Mobile Food Vendors Association, with its 130 member food trucks, runs five food truck lots. They're currently in talks to develop additional lots, many in partnership with institutions such as the California Heritage Museum. What could be more perfect than institutions with tons of visitors offering better-quality, diverse food? That's what food trucks are all about. Because food trucks are mobile, they don't have to wait for opportunity to find them; they can go out and look for it themselves!

BEEP! BEEP!

Food truck lots are often the target of city health departments. They're an easy way for inspectors to review multiple trucks in a short period of time. If you choose to be involved in a lot, make sure you're prepared. Make sure the lot meets the local health department requirements as well. They will go after the vendor, not the organizer.

Developers use food truck lots as short-term ventures to attract interest in the properties, just as they do with pop-up restaurants and flea markets. Once the area develops and there are more lucrative options for the properties, the food trucks will have to move on to other locations. The key to your success as a truck operator will be to find the best opportunities and exploit them to the best of your ability. But that's why you have a restaurant on wheels, right?

TRUCK TALES

In Austin, Texas, they call their food truck lots food truck trailer parks. Feed the Soul, a lot run by St. Martin's Evangelical Lutheran Church, houses food trucks such as Latasca Tapas, OneTaco, Evil Weiner, and Way South Philly. The organizers have been in a constant battle with the city to keep the park open. Where there's a will there's a way. Keep feeding our souls and fighting for the rights of food trucks across the country!

Television

Long gone are the days of Julia Child and the Frugal Gourmet. The Food Network, founded in 1993, combined with the incredible talent of Emeril Lagasse, changed how Americans think about food forever. Although they're a relatively young industry, food trucks have found their way into your homes via TV. The lure of the mobile gourmet has been too great for TV executives to ignore.

Television is a great way to gain massive exposure for your food truck brand, but you want to make sure it's positive exposure. You wouldn't want to appear on local or national TV unless it was a positive portrayal of your product, brand, and self. There's no way to make sure of that other than to trust the people you're working with and control your actions while filming. If you have the opportunity to take your truck to the airwaves, be aware of everything you're saying while the cameras are rolling, and only do business with producers you feel make content that's in line with your beliefs. A positive TV piece should showcase your truck, not the conflicts and drama that go on within your organization. If you choose to go the way of a show like the *Real Housewives* series, producers will find a way to encourage drama and conflict. Don't be naive. Protect your business at all costs.

BEEP! BEEP!

Television can be a very powerful tool to promote your business, but make sure you aren't doing it for your ego. Any time you're focused on promoting yourself, the viewer will know. The camera never lies.

The following sections offer a sampling of the greatest moments in food truck television to date.

The Great Food Truck Race: Season 1

The Great Food Truck Race premiered on August 15, 2010, on the Food Network. Hosted by celebrity chef Tyler Florence, seven specialty food trucks competed in a multi-week competition in different locations including San Diego, New York, a truck stop, and a farm. The trucks traveled across the country from west to east, selling their food and competing for the highest total revenues. The truck that earned the least amount of money each week was eliminated. The winner of the competition received a cash payment of $50,000, along with many prizes given out throughout the competition.

Season 1 teams included:

- **Austin Daily Press:** Originally from Austin, Texas; serves hot sandwiches wrapped in a sheet of newspaper from the Onion.

- **Crepes Bonaparte:** From Fullerton, California; serves Parisian style crepes.

- **Grill Em All:** From Los Angeles, California; serves gourmet burgers.

- **Nana Queens:** From Culver City, California; serves banana pudding and chicken wings.

- **Nom Nom Truck:** From Los Angeles, California; serves Vietnamese style sandwiches and tacos.

- **Ragin Cajun:** From Hermosa Beach, California; serves Cajun cuisine.

- **Spencer on the Go!:** From San Francisco, California; serves French cuisine. Through a legal loophole, Spencer can set up chairs so customers can sit down to eat in front of the truck.

Top Chef

On Episode 8 of Season 3, Guilty Pleasures, each team was given a food truck and asked to create late-night grub at the Miami nightclub Nikki Beach. Contestants used their trucks to create items such as Oysters in a Half Shell with a Spicy Watermelon Ceviche Taco and Bacon Wrapped Shrimp with Cheese Grits and Tomato Chipolte Butter. Chef Sara Nguyen was eliminated for her take on Beef Sliders, while Chef Tre Wilcox won the competition. He took home a first edition signed copy of guest judge Chef Govind Armstrong's book and a platinum access card to all Nikki Beach locations.

Throwdown! with Bobby Flay

The premise of this Food Network show is that celebrity Chef Bobby Flay has an impromptu cook-off with a chef or restaurateur known for a specific food item, such as meatballs or hamburgers. The contestant thinks he's going to be on a Food Network show and instead is challenged by Chef Flay in front of a large group of people, many times the contestant's closest friends and family, and Flay and his team create their own version of the food item. The episodes follow the cook-off, and dishes are judged by two local chefs to determine the winner. Since commencing the show, Flay has challenged two trucks.

First, Bobby was challenged by Jerome Chang and Chris Chen's Dessert Truck to make a better chocolate bread pudding. The Dessert Truck boys put Bobby to shame; the contest wasn't even close!

In his second food truck challenge, Bobby took on the boys of Wafels & Dinges. Once again the truck bested Bobby, as Chef Thomas DeGeest made his famous Liege Belgian Waffles. Doesn't Bobby know not to try to out-do a Belgian when it comes to waffles?

What's Next?

The food truck revolution is just beginning. Although big cities like Los Angeles and New York are saturated with food trucks, secondary cities are just beginning to be hit by the wave. The opportunity for new trucks now lies in these areas. Established brands, like Kogi, Korilla, Souvlaki GR, Rickshaw Dumpling, Mexicue, and many others also have the opportunity to open new trucks or offer licenses and franchises in these cities.

It's incredible to think that what started as a way for people to enter the business with a small investment has become a booming industry all its own. And with many of the successful trucks opening their first bricks-and-mortar locations, it's not crazy to think that the next big fast-food restaurant could come out of what once was a food truck.

In major cities, food trucks are in what I call generation 2.0. The streets are saturated and backlash is rampant; but despite all this, many trucks are still thriving. How? The opportunity lies in events and catering. You work in the streets to pay your expenses, generate a modest profit, and pay your staff, but establishing a catering or events business is the way to profitability. Restaurants have known for a long time that catering is where the big money is.

Now that the truck business is maturing in major cities and there's more competition, trucks need this second revenue source. You can generate the same profits from catering one corporate function or working a day at a music festival as you can an entire week on the streets. It is especially important to promote your catering services in November and December. This is when businesses are looking to spend, and you should maximize your share of the pie by making direct contact by phone, using social media, and sending e-mails to your targeted list.

The Least You Need to Know

- Food truck festivals can be a great way to become better known in your area, but be sure you have the details ironed out before you sign up.
- Empty lots given over to an assortment of food trucks are a cheaper way to go than festivals, and your presence there can lead to a bricks-and-mortar location as a neighborhood develops.
- If you have the opportunity to become involved in a food truck reality-type TV program, your involvement should benefit your business, not be an ego trip for you personally.
- Catering is the way to larger profits. A truck can make as much money in one day at a corporate event as a whole week on the street.

One Truck or More?

In This Chapter

- Determining if and when it's time to expand
- The pros and cons of expansion
- Selling up

To expand or not to expand? Once you have one successful truck, that question will inevitably start popping up. But expansion is serious business and brings with it some very important questions.

Is expansion the right thing for you personally? Is your business ready for expansion? Does the demand exist for multiple trucks? Do you have the infrastructure to support more than one truck? If not, how would you need to build or change your infrastructure to support this expansion? Are there enough parking spots in high-traffic areas to support the expansion of your fleet? These are only a few of the questions you need to ask yourself before considering an expansion of your food truck business.

In this chapter, I discuss the profits and pitfalls involved in an expansion of a food truck business.

Lifecycle of a Hospitality Business

Before considering expanding, you need to understand the lifecycle of a hospitality business. By grasping the stages a truck goes through, you'll be able to make more educated decisions about a potential expansion of your truck empire.

Stage One: Market Introduction

The first stage in the life of any hospitality product is the market introduction. That's when you're launching your truck and making the market familiar with the product you're offering. There are no shortcuts; you may have the most amazing concept in the history of food trucks, but you can't avoid the introduction phase.

During this period, which can last from three months to a year, you're performing a delicate dance with your customers and the press to create positive buzz about your truck. Every customer experience is magnified because these people are the seeds of your word of mouth, the major source of your buzz. Every mention in a local newspaper and food blog forms the public perception of your business.

The characteristics of the introduction phase are high costs, low sales volume, and minimal direct competition in your niche. In this stage, there's little existing customer demand, and you need to create that demand. At this point you'll most likely be making little or no money. You may actually be losing money because of all you're spending on marketing to drive sales and operations to establish a great product.

Stage Two: Growth

The characteristics of the growth stage are reduced costs, increased sales, moderate profitability, and increased customer awareness. As the business grows, you're becoming more efficient and shedding the costs related to launching and training. This, combined with increased sales, should lead to some level of profitability. Expect this stage to begin at the end of year one, perhaps continuing into years two and three.

As the market becomes more aware of your product, you may find you have increased competition within your niche and parking locations.

TIP

When thinking which stage your business is in, you must also consider the stage of the food truck industry in your area. The food truck business may be a mature industry in Los Angeles, but in a city like Indianapolis food trucks may still be in a growth stage. If you had the first food truck in Indianapolis, you might be in the growth stage because the overall market is growing.

Stage Three: Maturity

You've reached the maturity stage when your truck is a known brand and has a consistent customer flow. You may be able to go on your first vacation during this stage. The key in the hospitality business is to maximize the length of the maturity stage and rake in the profits. Your costs should be at their lowest and your sales at their highest. Your hard work is paying off and the customers are showing up with minimal money being spent on marketing. This stage should begin in year three and continue as long as possible.

If you've reached the maturity phase it's because you're successful. You should expect increased competition, which may force you to lower your prices or offer more value, cutting into your margins. Your most important initiative at this point is to be creative in implementing programs that differentiate your brand from the rest of the pack. It could mean new menu items, weekly special events, or partnering with artists to do installations on your truck's façade. Whatever you choose, it must appeal to your audience, giving them a reason to talk about and visit your truck.

Stage Four: Decline

The final stage in the life of a hospitality business is the decline. There's not too much to say about it, and I hope you never reach it. If your truck arrives here, I have only one good piece of advice: don't hold on too long. Sell if you can, so you can leave gracefully and with a couple of bucks in your pocket. Shutting down a business you've put so much of yourself into is more painful if you build up debt while hanging on too long.

You're in the decline phase when your costs become too prohibitive to continue operating your truck. If you're selling corn and all of a sudden the price goes up 10 times with no signs of falling you might as well shut down unless you're able to increase your retail price 10 times. The other way you'll know you're in decline is a consistent decrease in sales volume. If your sales are dropping regularly over a three- to six-month period, you have a major problem.

Making a Living from a Food Truck

Making money from your truck needs to be your main goal. It's a simple matter of getting a reward for your hard work. Passion is important and admirable, and enjoying your work is great as well, but your excitement will disappear very quickly if you aren't generating enough profit.

What constitutes "enough"? That's a very personal question. Let's define enough profit as the maximum income you can generate working in a business you enjoy. So if you love being in the food business and you can make $60,000 working in a restaurant and you're only making $20,000 running your own food truck, you aren't making "enough" profit. If your truck is reaching its full capacity and generating only $20,000 in profits, you need to either expand or get out of the business.

Let's assume you want to expand. One truck is never going to make you rich. A food truck business at its most profitable will generate $500,000 in gross revenues annually. With that kind of revenue you'd be considered an extremely successful operation. At that level your profit margin would be no greater than 15 percent (I'm being generous here). That means you'd be making about $75,000 before paying taxes, so your take home would be around $60,000. It's a respectable income, but after paying back the initial investment, and especially if you're sharing that money with partners or investors, is that enough? You can increase your income by working the truck and paying yourself a salary, but that isn't a strategy for expansion, which requires delegating authority effectively to your employees. Trying to do everything yourself is a recipe for disaster.

Assuming you live a middle-class lifestyle—or aspire to—and you're planning to support yourself from your food truck business, you'll almost definitely have to expand your operation. But if your truck is an investment or passion project, expansion probably isn't the best option for you. It will quickly make this more of a grind and less about pursuing your dream. The stakes will go up, and so will the stress.

The key to deciding whether you should expand is to determine whether expansion is in line with your goals as an individual and a business owner. There's no way to expand without increased stress and responsibility.

TIP

Some people aren't motivated by material wealth. Anthony Mangieri, the owner of Una Pizza Napoletana, was noted for his obsession with his craft, his high-quality product, and his dedication to classic Neapolitan pizza. After reaching the height of his popularity in New York, Mangieri abruptly shut down his parlor and moved to San Francisco. He could have stayed and reigned supreme over pizza in the biggest city in the world or expanded to multiple locations, but Anthony walked away because he had different goals for himself. He opened a small pizzeria in California and followed his desire to spend more time with nature. Mangieri's personal plan didn't call for a multi-unit expansion.

Am I Ready to Expand?

If you've decided that expansion is right for you and your business, the next thing to determine is whether you're ready. Every truck you add will require more staff, inventory, prep time, maintenance, gas, cooking fuels, insurance, and the list goes on.

Demand

The first issue that you need to consider is demand. Is there enough demand to support an expansion of your product? You can find out the answer to this question pretty easily by answering some follow-up questions:

- Is there always a line for your truck?

- Do you have more locations at which you think you can generate high revenues in one day?

- Are you getting more catering requests than you can handle?

If the answer to all of these questions is yes, then there's enough demand for you to expand. If it's not, think twice about it and thoroughly analyze your business. If you're not operating your first truck perfectly, what makes you think you can operate two?

BEEP! BEEP!

Look at the macro environment before seriously considering an expansion. If the economy is in recession or local businesses are closing, it may not be a good time to expand. Speak to local businesspeople about their performance for more insight into the general marketplace.

Capital Resources

The first question you need to ask yourself is whether you have the capital resources to support an expansion. As a rule of thumb, you should have a minimum of two months' operating capital in the bank to support your business. That can be hard for many people, but if you want to expand it's an absolute necessity. You should have that capital in addition to the fixed costs related to expanding, including an additional truck, commissary, insurance, and other costs that don't vary with consumer demand.

Let's say a second truck costs you $50,000 plus an additional $10,000 to operate it for a month. You'd need $20,000 a month to operate both trucks, so that means you need $40,000 in the bank at launch to cover the introduction of the second truck and the operation of both trucks for the two months after expansion. And that assumes you'll be generating positive cash flow within the first couple of weeks of the new truck's operation.

Staff

Once you know the capital requirements of expansion, you need to make sure you have enough great people to expand your operation without negatively affecting the original or expansion product. An expanding enterprise immediately comes under the watchful eye of consumers and the media. Your competition and critics will be waiting for you to make a mistake, so you need to be entirely confident that you, your management, and your facilities can handle the increased capacity.

BEEP! BEEP!

During an expansion you'll be putting much more stress on your business, staff, and systems. A poorly planned expansion can end up ruining a thriving enterprise. Make sure you protect your core with a strong capital and talent base before thinking about any growth.

Systems

In addition to great people, you also need foolproof systems. As you expand, you'll have less time to oversee the day-to-day operations of the truck; the only way to make sure your customers' experience is the same every time is to implement systems for all aspects of your trucks' operation. Systems will also protect the costs of goods sold and transportation, keep waste at manageable levels, and protect you from employee theft.

Adding a Bricks-and-Mortar Location

Expansion doesn't necessarily refer to additional trucks; it can also mean a bricks-and-mortar location. One of the best parts of being in the truck business is that you have a chance to showcase your talents with a minimal initial investment, something that's never been available in the food business before. Right now the media loves food trucks, so it's an optimal way for you to build your brand. Once the public recognizes your name, it has value and can be used for expansion. Opening an actual restaurant can be an optimal way to expand.

> **TIP**
>
> Other potential expansion opportunities could include licensing/franchising, packaged food products, and catering services.

A bricks-and-mortar expansion is complementary to your food truck business. You're already paying for a commissary, storage, and staff, as well as infrastructure costs like an accountant and a lawyer. A bricks-and-mortar location would share those costs, and in many cases, absorb them. Excess food could be used in the restaurant before it spoils, and cooks can prepare in the morning for both truck and restaurant. This will vastly decrease your operating costs for the truck and might increase its profitability by 25 to 50 percent. The restaurant on its own should be a profitable venture because of the positive brand association with the truck and your built-in following.

Finally, when you have a restaurant, rainy days are nonissues. You don't have to take the truck out when the weather's bad and customers don't want to stand in line on the street, so days that would have created a loss for you in the past are no longer a problem. With two sources of income, you only have to take out the truck when the demand exists. When it doesn't, you can ride out the storm in the comfort of your very own restaurant.

> **TIP**
>
> If you do expand into a bricks-and-mortar restaurant, make sure you open in a high-traffic location. If you've learned anything from food trucks, it's that location is one of the most important aspects of a successful hospitality business.

Identifying the Benefits of Expansion

Expanding your food truck business has the potential of bringing you increased sales for higher profits and further expansion. A successful expansion plan combined with high consumer demand will most definitely add profit to your bottom line. Those profits, combined with additional exposure, will help further establish your brand in the marketplace, which will assist in extending the life of your business. The additional profits and branding will also make your business more attractive for a potential sale.

BEEP! BEEP!

Avoid the ego trap. Expand because you think it's the best thing for the health of your business, not because you want to have the biggest truck fleet on the road. Many of the most successful businesspeople I know made the most money when their companies were small and regret expanding. They ended up with more revenues, less profits, and a bunch of headaches.

Watching for the Pitfalls of Expansion

If it were easy to build an empire, our society wouldn't spend so much time celebrating those who succeeded. Your expansion will come with increased expenses, stress, and a more complicated organizational structure, which means you'll need more capital and better management. Proper capitalization and the hiring and training of new staff will be critical. After that, you'll need to worry about maintaining the quality of your food and service. But the biggest concern is the exposure you're creating by leveraging your current business. Your expansion is putting additional stress on the original operation, and if it isn't successful it will threaten the health of the entire enterprise.

Before you choose to expand, examine every part of your organization, determine what point of the truck's lifecycle you're in, gauge consumer demand, and put together a clear plan. Once you've prepared the plan, sit with it for at least a month. Speak to your staff, trusted advisers, other operators, and take some time to think. If expansion still feels like a good idea after that, go for it!

Selling Your Business

Whether your truck is a great success or runs into difficulties, the most viable exit strategy is to sell your business. If your truck has been a success, you can sell it for the value of the business plus the value of the truck. If the business hasn't been profitable, you'll only be able to sell it for the value of the truck.

My rule of thumb for determining the value of a food truck business is 40 percent of annual revenues: that's what your brand, website, trademarks, concept, customer lists, databases, and anything else related to the business other than the truck itself is worth. If your truck is making $500,000 in revenue, the value of the business side of things is $200,000. If your truck is worth another $50,000, you should price the entire operation, including equipment, at $250,000.

To determine the worth of the truck itself, reference the Kelly Blue Book, Edmunds, or another guide to valuing automobiles. These guides price used automobiles by their make, model, year, and mileage/condition. Once you've done your homework, it's time to visit some truck dealers. Get a proposed valuation from at least three. They'll let you know whether they're interested in brokering a sale or purchasing your truck. Dealers may know people looking for trucks and will put the two of you together for a percentage. There's no standard for that, but the fee shouldn't exceed 10 percent.

Try online bulletin boards like ROADSTOVES.com, auction sites like eBay.com, and classified sites like craigslist.com to sell your business and truck. Putting them up on these sites will help you test the market. You can gauge interest at different price points and get a good feel for the questions potential buyers will ask.

BEEP! BEEP!

Don't put the name of your food truck on websites if you're still running your business. Word travels fast, and your business could be negatively affected if people know you want to sell. Keep all your strategic alternatives open by revealing only the necessary information.

The guidelines I've provided for the valuation of your business and truck are only that—guidelines. Also take into account the unique attributes of your particular truck and the motivations of potential buyers. There are things that can drive up the value. For example, if you have a pending contract to serve as the exclusive vendor for a local stadium or arena, your business could be worth more to buyers, and selling for 40 percent of annual revenues might be too low. Some buyers want to purchase a food business to fulfill a life-long dream, and that could mean they'd be willing to pay a higher price because the intrinsic value is more than the market value.

Here's a brief list of the steps you'll need to take if you're considering selling your food truck business:

1. **Initial review.** Discuss potential pitfalls with your lawyer and your accountant. They'll give you an outline of the process and what legal and tax issues you need to take into consideration. Once you have that information, you can do the market review already discussed.

2. **Valuation.** Check out the automobile guides, speak to truck dealers, and review your financials and other items that may add value to your truck operation. Now's the time to decide what you think your business is worth.

3. **Locate a buyer.** Utilize your personal network, place advertisements online, and speak to customizers, truck dealers, and other operators who may be interested in buying your truck or know people who might be. Be discreet!

4. **Structure a deal.** Get as much money as you can up front. The only benefit to not getting all of your money ahead of time is that if the new operator defaults on payments you can take back your truck. But if you're selling your truck, you don't want it anymore, so it's best to get all of your money and be done with it!

5. **Complete the deal.** Sign a letter of intent immediately upon agreeing on terms. Both sides can then perform their due diligence while creating the purchase agreement. At the closing contracts are signed, checks are exchanged, and you're off to the next stage of your business career.

The Least You Need to Know

- An understanding of the lifecycle of all hospitality businesses will give you a greater understanding of whether you should consider growing your food truck enterprise.

- An expansion puts stress on every part of your business, but it also has its benefits. You need to carefully assess the pros and cons of expansion before moving forward.

- Adding a bricks-and-mortar restaurant can be the perfect way to expand your business.

- Selling your business is the best exit strategy, whether you've been doing great or are having difficulties.

Glossary

added value   Characteristic of a product or service that has exceeded the customer's expectations by providing something more at little or no cost.

aspirational   A product or service a user believes has positive characteristics, inspiring a strong desire to obtain or to associate with it.

assembly line   The process in which parts are added to a product in sequence.

average cover   The typical amount of money a customer spends to feed one person.

blog   A website or part of a website maintained by an individual containing commentary, descriptions of events, and sometimes graphics or video.

blogger   A person who writes a blog.

bricks and mortar   A business that serves customers from a permanent physical structure.

cash flow   The rate at which money enters and leaves a business.

catering   Providing food to a customer remote site or preparing prepackaged food for a large group of people.

check average   In the food business, the typical amount of each customer's check.

commissary   The location at which a food truck operator parks, cleans, and stocks a truck; often also the location of the kitchen.

compounding cycle   A marketing cycle combining public relations, advertising, social media, experiential follow through, and personal relationships to reinforce a singular message to a target market.

consistency   In the food business, the delivery of a product in the same way over an extended period of time.

cook time   How long an item takes to cook.

corporation   A legal entity that has its own privileges and liabilities distinct from its members.

cost of goods sold (COGS) report   A report that measures the true food cost percentage for a menu and inventory as a whole.

cross-contamination   When foods and surfaces that might be contaminated with bacteria come into contact with other foods and surfaces that otherwise wouldn't be a potential threat.

cultural perspective   The underlying message your truck communicates to the customer. Also known as *point of view*.

customer relationship management (CRM)   A widely implemented strategy for businesses to manage their relationships with their customers.

customized truck   A truck that's made to your specifications for the use of your business.

delivery sales   Sales made when a customer orders through the phone or Internet and the food is delivered to their location.

demand   The willingness of a consumer or group of consumers to make purchases at any given time.

dry goods   Items such as tea, coffee, sugar, flour, and paper products that don't require refrigeration.

eighty-six   Restaurant lingo for taking an item off the menu. Generally refers to taking it off temporarily because you ran out of the item, but it can also refer to removing it permanently.

emotional attachment   A feeling of closeness developed through a long-term relationship.

enlightened hospitality   The positive feeling that the delivery of your hospitality product, a.k.a. food from your truck, makes the recipient feel due to the positive and generous way you operate your business and share your passion.

expeditor   The person in charge of organizing orders.

fan page   A page on Facebook dedicated to promoting a commercial interest such as a business or celebrity.

fifty one percenters   Employees who will go the extra step every time to get the job done, with skills divided 51 to 49 between emotional hospitality and technical excellence.

fixed costs   Business expenses that aren't dependent upon the level of goods or services produced.

Food Code   A document created and published by the Food and Drug Administration (FDA) every four years as an example for health departments nationwide. It includes the best practices for storing, preparing, and handling of food as recommended by the federal government.

food truck   A mobile kitchen, canteen, or catering truck that sells food or drinks.

foodie   Aficionados of food and drink who don't work in the food and beverage industry professionally.

forecast   The process of making educated guesses or statements that predict events not yet observed.

general liability insurance   Specific coverage, for property and bodily injury, for instance, in a single policy.

gourmand   A person who takes great pleasure in food.

income statement   A monthly report that reviews a business's sales, expenses, and profits. Also known as a profit and loss statement.

inventory   The amount of food, beverage, and other saleable materials a business has on hand at any given time.

labor costs   The amount of money spent on labor to run a business over a set period of time. This can be turned into a percentage by dividing the total labor cost by the total revenue.

layered marketing   A method in which multiple marketing techniques are utilized in one campaign to reinforce the brand's message and intentions.

lead generator form   A form on your website customers can fill out to request information on your business. It's one of the simplest and most effective ways to turn Internet marketing into actual customer connections.

menu mix   The calculation of how much of your gross sales each item accounts for.

niche   The subset of the market you're focusing on to sell your goods.

on-truck cook   The person in charge of preparing the food to be served to your truck's customers—similar to a line cook in a restaurant.

operating capital   The amount of money you need to have on hand to run a business.

operating costs   Expenses related to daily operation of a business, including fixed and variable.

par   The level of stock needed to service a business over a set period of time.

partnership   Two or more persons agreeing to carry on a business, each sharing the profits and losses.

plating   The act of placing prepared food onto a serving dish to be presented to a customer.

Point of Sale System (POS)   Manages and monitors the checkout process, sales, and financial reporting of a business.

prep   Work such as chopping vegetables or marinating meat that's done prior to service.

prep cook   A kitchen employee who prepares food for service.

prep time   The amount of time it takes to prepare ingredients for service.

price-value relationship   The connection consumers make between the price and quality of a particular product or service.

profitability   The efficiency of your business at generating net earnings.

reverse truck   A food truck business that began as a bricks-and-mortar food operation.

service recovery   The paradox that a service or product failure can offer the opportunity for a business to receive higher customer satisfaction than if the problem had never occurred.

simple food cost   The wholesale cost of the food purchased for a business. This can be turned into a percentage by dividing the total by gross sales.

sole proprietorship   A business owned and run by one individual who assumes responsibility for all profits, losses, and liabilities.

start-up capital   The amount of money needed to begin and continue to operate a business.

steps of service   The basic steps employees perform in a food business.

target market   A defined group of customers to whom a business is pitching its product.

trademark   A legal term for a distinctive sign or indicator owned and used by an individual, business, or legal entity to identify products and/or services to consumers.

true food cost   Food cost that incorporates factors such as waste, menu mix, and discounts.

up selling   Casual suggestions made by service employees to customers to attempt to increase the amount of money spent.

variable costs   Expenses that change in proportion to the activity of your business.

volume   The amount of product your business sells in a given time period.

Resources

In this appendix I provide resources to help you navigate the world of food trucks and help you run a small business. I've also included some direct links to notable trucks and websites for the latest news.

Websites

www.eater.com

Food blog with a national site and 13 city sites: New York, Los Angeles, Miami, Washington, D.C., Atlanta, New Orleans, Chicago, Dallas, Houston, Austin, San Francisco, Portland, and Seattle.

www.findlafoodtrucks.com

Centralized site for Los Angeles food truck twitter feeds, as well as a blog.

www.foodtruckfiesta.com

A real-time automated food truck tracker for the Washington, D.C., market.

www.Grubstreet.com

National food blog specializing in the culinary scene in New York, Los Angeles, San Francisco, Chicago, Boston, and Philadelphia.

www.MidtownLunch.com

Food adventures for your urban lunch hour in Midtown and Downtown NYC, Philadelphia, and Los Angeles.

www.mobimunch.com

The self-proclaimed center of the food truck universe.

www.mobile-cuisine.com

A complete online resource for the mobile food industry.

www.roadstoves.com

A business-to-business site for food trucks, including trucks for sales, events, and promotional opportunities.

Food Trucks

Antojitos Mi Abuelita

www.facebook.com/pages/antojitos-mi-abuelita-in-north-hollywood-ca/351837201356
Mexican cuisine, Los Angeles

Big Gay Ice Cream Truck

www.biggayicecream.com
Exotic soft-serve ice cream, New York

Dessert Truck

www.dt-works.net
High-end desserts, New York

Eddie's Pizza Truck

www.eddiespizzany.com
Thin-crust pizza, New York

Flirty Cupcakes

www.flirtycupcakes.com
Cupcakes, Chicago

Fojol Bros. of Merlindia

www.fojol.com
Indian and South Asian, Washington, D.C.

Fresher Than Fresh Snow Cones

www.ftfsnowcones.com
Snow cones, Kansas City, MO

Gastropod

www.gastropodmiami.com
Molecular haute cuisine, Miami

Grill Em All

www.grillemalltruck.com
Burgers, Los Angeles

Kogi BBQ

www.kogibbq.com
Korean BBQ, Los Angeles

Korilla BBQ

www.korillabbq.com
Korean BBQ, New York

Mighty Cone

www.mightycone.com
Cones and sliders, Austin, TX

Nom Nom

www.nomnomtruck.com
Vietnamese Bahn Mi and tacos, Los Angeles and San Francisco

On The Fly

www.ontheflydc.com
Organic food, Washington, D.C.

Rickshaw Dumplings

www.rickshawdumplings.com
Gourmet dumplings, New York

Roxy's Grilled Cheese

www.roxysgrilledcheese.com
Grilled cheese, Boston

Skillet

www.skilletstreetfood.com
Seasonal comfort food, Seattle

Souvlaki GR

www.SouvlakiGR.com
Greek, New York

Spencer on the Go

www.spenceronthego.com
French, San Francisco

Taim Mobile

www.taimmobile.com
Falafel and smoothies, New York

Van Leeuwen

www.vanleeuwenicecream.com
Artisan ice cream, New York

Wafels & Dinges

www.wafelsanddinges.com
Belgian waffles, New York

Truck Customizers

AA Cater Truck

750 E. Slauson Avenue
Los Angeles, CA 90011
323-235-6650
www.aacatertruck.com

Armenco

8526 San Fernando Road
Sun Valley, CA 91352
1-800-345-0104
www.cateringtruck.com

Food Cart USA, Inc.

Miami, FL
www.foodcartusa.com
866-274-6935

Shanghai Stainless

78–82 Gerry Street
Brooklyn, NY 11206
800-253-4815
www.shanghaistainless.com

Worksman Cycles

94–15 100th St
Ozone Park, NY 11416
1-800-BUY-CART
www.worksmancycles.com

Hospitality and Small Business Organizations

Legal Zoom

www.legalzoom.com
An online legal documentation service that provides low-cost legal services for processes such as trademarking and copywriting.

National Restaurant Association

www.restaurant.org
The largest organization of restaurant and food businesses in the United States.

New York Food Truck Association

www.nycfoodtrucks.org
An organization representing over 30 food trucks in New York.

Small Business Administration

www.sba.gov
A government organization that provides support to entrepreneurs and small businesses.

Southern California Mobile Food Vendors Association

www.socalmfva.com
An organization representing food trucks and street vendors in Southern California.

Street Vendor Project

www.streetvendor.org
An organization dedicated to protecting and promoting street food vendors, including food trucks. They also are responsible for the Vendy Awards, a New York–based food truck awards event.

United States Patent and Trademark Office

www.uspto.gov
The agency within the Department of Commerce that issues patents to investors and businesses for their inventions, and trademark registration for product and intellectual property identification.

Truck Tales

Our society has an obsession with telling the stories of brave pioneers and their journeys from relative obscurity to fame, fortune, and success. Watching shows like *Biography* and *60 Minutes*, we mimic these pioneers and entrepreneurs to get closer to achieving our own dreams. The world of food trucks is no different. There are stories that include great success, tremendous obstacles, unique partnerships, creative genius, and sometime catastrophic failure. In Appendix C, we will share the stories of some notable trucks. Take some time to examine the stories and glean as much information as you can. You may find something that makes the difference between your success and failure. As the Greek writer Euripides said, "leave no stone unturned."

The Big Gay Ice Cream Truck

Does the name sound funny to you? You're definitely not the first person to enjoy a giggle or smile when hearing it. But when it comes to ice cream, the Big Gay Ice Cream Truck is as serious as it gets. Doug Quint, the founder of this gourmet ice cream truck, is actually a classically trained musician. After earning degrees from the Manhattan School of Music and Juilliard, Doug decided to follow his passion. He purchased an ice cream truck from a flutist who played in an orchestra with him and set out to make ice cream even more delicious.

After taking some time to customize his truck, Doug went from musician to ice cream man with partner Bryan Petroff in early 2009. And the name? It came from the way they used to refer to their truck during its creation. One day when setting up the truck's Facebook page, Doug said to a friend, "it's just me and my big gay ice cream truck," and the brand that launched a thousand cones was born. Doug figured that even if the truck failed, people would walk by and laugh. But that ended up being far from the case. The Big Gay Ice Cream Truck spawned an ice cream empire, and their biggest problem became keeping up with demand.

Doug's truck is part old-school Mr. Softee and part mad flavor science. The Big Gay Ice Cream Truck is known for its wacky combinations and even wackier names. Would you like a Bea Arthur—vanilla soft serve, crushed Nilla wafers, and dulce de leche—or a Salty Pimp—vanilla ice cream, sea salt, dulce de leche, and chocolate dip? The truck pairs creamy soft serve ice cream with even crazier toppings such as sriracha hot sauce, bacon marmalade, and crushed wasabi peas. The truck has become so popular that Doug and Bryan recently expanded to their first bricks-and-mortar shop in downtown Manhattan. On top of that, they've become media darlings with feature segments on Anthony Bourdain's *Layover* and the *Rachael Ray Show;* a write-up in *The New York Times;* and attention in many of the biggest media outlets in the food universe.

Through a combination of creativity, personality, and plain old-fashioned deliciousness, the Big Gay Ice Cream truck has become big business.

Soul Patrol

When you think of Hawaii, what comes to mind? Beaches? Luaus? Pineapples? Definitely not fried chicken, right? Well, chef Sean Priester plans on changing that with his truck, Soul Patrol. In 2009, Sean was working as a chef at *The Top of Waikiki*, one of Hawaii's most popular fine dining restaurants. He had a big salary, stability, and acclaim, but his true destiny was about to find him in the form of a truck.

That destiny showed up as his friend Utu in a white lunch box truck that serviced the needs of his community. Utu founded an agency called H5 (Hawaii Helping the Hungry Have Hope) that used a truck to deliver meals to the homeless in poverty-stricken neighborhoods. Sean got involved with the program and began to help out in his free time. However, the part-time gig became full time, as Sean got addicted to helping others. When his friend saw his passion, he purchased a second lunch truck and said, "here you go." With that, Soul Patrol was born.

In the beginning, Sean tried to keep his job in fine dining, but the time constraints made the decision for him. So Soul Patrol, the truck with a humanitarian mission, became a full-time gig serving the most revered soul food in the south Pacific.

Sean is an army brat whose family moved from place to place, but he has roots in South Carolina. The food on Soul Patrol is 99 percent Southern cooking with a little Hawaiian influence. For instance, the "Southern Sampler Plate" is inspired by a classic Hawaiian luau plate. The fried chicken replaces laulau and collard greens replace poke, but the yum factor remains the same. Sean's menu is a heartfelt ode to Southern cuisine with signature items like Carolina-style pulled pork and crunchy shrimp po'boys. This food is without question the best Southern food the islands have ever seen, and that's because it is made with love. Sean has always made tasty food, but it turns out he had to return to his grandmothers' recipes and family roots to find greatness. Most recently, Sean has added to this soul food empire by opening a bricks-and-mortar restaurant called Soul in Honolulu.

Sauca

Sauca is serious business. Just ask Farhad Assari, the owner. He will tell you that Sauca is a "global lifestyle brand that combines food, travel, music, and fun into the most interesting new concept to hit the streets." Can you say big dreams?

Farhad knows a thing or two about big business. Of Iranian descent, Farhad went to college at NYU and Wharton. He then followed that up with 20-plus years in the investment banking business. When his mother became ill, he moved back to Washington, D.C., and had to figure out his next move. After thinking long and hard about something that could be exciting and involve the world of food, he came up with a food truck called Sauca. The name is a variation on the word "sauce," but because sauce couldn't be trademarked he settled on Sauca. The truck serves globally inspired flatbread wraps that combine proteins like Mumbai butter chicken, Mexicali fish taco, and pork bahn mi with an array of sauces like world hot sauce, tahini, and garlic chili. The protein and sauce are combined in a Lebanese flatbread for a scrumptious combination of flavors that traveled the globe to get into your hands.

In addition to food, Sauca aims to offer a complete experience to its customers. Some of the add-ons they offer are karaoke, global TV from a satellite, and a phone service called "token time." This service allows customers to call all over the globe with tokens earned by making purchases at the truck. Why? Because Farhad wants Sauca to be a lifestyle brand, not just a truck. He wants to connect people through this brand and build an international business in the process. And it seems to be working: currently four Sauca trucks operate in the D.C. area, and Farhad has plans for a national roll out.

Whatever the long-term results of Farhad's plan, he has clearly combined his passion and business acumen to become a compelling force in the world of food trucks.

Schnitzel & Things

While the recession hit many companies hard, some people used their unemployment as a chance to start their own business. Oleg Voss was one of them. The Ukranian-born Voss went from international investment banking to food trucks. Currently in his late twenties, Voss got his start in the hospitality business at a restaurant, but he "hated it." So he decided to get his business degree from NYU instead. He had an opportunity to go to Austria to become an investment banker and took it. He packed up his fancy suits, expensive watches, and was all set to become an international businessman, but six months in the crisis hit and he was unemployed. "Last one in, first one out" is how he puts it.

So he started researching the food truck trend and came up with the idea for a Schnitzel truck because "who doesn't like a fried piece of chicken or pork." With that, Schnitzel & Things was alive and frying—frying so well, in fact, that the truck won Rookie of the Year in the 2009 Vendy Awards. Oleg's menu consists of four types of schnitzel including chicken, veal, pork, and cod, as well as German-style bratwurst sausage and his very own deep fried Schnitz Burger. The schnitzel is served Austrian style with sides such as potato salad, beet salad, cucumber salad, and even Oleg's own sauerkraut. Combine that with a little spicy sriracha mayo or ginger scallion relish, and you have one of the most delectable lunches in Manhattan.

But this isn't a hobby for Voss, it's his business, and he's in it to make money. With that in mind, Oleg recently expanded from the truck into a bricks-and-mortar location in Midtown Manhattan. Schnitzel and Things is a perfect example of taking something that you love and turning it into food truck gold, and I am not talking about the crispy skin on your Schnitzel.

Mmmpanadas

Empanadas are fried pastry from Latin America that are stuffed with meats, cheeses, fruits, vegetables, and any other edible delicacy you can dream up. Mmmpanadas is a food truck in Austin, Texas, founded by Cody and Kristen Fields, a couple who absolutely love empanadas. Cody fell for the pastry while building wastewater plants in Costa Rica. After working the grind at a local bank, the Fieldses began to think of ways to become self-employed. That's when fate came knocking on their door. While speaking to a bar owner, he mentioned that his empanada guy fell through, and the Fieldses offered to provide the product. They delivered six dozen, and the bar owner and his customers instantly loved them. From that one account, they began a business as wholesalers of fresh empanadas. From there, it took only six months for the couple to enter the food truck business.

The Fields' truck was originally a pizza truck that they purchased off eBay. They replaced the pizza oven with a convection oven and installed warming cabinets to hold their cooked empanadas. For the first year, Cody worked every single shift that the truck operated. He learned a lot, becoming an expert on things like fixing a diesel engine. Most importantly, he always trusted his belief that the empanada was the perfect street food.

Since then, they have served Green Chile Chicken and Spicy Black Bean Empanadas to luminaries such as the Stone Temple Pilots and Matthew McConaughey. They even serve experimental items such as the "ham and cheese experiment" and a sweet empanada based off of S'mores. My mother used to always say "find what you love and get someone to pay you for it," and that's exactly what the Fieldses have been able to achieve.

Spencer on the Go!

Oh the joy of sitting at your neighborhood bistro sipping a café au lait. That may be what you had in mind, but the guys at Spencer on the Go! have a much different idea of the classic French bistro. Chef Laurent Katgely started parking his bistro truck in downtown San Francisco in 2009, serving delicacies such as Escargot Lollipops and braised lamb cheek sandwiches.

Originally from the French Alps, Chef Katgely started cooking when he was just 14 years old. He apprenticed at Alain Chapel under a three-starred Michelin chef, and followed that by working at famed restaurants like Lespinasse in New York and Pastis in Los Angeles. From there, he went on to open Chez Spencer in 2002 in San Francisco with his wife. The restaurant, as well as the truck, is named after their son, Spencer.

Katgely found his food truck by going out for lunch. He was a regular visitor to a taco truck down the street from Chez Spencer and used to joke about opening a food truck to compete with them. Those jokes became serious when he recognized opportunity for his idea. He found a used truck for $15,000 from a defunct burrito seller, and opened for business seven blocks from his restaurant. He decided to focus on being a fun and affordable alternative to high-end French dining. The truck serves incredible French items like Ratatouille and Truffled Boeuf Bourginion for less than $12 a plate. Spencer on the Go! received national recognition when it was featured on the Food Network's *The Great Food Truck Race* and has recently developed a growing catering business.

Spencer on the Go! demonstrates that food trucks can be a great way of expanding a business, not just a way to start a new one.

Skillet

Every food truck has elements of the city in which it was founded. Seattle is known for rain, coffee, and grunge rock. So what type of food trucks does this city produce? The answer is an awesome one named *Skillet*. Way back in the beginning of the food truck revolution (circa 2007), Josh Henderson founded Skillet, an airstream trailer serving high-end American comfort food using the best local ingredients available. And boy is it good!

Josh spent the years prior to launching Skillet finding his way. For a while he worked in restaurants and hotels, but was tired of working long hours and "missed his dog." So he spent the next couple of years working with photographers handling the food for photo shoots in faraway locations like the Mojave Desert. Even though he loved the experiences, he knew he needed something closer to home. With that in mind, he began searching for something, and stumbled upon a truck while browsing Craigslist. Once he struck a deal, it was off to the races.

For Josh, it has been a downhill journey. From the moment the doors opened, there has been an onslaught of press and lines of people. The main battle for Skillet has been getting the city of Seattle to change their legislation and make it friendly for food trucks to operate. This finally happened three years into their operation. The city used to only allow trucks to park on private property, but with Skillet's help, food trucks now can park virtually anywhere with the right permits.

Skillet still operates today, but has expanded with a bricks-and-mortar location, the Skillet Diner, and a line of products including Bacon Jam and Pumpkin Sauce. Josh also recently released *The Skillet Cookbook: A Street Food Manifesto*. In a 2011 interview with *Seattle Weekly*, Henderson said, "street food was never going to be the foundation of at least a financial empire—it'll be the foundation of our business and the brand and who we are as DNA, but it's never going to take us to our Bacon Jammer Yacht we planned." This is a clear example of how important it is to use your food truck to expose your skills and establish your brand so that you can generate supplementary opportunities.

Marcelo's Ceviche

There's nothing more refreshing and tropical than a well-prepared ceviche. And there are many things that are more refreshing than losing your job. That's exactly what happened five years ago to Marcello Florindez when he went on vacation from his position at a Miami restaurant. After that gut check, Marcelo, the eternal optimist, wanted to open his own restaurant. But a restaurant was too expensive, so he decided to take his idea mobile. And are we happy he did!

Marcelo's first step was to purchase and build the vehicle, which he did completely by himself. Next he had to obtain a license, something that most ceviche trucks in Miami don't usually take the time to obtain. Marcelo is by most accounts the only licensed ceviche truck in Miami, and he has a stellar record with the health department. That is something any truck would take pride in, but it is especially difficult when you are serving raw fish. Marcelo operates the truck alone or with one employee four days a week and also caters private events.

All the ingredients that Marcelo uses, aside from the fish, are sourced from Peru, the ceviche capital of the world. The fish are sourced from Costa Rica and Panama, as well as some local suppliers. Marcelo's fish ceviche is marinated in lime juice, cilantro, red onions, and Rocoto chiles. All of the ceviches are made to order, and he makes custom items based on special requests.

Marcelo's ceviche is an example of taking darkness and turning it into light. He was given a challenge when he lost his job, and he turned it into opportunity. In the process, he established a market-leading product that is nationally recognized. Gooooo Marcelo!

Mexicue

What do you get when you combine the spicy deliciousness of Mexican food with the smoky goodness of BBQ? The answer is Mexicue. Founded by David Schillace and Thomas Kelly, Mexicue got its start when the owners started experimenting mixing spicy and smokey flavors in their Brooklyn kitchen.

Prior to deciding to start the truck, Dave was at a corporate sales job and looking for something different. He had spent some time in Los Angeles and was inspired by watching Kogi explode onto the scene. David and Thomas were close friends, and Dave knew that Thomas was very talented in the kitchen and was also looking to make a change. So Dave approached him with the idea, and they both knew it was the perfect opportunity. But what type of truck would it be?

The first step was to find a truck, and they had a rough time of it. Eventually they located one that was partly built on eBay. After bidding online, they traveled a few hours to Woodstock, New York, and picked up their rig. They spent the next four months testing, planning, and customizing their truck in Long Island City, just outside of Manhattan. The original concept was tamales but as Thomas began experimenting in the kitchen, he decided to expand the menu. After finalizing their Mexican BBQ fusion concept, they expanded to a commissary kitchen on the lower east side of Manhattan and developed a system to prepare their signature smokes and braises.

When Dave and Thomas were finally ready to launch the truck, they decided to spend their first day in Park Slope, in Brooklyn. The traffic was light that first day, and so the next day they felt ready to challenge themselves by heading into the midtown business district. They had no idea what was waiting for them. From the minute they started serving, a line developed. It got so busy that during the lunch rush, it reached three city blocks long. That shocked their system, and they knew it was time to develop operational procedures. Once they got the system in place, things became much easier, so much so that after only six months they launched their first bricks-and-mortar location. Currently they have a second one planned and believe the future of their business is in fast, casual, quick service restaurants.

When asked what the key to their success was Thomas said, "My personal tip—what has been most beneficial for us—is to develop a strong brand, the sky's the limit, then you can take that brand and do whatever you want with it." Moral of the story: think through your branding and marketing efforts at the beginning to maximize your long-term value.

Maximus/Minimus

An enormous travelling steel pig—that's one way to describe Maximus/Minimus; deliciously brilliant is another. Kurt Beecher Dammeier came up with the idea for Maximus/Minimus in 2008 when he was making pulled pork sandwiches to feed his office workers. The sandwiches were a huge hit, so much so that people at the office wished they had a place to get them every day. He started looking for locations, but there was nothing perfect for his concept available near the office. So he decided on a food truck that he could park in a lot just down the block.

But finding his location was just the start. Kurt needed a name and a killer design for his truck. For the name, he turned to his son and an excellent branding gimmick. His son's name is Maximus, and the sandwiches were going to either be spicy or sweet. Maximus, the spicy, needed an opposite end of the spectrum to represent the sweet, hence Minimus.

For the truck design, Kurt worked with local designer Colin Reedy. The duo turned an Alaskan Hot Dog truck into an "urban assault pig" straight out of the movies—a metal sculpture that roams the Seattle streets spreading deliciousness everywhere it turns.

The truck finally launched to much acclaim in June 2009 and has been operating from April to October annually ever since. The food on the Maximus/Minimus includes pulled pork sandwiches, veg sandwiches, grilled chicken sandwiches, Posole (a Columbian soup) and pork, and mac & cheese. All the items are available Maximus—spicy—or Minimus—sweet. Even the drinks have two iterations, the Maximus ginger lemonade, and the Minimus hibiscus nectar tea. Kurt is also the owner of Beecher's Handmade Cheese, which makes his mac & cheese an extra special combination of handmade cheese and Maximus sauce.

What is the most ironic part of this amazing story? Kurt Beecher created the truck and made a success of it based on pure passion. When Beecher was 38 years old, he sold his family's printing business for $85 million dollars. He could have easily retired, but in his own words, he "didn't like golf." Money definitely makes things easier, but a great way to know if you're pursuing the right path is to ask, would I be doing this if I didn't need money? If the answer is yes, you have found your path.

Crepes Bonaparte

Gaston. You may think that is the name of the owner of Crepes Bonaparte, but that's actually the name of the truck. The brains behind this creative stunt are Christian and Dannielle Murcia, a husband and wife team from Fullerton, California. The Murcias started Crepes Bonaparte as a catering company in 2008, providing French crepe stations to private events. After seeing the opportunity and growth in the food truck business, the Murcias decided to join the party in 2010.

Christian and Dannielle purchased Gaston, their Morgan Olson Stepvan, from a local Chevy dealer. After finding the rig, they worked with MSM Catering Trucks in Southern California to customize it. Some of their special requests included a crepe grill and service window large enough to allow customers to see their crepes being prepared. According to Christian, the most important step the Murcias took was to include a clause in the contract requiring MSM to finish the job in three months. They chose to go with a completely custom interior for the truck because pre-fab trucks came with a lot of materials they wouldn't need to execute their menu. By customizing the truck and purchasing the chassis, Christian estimates they were able to save $30,000 to $40,000 dollars.

The Murcias offer their delicious sweet and savory crepes throughout Los Angeles and Orange County. Their menu consists of breakfast crepes, savory crepes, dessert crepes, and traditional crepes. The most requested crepe is the "HazelBerryAnna," a classic sweet crepe filled with strawberries, bananas, and Nutella. Christian's favorite crepe is the "PCH" a decadent mix of peanut butter, Nutella, and honey, which he prefers with a big scoop of ice cream. They say the biggest challenge is working out of such a small space. Not only do they serve their customers from the truck, the Murcias actually run their catering business from the truck as well. This makes for major storage issues, especially when it comes to refrigeration. But good operators make the best of situations, and that's exactly what the Murcias are.

Even with the challenges, Crepes Bonaparte is flourishing. The Murcias goal is to provide crepes like they do in France, "simple, cheap, and on-the-go." Their commitment to this goal has made them a leader in the business and carried them all the way to become a contestant on *The Great Food Truck Race* with celebrity chef Tyler Florence. Even though they only made it to the third round of the competition, the exposure has increased business and helped make them local celebrities. With huge amounts of media exposure, passion, and a great product, Crepes Bonaparte should be satisfying people's crepe cravings for years to come.

Index

F

T

U–V

W–X–Y–Z

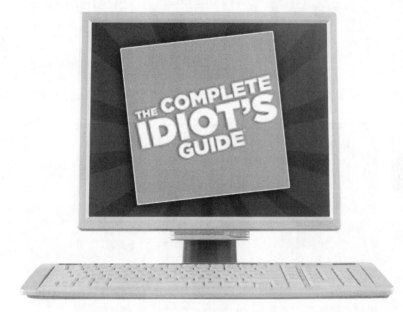